The French Deputy

The French Deputy

Incentives and Behavior in the National Assembly

Oliver H. Woshinsky
University of Maine at
Portland-Gorham

Lexington Books
D.C. Heath and Company
Lexington, Massachusetts
Toronto   London

Library of Congress Cataloging in Publication Data

Woshinsky, Oliver H.
    The French deputy: incentives and behavior in the National Assembly.

    Bibliography: p.
    1. Legislators—France. 2. Political participation—France. 3. Political
psychology. 4. Incentive (Psychology) I. Title.
JN2865.W67   329   73-7960
ISBN 0-669-90159-8

                                                        LC

Published simultaneously in Canada.

Printed in the United States of America.

International Standard Book Number: 0-669-90159-8

Library of Congress Catalog Card Number: 73-7960

To
Ada Ruth Hanson Woshinsky
and
Harry J. Woshinsky

Contents

List of Tables ix

List of Abbreviations xiii

Preface xv

Chapter 1 Incentive Analysis and French Politics 1

Chapter 2 Portrait of Four Deputies 29

Chapter 3 The Mission Participant 61

Chapter 4 The Program Participant 81

Chapter 5 The Obligation Participant 97

Chapter 6 The Status Participant 111

Chapter 7 Behavioral Differences Among Incentive Types (1): Behavior in the National Assembly 127

Chapter 8 Behavioral Differences Among Incentive Types (2): Political Careers of French Deputies 143

Chapter 9 Toward an Incentive Analysis of French Politics (1): Incentives and the French National Assembly 153

Chapter 10 Toward an Incentive Analysis of French Politics (2): Incentives and French Political Parties 169

	Appendixes	181
Appendix A	Summary Description of the Four Incentive Types in France	183
Appendix B	Construction of the Index of Disruptiveness	185
Appendix C	Construction of the Index of Legislative Leadership and Initiative	187
Appendix D	Interview Schedule and Procedure	189
	Notes	195
	Selected Bibliography	213
	Index	223
	About the Author	233

List of Tables

1-1   Overview of the Observed Incentive
        Types   4

1-2   Suggestive Comparisons: Some
        Personality Types or Motivations
        Described by Other Investigators
        Which May Correspond to Incentive
        Types Observed in France   7

1-3   Profile of the Four Incentive Types
        in the French National Assembly   16

1-4   Turnover in the National Assembly:
        The Rate of Return Among Deputies
        Since 1951   24

1-5   Representativeness of the Sample:
        Party Distribution Among All
        Deputies, Deputies in Sample, and
        Deputies Interviewed   25

1-6   Distribution of Incentive Types
        Among French Deputies   27

3-1   Distribution of Mission Participants
        by Legislative Party Group   62

4-1   Distribution of Program Participants
        by Legislative Party Group   82

5-1   Distribution of Obligation Participants
        by Legislative Party Group   98

6-1   Distribution of Status Participants
        by Legislative Party Group   112

7-1   Differences Among Incentive Types:
        Speaking on the Floor of the
        Assembly   128

7-2	Differences Among Incentive Types: Legislative Speech-making	130
7-3	Differences Among Incentive Types: Expertise and Specialization	131
7-4	Differences Among Incentive Types: Experience in the Legislature	133
7-5	Differences Among Incentive Types: Proportion of Plenary Session Work Spent on Matters Requiring Legislative Expertise	134
7-6	Differences Among Incentive Types: Number of Committee Meetings Attended	136
7-7	Differences Among Incentive Types: Percent of Committee Meetings Attended	136
7-8	Differences Among Incentive Types: Number of Written Questions Submitted to Cabinet Ministers	138
7-9	Differences Among Incentive Types: Scores on Index of Disruptiveness	139
7-10	Differences Among Incentive Types: Scores on Index of Legislative Leadership and Initiative	141
8-1	Differences Among Incentive Types: Ages at Important Career Stages	145
8-2	Differences Among Incentive Types: Seniority in the Legislature	146
8-3	Differences Among Incentive Types: Time Spent in Politics	148
8-4	Differences Among Incentive Types: Party Activity	149

8-5   Relation Between Mission Incentive
           and Urbanism   151

9-1   Typology of Legislatures Based on
           Numbers of Conflict-Reducing and
           Conflict-Provoking Incentive Types   156

10-1   Incentive Distribution by Party   169

10-2   Party Distribution of Program Deputies   171

10-3   Distribution of Program Deputies:
           Right, Left, Center   172

10-4   Distribution of Program Deputies:
           Right   172

List of Abbreviations

UDR	Union des démocrates pour la république (Gaullist Party)
RI	Républicains indépendants (right-of-center party)
PDM	Progrès et démocratie moderne (Centrists)
FGDS	Fédération de la gauche démocrate et socialiste (Socialists and other left-of-center elements)
PC or PCF	Parti communiste or Parti communiste français (Communist Party)
Non-Ins	*Non-inscrit* (not enrolled in a party group at the National Assembly)
app	apparenté (attached to, but not a full member of, a party group at the National Assembly)

NOTE: These abbreviations used throughout the book refer to terms or political groups in existence during the time of the research (1968-69).

Preface

This book represents an extensive revision of my 1971 Yale University doctoral dissertation. The basic field research was conducted during a thirteen-month stay in France in 1968-69. During that time I talked with dozens of French political leaders. The conclusions reached in this book derive from interviews with fifty of them—all Deputies in the National Assembly in 1969. I completed writing the present version in August, 1972. The legislative elections of March, 1973, occurred shortly before final preparation of the manuscript for publication, and I have not made any attempt to relate those results to the findings presented below. It may be premature to say, but I do not believe the election outcome would lead me to alter the basic conclusions reached in this book.

This book could not have seen the light of day without help from many people. I am deeply indebted to the many French political leaders who interrupted their busy schedules to talk with me about their life in politics. I wish I could name and thank each of them individually, but my promise that they would remain anonymous must be respected. (In fact, I have gone to some lengths to guarantee this anonymity. In describing or quoting my respondents, I have when necessary made slight alterations in factual material which might give away their identities.)

During my research on this project a number of people gave me the benefit of their insights or in various ways provided material aid and comfort. Among those whose help was especially valuable are: Pierre Avril, James Barber, David Caputo, Roland Cayrol, Mark Kesselman, Joseph LaPalombara, Jean-Luc Parodi, Annick Percheron, Robert Putnam, Paul Schmitt, Nicholas Wahl, and Colette Ysmal.

Sidney Tarrow and Fred Greenstein both served as dissertation advisers and both were invaluable. Throughout my work they guided my research efforts, gave freely of their time, and shared with me their deep knowledge of people and politics.

My debt to James Payne cannot be exaggerated. My interest in incentives developed after long conversations with him and a careful reading of his study of Colombian politics. His encouragement of my efforts and his lengthy critiques of my various drafts contributed enormously to the writing of this book.

A grant from the Yale University Council on Comparative and International Studies allowed me to undertake the research on which this book is based.

I am grateful to Edna Durdan, who typed the final manuscript flawlessly; and to Georgia Lamb and Elizabeth Crowley Audette for typing and research assistance.

Barbara Woshinsky shared this project with me from the beginning—often learning more about it than she cared to know. It would be futile to enumerate the ways in which she guided and encouraged my work. Still, I cannot resist mentioning that she has taught me more about France, the French, and the French language than anyone I know.

Portland, Maine
June, 1973

The French Deputy

1 Incentive Analysis and French Politics

Few people enjoy politics. Most citizens devote little of their time even to thinking about politics, let alone to engaging in political life. Yet a small number of people in every society devote most of their waking hours to politics and derive great satisfactions from it. As a consequence they have a much greater impact on political institutions and policies than the average citizen.

What do these activists gain from their political participation? An answer to this question may shed vital light on the political process, which these men strongly influence. Understanding the motivation of political leaders in any system will help explain why these men act as they do and, ultimately, what political institutions they create.

This book focuses on the motives and actions of political leaders in one modern nation: France. The findings, it will be argued, have implications for understanding politics in many other settings.

My interest in French politicians (and in particular, French Deputies) was stimulated by a specific argument among French specialists. Two major interpretations of French politics have given radically different reasons for parliamentary instability and intense political conflict in France. One holds that French politicians are highly ideological. Their unresolvable conflicts result from strong commitments to opposing social classes and political faiths. This is, of course, the traditional interpretation of French politics.[1]

This ideological interpretation has been disputed by a second thesis which holds that French politicians are motivated by narrow personal goals. Legislative politics, in this view, is a game in which each man struggles against all others for positions of power and prestige, thus making any existing majority unstable. This viewpoint is best expressed in the works of Nathan Leites,[2] but the belief that Deputies primarily seek positions of prestige is widespread in France. One encounters it everywhere: in private conversations, in newspapers, in magazines, and in serious political writings.

There exist, then, two very different interpretations of French politics. French politicians are ideologues, expressing the extreme social cleavages of a divided country. French politicians are opportunists, seeking simply to enhance their own personal position in society. These opposing theories of French politics raise intriguing questions. What are French politicians really like? What does motivate men to engage in politics in France? Is there any relationship between these motives and the bitter devisiveness of political struggles in that country? The research undertaken among French Deputies was designed to answer these questions.

1

What is "Incentive Analysis?"

The questions which stimulated my interest in French politics concern the motivations of French political leaders and the relation between these motivations and political behavior. Because of this focus, an approach to the study of politics which can be termed "incentive analysis" seemed to offer a fruitful way to study these questions. James L. Payne was the first to formulate and use incentive analysis in his 1968 study of Colombia.[3] Since that time Payne, myself, and others have engaged in research which has added to and refined the incentive approach.[4] The formulations which follow draw heavily on a recent Payne-Woshinsky *World Politics* article which summarizes this approach and the main findings to date.[5]

Politics, in most systems, is an entirely voluntary activity. Men do not *have* to engage in it. If they do so, and continue to do so, they must gain certain basic satisfactions from their activity. It seems reasonable to suppose that they will act in politics so as to maintain or increase this level of satisfaction. Presumably, if a man hated political activity—i.e., got no satisfaction from it—he would not remain long in politics. Hence, a man's actions in politics are dependent on his reasons for being in politics. Incentive analysis, therefore, focuses on answering the question: what satisfactions do men gain from full-time political activity?

The decision to focus on this question grew out of extensive field research and observation of numerous political leaders.[6] Observing these men carefully, one becomes struck at the enormous amount of time and energy they expend in political activity. One wonders what they gain to compensate for the costs they must pay. Neither the specific rewards they receive nor their formal statements of purpose seem able to explain why they voluntarily commit themselves to years of work which is physically exhausting, intellectually tiring, emotionally fatiguing, and at times dangerous. As Payne and Woshinsky state: "Our respondents miss meals, neglect children, and lose sleep for politics. For them, politics is a central, vibrant, and continuing preoccupation. Formal statements of purpose cannot adequately account for their involvement."[7]

It is clear that political activity brings these men deep, intense satisfactions. These satisfactions are so strong that one may usefully think of them as representing emotional needs. If these men could not participate in politics, they would feel empty or frustrated. Politics provides them with an outlet in which to satisfy certain strong inner compulsions.

Incentives, then, are considered as deep human needs or satisfactions:

We have defined incentives, therefore, as the emotional needs which individuals seek to fill, or the satisfactions they get, through political participation. . . . This definition is novel, since we usually think of motives as specific desired "things out there" (money, "power," laws, reforms) rather than as needs or compulsions that the individual constantly carries around in himself. If the definition seems strange, we can only note that we did not select it arbitrarily at the outset. After several years of research, we came to feel that it provided the most accurate summary of our findings.[8]

This theory does not represent an isolated position in political science. Numerous other scholars have independently come to the same conclusion: active political participation must be explained by internal motivational forces.[9]

Since incentives are strong inner needs, it seems reasonable to assume that they will influence political behavior. Men will undertake actions which help them to satisfy their needs and avoid actions which frustrate those needs. Hence, men with different incentives will often behave differently in the same situation.

This idea of different incentives provides the key to the value of incentive analysis. Merely to say that men are influenced by their motives does little to increase our knowledge of politics. Incentive analysis aims at identifying specific incentives and discovering the behavior patterns associated with each.

The scholar using incentive analysis seeks to classify political leaders according to their primary incentive for politics. He next learns the behavior associated with each incentive type. To date, seven different types of political leader have been identified, and marked attitudinal and behavioral differences appear among them. Each type has been described by more than one scholar and observed in more than one setting.

Although a final classification is far from established, the fact that different observers can investigate political motives and discover the same phenomena is significant. It underscores the likelihood that the observed incentive types "are quite widespread; other investigators may expect to find them in other settings."[10]

Altogether six of the incentive types have been fully described. The six incentives have been labeled as: status, program, mission, obligation, game, and adulation. Each incentive type is briefly defined in Table 1-1. This table also lists the observers of each type, the places where they have been observed, and the written material describing the results of these observations. Only the first four of these types were observed in France. Hence, there is no prolonged discussion of the game or adulation incentive in this book. Attention is centered wholly on mission, program, obligation, and status participants—the four incentive types found among French Deputies. A short description of each type is found in Appendix A. A complete comparison of the attitudinal and behavioral differences among these types is shown in Table 1-3.

A seventh type has been observed and is listed in Table 1-1. The incentive has been labeled conviviality: expressing a need for friendly interaction with, and acceptance by, others. This type has not yet been observed in sufficient numbers to produce a clear-cut definition or to warrant inclusion in the present classification scheme.[11]

The work of numerous other scholars suggests the validity of incentive types. Others have seen the same kind of men or analyzed the same kind of incentives.

Table 1-1
Overview of the Observed Incentive Types

Incentive Type	Brief Description of Incentive Type	Where Observed	By Whom Observed	Where Reported[a]
1. Status	Seeks to enhance his social prestige by gaining high-ranking political positions.	Colombia	Payne	*Patterns of Conflict*
		Connecticut	Barber ("The Advertiser")	*The Lawmakers*
		Connecticut	Woshinsky	"Incentives to Political Action"
		Dominican Republic	Payne	*Incentive Theory*
		France	Woshinsky	"French Deputies"
2. Program	Seeks to manipulate his environment and solve problems in it; in politics he seeks to work on and influence public policies.	Antioquia, Colombia	Payne	*Patterns of Conflict*
		Connecticut	Barber ("The Lawmaker")	*The Lawmakers*
		Connecticut	Woshinsky	"Incentives to Political Action"
		Dominican Republic	Payne	*Incentive Theory*
		France	Woshinsky	"French Deputies"
3. Mission	Seeks to give meaning to his life by serving a transcendental cause; joins a political movement which serves as a secular religion for him.	Dominican Republic	Payne	*Incentive Theory*
		France	Woshinsky	"French Deputies"

Type	Description	Location	Author/Study	Source
4. Obligation	Seeks to alleviate feelings of guilt by acting strictly according to his moral beliefs; enters politics in order to fulfill his moral duty as a citizen.	Connecticut	Barber ("The Reluctant")	The Lawmakers
		U.S.–1964 Republican National Convention	Wildavsky ("Purists")	"Goldwater Phenomenon"
		Dominican Republic	Payne	Incentive Theory
		France	Woshinsky	"French Deputies"
5. Game	Seeks intellectually stimulating competition with other men in structured situations requiring calculated strategy-planning.	Connecticut	Woshinsky	"Incentives to Political Action"
		Washington, D.C.	Payne	—(no written report)
6. Adulation	Seeks the direct affection and praise of those he interacts with on a face-to-face basis.	Dominican Republic	Payne	Incentive Theory
		Brazil	McCullough	"Brazilian Congress"
7. Conviviality	Seeks acceptance, approval, positive support, friendly interaction, from those perceived as respected social leaders.	Connecticut	Barber ("The Spectator")	The Lawmakers
		Connecticut	Woshinsky	"Incentives to Political Action"
		Dominican Republic	Payne	Incentive Theory

aEach study mentioned here is cited in full in footnote 4 of this chapter. In addition, each of these types, except conviviality, is described at length in Payne and Woshinsky, "Incentives for Political Participation," and all but the game and conviviality types are described at length in Payne, "Determination of the Incentives of Political Participants."

Table 1-2 presents an overview of findings which parallel those on French Deputies. Political types seen by others are compared to those seen in France. The first five studies listed in this table present the core material on which the present incentive typology is based. The types described in each of those studies correspond exactly to one of the types of French Deputy. The remaining studies are listed for suggestive purposes. A precise correspondence between political types or motivations described in these works and incentive types in France cannot be proved. Some of the similarities, however, are striking. They encourage one to believe that the typology presented here is based on real clusters of attributes which have been seen and identififed by others.

As Table 1-2 makes clear, other scholars have noted types or motives which do not fit any known incentive category. This fact should stimulate additional study. Other incentive types surely remain to be investigated. On the other hand, some of the categories proposed by other scholars may simply not be useful for the study of political motivation. Final answers will not emerge until the completion of much additional research.[12]

The attentive reader may wonder why neither "power" nor "money" appear on the list of incentives. Neither of these terms appeared adequate for describing the fundamental needs of observed political leaders, despite widespread assumptions that power and money are both incentives for politics. These terms appear, instead, to connote *instrumental* values which men use to satisfy their fundamental needs (incentives). This conclusion emerges when one asks why political leaders might want power or money. It appeared that the respondents sought power or money, not for their own sake, but in order to achieve specific goals; and these goals in turn were desired because they helped to satisfy basic drives or needs.

In this view power and money are resources. Men use them to obtain their ends, the ends being dictated by their incentives. Thus, a program participant may seek to gain enough power to pass a certain bill, which will alleviate a social problem he has been working on. In this case power is sought to help satisfy the drive for positive involvement in social problem-solving. A status participant may seek money so that he can run a successful campaign for higher office. Here money is sought and used to obtain the satisfaction of gaining increased social status. Most political leaders, then, regardless of incentive, will at various times seek power or money, because these means can help them satisfy their needs. Power and money do not, however, represent the basic emotional needs themselves.

The Utility of Incentive Analysis

Central to incentive analysis is the assumption that incentives can help to explain aggregate patterns of political behavior. Indeed, the basic purpose of this

Table 1-2
Suggestive Comparisons: Some Personality Types or Motivations Described by Other Investigators Which May Correspond to Incentive Types Observed in France[a]

Investigator	Personality Type or Motivation Which Corresponds to:				
	Mission Incentive	Program Incentive	Status Incentive	Obligation Incentive	Personality Types or Motivations Described by the Investigator Cited, But Not Specifically Identified Among French Deputies
Payne[b]		Program Incentive	Status Incentive	Obligation Incentive	Adulation Incentive
Payne[c]	Mission Incentive	Program Incentive	Status Incentive		
Barber[d]		Lawmaker	Advertiser	Reluctant	Spectator Politicians
Wildavsky[e]					
Woshinsky[f]		Policy Incentive	Prestige Incentive	Purists	Game Incentive Conviviality Incentive
Fenton[g]		Issue-orientation			Job-orientation
Sorauf[h]	Ideology incentive	Policy-making Incentive	Political Career Incentive Personal Rewards Incentive		Patronage Incentive Preferments Incentive Economic Rewards Incentive Loyalty to Party Incentive
Wilson[i]				Amateur Democrat	

Table 1-2 (cont.)

	Personality Type or Motivation Which Corresponds to:				
Investigator	Mission Incentive	Program Incentive	Status Incentive	Obligation Incentive	Personality Types or Motivations Described by the Investigator Cited, But Not Specifically Identified Among French Deputies
Browning[j]		Policy-influencing Behavior	Status-orientated Behavior	Policy-concerned Behavior	Passive Behavior Organization-oriented Behavior
Matthews[k]			Agitator	Amateur	Patrician Professional
Duverger[l]	Devotee Party Member	Mass Party Member	Cadre Party Member		
Wahlke et al.[m]		Inventor		Ritualist	Tribune Broker
Wahlke et al.[n]		Facilitator (to pressure groups)		Resister (to pressure groups)	Neutral (to pressure groups)
Charlot[o]	Gaullistes de foi; Gaullistes doctrinaires	Gaullistes empiristes			
Riesman[p]				Moralizer	Inside-dopester Indifferent
Hoffer[q]	True Believer				
Tucker[r]	Warfare Personality				

	Externalization	Object Appraisal	Social Adjustment
Smith, Bruner & White[s]			
McClelland[t]	n Power	n Achievement	n Affiliation

[a] Categories in studies listed *above* the dotted line appear to correspond exactly to incentive types observed in France. Studies *below* that line are noted for suggestive and speculative purposes. An exact correspondence between types described in those studies and incentive types is unlikely, but there are many obvious similarities. (Studies below the dotted line are listed in a rough order, beginning with those whose findings seem closest to describing one or more known incentive types.

[b] Payne, *Patterns of Conflict*.

[c] Payne, "Determination of the Incentives of Political Participants."

[d] Barber, *The Lawmakers*.

[e] Wildavsky, "The Goldwater Phenomenon."

[f] Woshinsky, "Incentives to Political Action."

[g] Fenton, *People and Parties in Politics*.

[h] Sorauf, *Political Parties in the American System*.

[i] James Q. Wilson, *The Amateur Democrat* (Chicago: University of Chicago Press, 1962).

[j] Browning, "The Interaction of Personality and Political System."

[k] Matthews, *U.S. Senators*.

[l] Maurice Duverger, *Political Parties* (New York: John Wiley and Sons, 1954).

[m] Wahlke, et al., *The Legislative System*.

[n] Ibid.

[o] Jean Charlot, *L'Union pour la nouvelle république: étude du pouvoir au sein d'un parti politique* (Paris: Librairie Armand Colin, 1967).

[p] David Riesman, with Nathan Glazer and Reuel Denney, *The Lonely Crowd: A Study of the Changing American Character* (New York: Doubleday, 1953).

[q] Eric Hoffer, *The True Believer* (New York and Evanston: Harper & Row, 1951).

[r] Robert C. Tucker, "The Dictator and Totalitarianism," *World Politics* 17 (1965): 555-83.

[s] M. Brewster Smith, Jerome Bruner, and Robert White, *Opinions and Personality* (New York: John Wiley and Sons, 1956).

[t] David C. McClelland, *The Achieving Society* (Princeton: D. Van Nostrand Company, Inc., 1961).

approach is to explain why groups of men behave as they do. Incentives do not provide a deep enough portrait of the *individual* to explain his entire personality. One cannot predict all of a man's political actions, knowing his incentive for politics. Each individual is unique, with his own peculiar attributes and idiosyncracies. Incentive analysis cannot predict what each individual will do, but it may be able to predict how groups of the same type of individual will behave. That is, it can predict general tendencies, not specific actions. Hence, it is more useful for analyzing group behavior than the behavior of particular leaders. Incentives do not tell everything about a given individual. Thus, men holding the same incentive may differ on numerous other dimensions—intelligence, political beliefs, background. But the significant fact remains that along other important dimensions—career pattern, legislative activity, strength of party loyalty—incentive analysis does help to explain major differences among groups of political leaders.

The findings in incentive research suggest that different incentive types, acting to fulfill different needs, build different kinds of institutions and evolve different forms of social interaction. Incentives, therefore, seem particularly appropriate for studying legislatures as institutions. Legislatures do not *have* to adopt the same rules and procedures, the same informal customs and traditions. They are only partly constrained by "objective" external factors. In fact, legislatures exhibit remarkable differences in their formal and informal procedures for conducting business. Incentive analysis suggests that the norms and role expectations prevalent in a particular legislature depend at least partly on the incentives dominant in that body.

These suggestions will be explored at length in the final chapter. It may be illustrative at this point, however, to suggest concretely how different incentives help sustain different legislative norms.

Numerous studies of the U.S. Congress show that many of its members have the preoccupation with policy matters and the commitment to conflict-reducing norms characteristic of program participants.[13] In addition, the basic Congressional norms suggest the influence of program incentives. The norms of responsibility, courtesy, compromise, specialization, seniority, hard work, reciprocity, and depersonalization of conflict help reduce levels of conflict while insuring continuous work on policies. By making the legislature a smoothly functioning, working body, such norms increase its chances of being involved in the formulation of public policy. This involvement is the main aim of the program participant. It seems likely that he would help to introduce and sustain these norms, which assure him a role in the policy-making process.

Many incentive types have little interest in shaping public programs. A legislature dominated by one or more of these types should exhibit quite different characteristics from those of the U.S. Congress. This is a central hypothesis in Payne's work on Colombia.[14] Payne found the rules and customs of the Colombian legislature strikingly different from those of the U.S. Congress and traced these differences to the dominance of status participants in that body. According to Payne, the Colombian Congress is characterized by:

1. Chronic absenteeism in committees and votes
2. Low committee workloads
3. Few technical or research facilities for legislators
4. Disruptive, conflict-provoking patterns of behavior
5. A popular-demagogic orientation toward program policies[15]

This behavioral pattern prevents the legislature from playing a major role in formulating public policy. Payne hypothesizes that the pattern is related to the status incentive. Seeking to boost their own political positions, status participants enjoy fiery floor debates which gain them immediate publicity; unconcerned with program outcomes, they spend little time working quietly in committees on the technicalities of legislation. The legislative behavior of these men seems directly related to their intense desire to gain public prestige. The overall behavioral pattern of the Colombian legislature reflects the result of widespread attention-seeking behavior coupled with few continuous efforts to shape policies. This pattern may well be explained by the dominance of status participants in the legislature.

These brief comments suggest how incentive patterns might influence aggregate legislative behavior. In another study of political types Barber speculates about the impact of each type on the legislature.[16] These speculations are relevant to this study because the four types of freshman state legislator Barber discovered in Connecticut appear to correspond to four of the incentive types listed in Table 1-1. Barber's speculations reinforce the idea that different incentive types will produce different legislative customs and procedures.

For instance, discussing the contribution to the legislature of the "Lawmaker" (here judged to hold a program incentive), Barber states:

Broadly, it is clear that his presence [in a legislature] is likely to facilitate work on the major tasks, primarily because he brings a clear head and an intense interest directly to bear on legislation. . . . The Lawmaker's adjustive strategies reflect in many ways the practices that legislatures have developed to handle their tasks.[17]

The Lawmaker's work and "adjustive strategies" would appear to sustain the kind of norms already discussed as prevalent in the U.S. Congress.

In contrast, Barber identifies a second type—the "Advertiser." This man, apparently a status participant, would increase the level of conflict in the legislature:

Conflict in legislative debate becomes obstructive, irrational, or dysfunctional when (a) it is out of proportion to the importance of the issue, (b) it "gets into personalities," or (c) it "misses the point." . . . Advertisers are apt to contribute substantially to these negative aspects of legislative debate. . . . More fundamentally, the Advertiser, being basically uninterested in the substance of the issues, is unlikely to apply any very stringent criteria of relevance to his remarks. The important thing, to him, is that *he* is speaking, not that the issue is being clarified. . . . Furthermore, the Advertiser's participation in legislative debate is likely to be *ad hominem* in several directions.[18]

The Advertiser wishes to gain attention at all costs and is unconcerned about the substance of legislation. Barber, like Payne, suggests that the prevalence of such men in a legislature will minimize the chances for calm, rational evaluation of public issues.

The two other types of legislator described by Barber were fairly inactive in the legislature and might be expected to have little impact on it. Nevertheless, Barber did see some consequences of their presence. For instance, the "Reluctant," who apparently holds an obligation incentive, helps to reinforce the agreed-upon legislative rules and customs: "More than most other members, [the Reluctant] helps to ensure that the legislative rules of the game will be followed."[19]

Finally, the "Spectator," who holds the conviviality incentive, has a major effect on the legislature by helping to reduce political conflict and personal tensions:

It is in this tension-reducing task that the Spectators make their main contribution to the work of the legislature. Their orientation as applauding members of the legislative audience helps to maintain an atmosphere of affection, esteem, and respect which is encouraging to those who carry on the main tasks. Their optimism, mild humor, and politeness help to smooth over the interpersonal hostilities introduced by conflicting opinions on bills.[20]

The Spectator facilitates smooth personal relations in the legislature. But an overabundance of Spectators might have undesirable effects on any political body. As Barber puts it tersely: "A legislature composed entirely of Spectators would be a disaster—the work would grind to a halt."[21]

These remarks illustrate how incentive analysis can suggest explanations for the aggregate behavior of political groups. Actions consistent with incentives lead to different patterns of group behavior. It must be stressed, however, that incentives alone cannot provide a full explanation of individual or group action. One cannot know how men will behave simply by knowing their wants. One must also know the range of practical possibilities open to them in seeking to gratify those wants. And this range is determined by the political structures and institutions within which they must operate. When explanations of French politics are advanced below, they are based not only on knowledge of the incentives present in the National Assembly, but also on an understanding of the political structures of Fifth Republic France, which constrain and sometimes even dictate the political behavior of French Deputies.

The Identification of Incentive Types

The research undertaken in France aimed at discovering first the incentives of French Deputies, then the attitudes and behavior correlated with those incentives. A crucial step in the research process was clearly the classification of political leaders by incentives.

This differentiation of leaders was facilitated by use of a major simplifying principle: the assumption of one incentive for each political leader. That is, in incentive analysis it is assumed that each leader can usefully be classified as holding only one of the small number of basic emotional needs which have been found to induce extensive political activity.

This simplifying principle was adopted for two reasons. First, it encourages theory-building and hypothesis-construction. The assumption that political leaders are motivated by single, strong needs leads one to speculate about the behavioral consequences of each need and build testable hypotheses from these speculations. If, on the other hand, one assumes that men's motives for politics are multiple and complex, one cannot easily generate testable hypotheses about the behavior which might follow from these motives.

It is clear, of course, that the assumption of a single incentive for each political leader may not reflect the complexity of real-world motives for political participation. Yet any general or theoretical statement about human behavior is always a simplification. In attempting to construct elegant, complex theories, one always loses some ability to convey the full range of real human behavior. The question is whether the simplification is useful or not. The one-incentive-per-leader principle has been retained because it has led to fruitful hypotheses which are in fact supported by confirming data.

This data underscores the second reason for the one-incentive principle. It seems to "work." After interviewing scores of politicians in different countries, Payne and I found that it was useful to classify each individual as holding only one incentive. First, it "seemed right," intuitively, to say that one man was motivated primarily by, say, a status drive and another primarily by some other drive, such as the desire for adulation. Only one incentive appeared clearly during most interviews.

More significantly, definite attitudinal and behavioral differences did appear among men classified by different incentives. And these differences confirm hypotheses about the different kinds of behavior these incentives should generate. The one-incentive principle, then, has appeared useful in research to this date.

In attempting the actual classification of particular leaders, one must bear in mind an important distinction between incentives and their operational indicators. The incentive itself is a theoretical construct. One does not see the incentive but rather strong indications that some motivation exists which can best be described by the abstract incentive term. These indications are seen during in-depth personal interviews with political leaders—interviews in which respondents are encouraged to speak freely about their personal interests and satisfactions in politics, the things they like and dislike about politics, the reasons they entered and remain in politics. One assumes that, if properly encouraged, men will speak about those areas of their life which most interest and satisfy them.

One reasons backwards from these expressed areas of interest. If a man's primary focus during an interview is with X class of subjects, what can one infer about the basic satisfaction he derives from political activity? For instance, if the respondent shows an overriding interest in his chances for gaining higher office and the techniques he can use toward that end, one can infer that his basic satisfactions in politics derive from the enhanced social status he can gain through that activity. If a man speaks of nothing else in an interview but the public policies he is working on and the social problems these policies are designed to alleviate, one can infer that his real satisfactions come from working on programs which help solve problems he encounters in his environment.

The respondent is classified by incentive, then, on the basis of that general subject which, in interviews, most holds his interest, to which he frequently and voluntarily turns the conversation, and about which he is most knowledgeable and enthusiastic. The object of his spontaneous and intense interest, this subject matter is presumed to relate to his basic satisfactions. It thereby reveals his incentive for politics. This predominant interest area, as revealed by the focused interview, is termed in incentive analysis the *main identifying characteristic* of the incentive.

Ultimately, respondents were classified not by any specific statement they had made but on the basis of my own judgment about the area of their greatest satisfactions. This judgment was based on the overall interview and the general tenor of satisfaction-relevant statements in it. Statements quoted in the following chapters show the kind of remarks a respondent must make to be classified in the relevant incentive category. No respondent was classified on the basis of a single statement.

As yet no automatic, explicitly stated set of instructions exist for operationalizing the concept of the main identifying characteristic. Research is presently being conducted with the aim of building reliable criteria for classifying political leaders according to their incentives. Preliminary efforts at achieving reliability of incentive classifications have been encouraging.[22] The descriptions and quotes provided in the following chapters show how French Deputies were classified. This material should also help in the development of reliable incentive classifications. After studying it, other scholars could presumably come to independent agreement about the incentives which exist among any group of political leaders. (This statement assumes that the scholars would have for careful study transcribed, in-depth interviews with the political leaders they are trying to classify. No way, other than the in-depth interview, has yet been developed for discovering a politician's incentive.)

The quality of the French interviews ranged from excellent to poor. In a few of these interviews the Deputies did not cooperate in the attempt to explore their role satisfactions. Nevertheless, the decision was to use the material from each interview and classify each of these fifty leaders. Each interview did yield some information about the respondent's needs and motives, and the small number of respondents prompted me to use all the information that was collected. In future studies, however, I would recommend use of an "unknown" category for classifying participants whose incentives are unclear.

Despite shortcomings of the present study the evidence obtained was encouraging and suggests the real value of incentive analysis. The basic findings show: (1) *a host of attitudes and behaviors are associated with each incentive*; (2) *these attitudes and behavior are generally different for each incentive; and* (3) *the attitudes and behavior could have been predicted, and often were predicted, from knowledge of the incentive alone.*

This evidence is central to the study. The theory held that men will act in politics in ways consistent with their incentives, so as to obtain the basic satisfactions they seek. The evidence supports this theory. It appears that a particular cluster of attitudes and behavior is associated with each incentive type.

We call the elements in this cluster *attitudinal and behavioral correlates* of the incentive. A complete summary of the major findings is presented in Table 1-3. This table provides an overview of all the attitudinal and behavioral correlates of each incentive type observed in France.

These correlates strongly reinforce the likelihood that the incentive typology delineates real types. They indicate the importance of learning what incentives are prevalent in a given system—since one can predict how political leaders will act, and offer explanations for these actions, on the basis of incentive knowledge. These correlates, finally, can suggest explanations for aggregate patterns of political behavior.

One finds, for instance, as hypothesized, that program types are much more active in the legislature than status types; and that they are especially active in matters requiring detailed legislative expertise, while the status types, though generally inactive, become especially involved in formal debates before the whole Assembly. These findings precisely confirm incentive hypotheses elaborated long before the present study was undertaken.[23] And they suggest an explanation for cross-national differences in aggregate legislative behavior. A legislature full of program types, working assiduously to become experts on legislative policies, might develop very different internal procedures from those of a legislature full of status types, competing for public attention against each other's rhetoric.

Table 1-3
Profile of the Four Incentive Types in The French National Assembly

Dimension	*Incentive Type*			
	Mission Participant	Program Participant	Status Participant	Obligation Participant
I. Basic need or satisfaction.	Serve a transcendental cause.	Learn about and manipulate environment.	Gain prestige to avoid feeling inferior.	Act in a manner consistent with his moral principles.
II. Main identifying characteristic.	Concern with the ideology of his cause.	Interest in the substance of policy administration.	Interest in positions & techniques of position-getting.	Preoccupation with moral & normative aspects of politics.
III. Attitudinal correlates: 1. Expression of satisfactions which define other incentive types:				
a. Mission.	*Present.*	Absent.	Absent.	Absent.
b. Program.	Absent.	*Present.*	Absent.	Absent.
c. Status.	Absent.	Absent.	*Present.*	Absent.
d. Obligation.	Absent.	Absent.	Absent.	*Present.*
2. Attitude toward interview and interviewer.	Tries to convert interviewer or argue with him about ideas.	Tries to help interviewer learn what he wants to know.	Tries to avoid interview; in it, is rude & uncooperative.	Answers all questions perfunctorily but offers little real help.

3. Attitude toward "significant others":			
a. Leaders in higher positions.	Glorifies his own leaders; calumniates others.	Accepts leader who "can't get things done"; doesn't revere them.	Envies leaders for their positions; fears their power over him.	Idealizes "moral & principled" leaders; scorns others as politicians.
b. Other Political Activists.	Feels brotherly ties to those on his side; hates others, who are either "the enemy" or selfish opportunists.	Shows openness toward others; wants to work with them but is not dependent on them.	Denigrates others, is personally cool toward them & intensely competitive.	Suspects motives of others in politics & hence distrusts all but the few who can prove themselves "morally pure" in his eyes.
c. Voters.	Sees voters as supporters or potential supporters of his movement.	Shows sympathy & understanding for voters' problems; also sees voters in realistic political terms.	Takes patronizing attitude towards voters but sees their support as proof of his own superiority.	Voices abstract desires to "serve the voters," to bring them "social justice."
4. Conception of one's role in the legislature.	Act as the voice of one's movement; promote one's ideology.	Work for specific laws which deal with particular national problems.	Has no conception of playing a role; one's legislative position is just a means for obtaining higher position.	Work selflessly and uncompromisingly for "the public interest."
5. Attitude toward one's own party.	Sees his party as a united army of co-believers promoting a political faith.	Sees his party as a group of likeminded men working together for common ends.	Sees his party as a useful coalition of political leaders which can help him win elections & gain high office.	Believes his party *should* be a group of idealistic public servants, but feels maany party members compromise their integrity in politics and fall short of the ideal.
6. General orientation toward politics.	Shows an intense, lifelong dedication to political activities of every kind.	Enjoys politics greatly as long as he is involved in policy-making at some level of government.	Enjoys the prestige he gets in politics, but finds the process of fighting for it painful.	Dislikes the whole process of politics, seeing it as a "dirty world of self-serving opportunists."

Table 1-3 (cont.)

Incentive Type

Dimension	Mission Participant	Program Participant	Status Participant	Obligation Participant
IV. Behavioral correlates. 1. Legislative activities: a. Overall	More active than average	Much more active than average	Less active than average	Much less active than average
b. In plenary sessions	Average	Much more active than average	Average	Much less active than average
c. In formal debates	More active than average	Less active than average	Much more active than average	Less active than average
d. In areas requiring legislative expertise	More active than average	Much more active than average	Less active than average	Much less active than average
e. In actions which bring personal publicity.	More active than average	Less active than average	Much more active than average	Less active than average
f. Disruptiveness	More than average	Less than average	More than average	Much less than average
g. Leadership roles	More than average	More than average	More than average	Fewer than average

2. Political career:				
a. Age at entry into politics	Younger than average	Older than average	Younger than average	Older than average
b. After entry into politics, gains first public office . . .	Very slowly	Fairly quickly	Very quickly	Slowly
c. After entry into politics, reaches national legislature . . .	Very slowly	Slowly	Quickly	Quickly
d. Seniority in national legislature	More than average	Average	Average	Less than average
e. Total number of years in politics	Much more than average	More than average	Fewer than average	Fewer than average
f. Personal dedication to his party, as measured by years of active service	More than average	Average	Average	Less than average
g. Likely to seek high power position early in political career?	No	No	Yes	
h. Legislative district: likely to come from urban area?	Yes	No	No	No

Comparing Incentive Types

Exactly how do incentive types differ from each other? Answering that question formed a central goal of the research. Six *attitudinal* and two *behavioral* dimensions best serve to compare and delineate incentive types. In Chapters 3-8 each incentive type in France is compared with the other types on each of these dimensions.

The attitudinal dimensions include:

1. *Absence of the expression of satisfactions which define other incentive types*. The absence of expressed attitudes which define other types is an important correlate of each incentive. Most Deputies show a complete lack of interest in those subjects which provide intense satisfactions for, and thus reveal the incentives of, other Deputies. The status participant, for instance, finds his basic satisfaction in receiving the marks of high office. Comments by status participants throughout the interviews reveal their total indifference to questions of public policy, ideology, or morality—subjects of burning concern to program, mission, and obligation participants, respectively.

2. *Attitude toward interview and interviewer*. The way men behave in the interview situation gives important insights into their personality. Different incentive types handle interviewers differently. Status participants, for example, are rude and uncooperative, apparently feeling their status demeaned by the dependent role of interviewee. In contrast, mission participants are often quite expansive, apparently enjoying the opportunity to reaffirm their own beliefs and even hoping to make a convert. Consequently status participants grant shorter interviews than others. The average interview with status Deputies lasted fifty-five minutes, while mission Deputies allowed an average of ninety minutes for each interview.

3. *Attitude toward "significant others" in the political environment*. The way political participants regard other men affects the way they behave toward them. When one knows what a man thinks about other politicians and his constituents, one can speculate intelligently about how he will act in particular situations. The status type, for instance, is likely to emphasize the competitive aspect of his relations with those around him. The program type emphasizes cooperation. The delineation of each type's attitudes toward others will be divided into three sections: (a) attitudes toward higher leaders; (b) attitudes toward other political activists; and (c) attitudes toward voters.

4. *Conception of legislative role*. Role analysis has contributed much to an understanding of politics.[24] It rests on the insight that a person's expectation of how he ought to act in a given situation often determines his behavior. Numerous studies of the way legislators define their roles show that these role-definitions, and presumably the behavior associated with them, can differ radically. One weakness in the studies of legislative role analysis has been the lack of attempts to explain why different men define the same role differently.

Incentive analysis offers a simple but powerful explanation for this important phenomenon: men will adopt roles consistent with their incentives. Thus, the obligation participant, impelled by a concern for principles and correct behavior, may become a "ritualist"—a man skilled in legislative procedure—to insure the carrying out of legislative business in a proper, consistent manner.

The interviews with French Deputies are not coded for an existing set of role categories. Instead, an attempt is made to describe in general terms how each incentive type conceives of his work as a legislator, how he views interpersonal relations in the National Assembly ("the rules of the game"), and how he views the institutions of the Fifth Republic.

5. *Attitude toward one's political party*. Party loyalty is a key variable for understanding politics. And as it turns out, attitude toward one's party is closely related to incentive. Program participants like and support strong, cohesive parties which help them obtain their policy goals. Mission participants prefer militant, authoritarian parties, which seem to them best able to promote the cause to which they are dedicated. One would expect that the incentive types dominant within a party could explain much about the party's structure and operations. The fact that all six Communist Party Deputies interviewed were mission participants suggests a powerful explanation for the rigid, nondemocratic structure of the French Communist Party—and for the blind, intense loyalty of its old *militants*.

Incentive analysis also suggests that one could view intraparty struggles as conflict between different incentive types hoping to mold the party in mutually exclusive ways. The UDR, for instance, contains each of the four incentive types. The dissensions within the Gaullist bloc may be partially understood in terms of conflict among incentive types with very different conceptions of a political party and its uses.

6. *General orientation toward politics*. It is important to know how political leaders view their chosen world. Do they see politics as a stimulating game, a constructive business venture, or a dangerous jungle? These varying attitudes, which could help explain their political behavior, are definitely linked to incentives. Some incentive types like politics more than do others. Program and mission types like political activity immensely, while status and obligation types have mixed or even negative attitudes toward politics. One would expect these attitudes to relate to the amount of time they will spend in politics. The hypothesis is that mission and program Deputies will remain longer in politics than status and obligation Deputies. The evidence supports this hypothesis. From their entry into politics to mid-1969, mission and program Deputies averaged, respectively, 25.5 and 21.3 years of continuous political work. These figures compare with 17.0 years for status Deputies and 15.2 years for obligation Deputies.

This data suggests that a knowledge of incentives can help shed light on general processes of recruitment and turnover in a political system. Interesting, testable hypotheses can easily be built on these foundations. For example, one would posit that the more obligation participants in a given institution, the higher the rate of turnover in that institution.

Objective, noninterview data are used in Chapters 7 and 8 to correlate Deputies' incentives with their political behavior. The evidence is focused on two behavioral dimensions:

1. *Legislative activities.* Incentive analysis offers numerous hypotheses about how different incentive types will behave in a legislature. Many of these hypotheses are amply confirmed by the data presented in Chapter 7. For instance, incentive analysis hypothesizes that obligation participants, who like politics less than most participants, will participate less than others in political institutions which demand full-time commitments from their members.[25] They should, therefore, be less active than others in a national legislature. The evidence shows that obligation participants, indeed, are the least active of the four types in France, being coded as "less active" or "much less active" than average on the seven indices of legislative activity. Much of the data on legislative activities confirms this strong relationship between a Deputy's incentive and the way he behaves in the National Assembly.

2. *Political career.* Theoretically, incentives should be intimately linked with men's political careers. The kind of satisfactions they seek will influence what positions they want, how rapidly they try to rise, and how long they will remain in politics.[26] For instance, one of Payne's first hypotheses held that status participants, being more concerned than program participants with achieving "success" rapidly, will enter politics at an earlier age than program participants.[27] This hypothesis is fully confirmed by the French data. Status Deputies entered politics at the average age of twenty-six, while program Deputies were well over thirty-two years old, on the average, before taking their first step into politics. The data presented in Chapter 8 confirms numerous similar hypotheses concerning the type of career each incentive participant will follow. Taken as a whole, the findings presented in the following chapters strongly suggest that many of the attitudes and actions of men in politics are related to, and explained by, their political motivations.

Conduct of the Research

The original research design called for a study of Deputies who had been elected to the National Assembly in March, 1967. This Assembly had been the first elected under relatively calm conditions in France for years. The result was a near victory for anti-Gaullist Left and Center-Left forces which had momentarily combined in an electoral coalition. At the time it appeared that the pendulum was swinging back from the unusually strong showing of Right-of-center parties in the first two parliamentary elections of the Fifth Republic to the more traditional French voting pattern favoring the Left.

Political events in France have a way of upsetting one's expectations. The revolutionary disorders of May, 1968, and the subsequent Gaullist sweep of the June legislative election changed the face of French politics. The 1967 Assembly may now come to be seen as a fourteen-month aberration in the history of the Fifth Republic.

On the other hand, the 1968 election produced the most unusual Assembly in France's history. One party (the Gaullist UDR) obtained an absolute majority of Assembly seats. This development presented me with a serious problem. Given my desire to generalize about all Deputies in a particular legislative session, should I select for study the unusual 1968 group of Deputies or the defunct 1967 group? The 1968 Deputies were finally chosen for reasons which follow.

When I began my research in the late summer of 1968, it was possible to argue that the 1968 election—although undoubtedly an extreme case—reflected a general trend in French politics. The election was one more step in the continuing decline of the non-Communist Left, as well as one more step in the consolidation of a strong conservative party, which might for decades play the role of major governmental party in a fragmented party system where the only real opposition could come from the Communists. The 1968 election might be seen as solidifying in France a political pattern strongly reminiscent of post-World-War-II Italy. It was, and still is, too early to know.

Since it was impossible to say which Assembly was more representative of present or future French politics, it seemed logical to conduct field research on the present legislature. Incentive analysis focuses on the satisfactions of active political leaders. It was important, therefore, to talk with men currently holding a major political position. A study of the 1967 Assembly would have entailed interviews with a large number of men who had been defeated for re-election. It appeared unjustified to compare the satisfactions of men daily engaged in legislative work with the remembered satisfactions of men who would view their former activities through the haze of time and the bitterness of defeat.

A final consideration entered into the decision to concentrate on the Assembly elected in 1968. In terms of personnel turnover the 1968 Assembly is not as unusual as one might believe. Somewhat *more* Deputies than usual with past legislative experience were elected that year, as Table 1-4 shows. The return rate was double in 1968 what it had been in the strikingly unusual 1958 election—the first of the Fifth Republic. The basic difference between the 1968 election and those of 1951, 1956, 1962, and 1967 was that nearly all the new members of the Assembly in 1968 belonged to the same *tendance*—a fact which made the change in personnel seem more unusual than it actually was. A random sample of this Assembly would normally produce the same percentage of legislative veterans that one would expect to find in most Assemblies of modern France. Generalizations about French politics based on this sample would therefore not be biased by an excessive number of inexperienced legislators. This fact produced the final argument for studying the 1968 Assembly. (And as it turned out, seventy percent of those interviewed had served previously in the Assembly—nearly the same percentage as that for all Deputies.)

Table 1-4
Turnover in the National Assembly: The Rate of Return Among Deputies Since 1951

Election Year	Percent of Deputies Elected Who Had Previously Served in the National Assembly	Election Year	Percent of Deputies Elected Who Had Previously Served in the National Assembly
1951	64.5%[a]	1962	64.1%[c]
1956	70.4%[a]	1967	71.3%[d]
1958	35.1%[b]	1968	77.4%[e]

[a]Calculated from data in Mattei Dogan, "Les candidats et les élus," in Maurice Duverger, François Goguel, and Jean Touchard, eds., Les élections de 2 janvier 1956 (Paris: Librairie Armand Colin, 1957), pp. 425-67. Relevant data on pp. 446-47.

[b]Calculated from data in Mattei Dogan, "Changement de régime et changement de personnel," in Association française de science politique, Le référendum de septembre et les élections de novembre 1958 (Paris: Librairie Armand Colin, 1960), pp. 241-79. Relevant data on pp. 261-63.

[c]Calculated from data in Mattei Dogan, "Note sur le nouveau personnel parlementaire," in François Goguel, ed., Le référendum d'octobre et les élections de novembre 1962 (Paris: Librairie Armand Colin, 1965), pp. 429-32. Relevant data on p. 429.

[d]Calculated from election statistics in L'Année politique, 1967, pp. 400-430. See also footnote e, this page.

[e]Calculated from election statistics in L'Année politique, 1968, pp. 395-425. This figure and the figure for 1967 exaggerate somewhat (by at most five percent) the actual percent of sitting Deputies during the third and fourth legislatures of the Fifth Republic who had had prior service in the National Assembly. This exaggeration results from the fact that twenty-five to thirty of those Deputies who were elected in 1967 and in 1968 and who had had prior Assembly experience assumed Ministerial positions soon after these elections and therefore were required by law to resign from their seats in the legislature. These seats were then taken by their suppléants (alternates). The great majority of these suppléants had not had prior legislative experience. The small numbers involved here do not alter the fact that 1958 is the unusual electoral year and that slightly more Deputies than normal were returned to the Assembly in 1968.

Having decided on what group to study, I then drew a random sample of 100 of the 470 members of the Assembly representing the ninety-five départements of metropolitan France.[28] Unfortunately, I was able to interview only fifty of these Deputies. My time schedule was greatly disrupted by de Gaulle's unexpected Referendum of April, 1969, and the subsequent Presidential election after his defeat and resignation. I had planned to conduct most of the interviews during the normally slow spring session of the National Assembly. Those months, however, became a time of constant political campaigning. Deputies were suddenly very difficult to reach. Only after persistent prodding and travel around France was I able to track down and talk with half the members of my sample. Since I was obliged to leave France soon after Pompidou's election in June, 1969, I considered myself fortunate to depart with fifty complete interviews.[29]

Both the original sample of 100, and the group of fifty interviewed Deputies, appear fairly representative of the 1968 Assembly, as Table 1-5 shows. In both the sample and the group of those interviewed, Gaullists are somewhat underrepresented and Communists somewhat overrepresented. This fact may be seen as a positive advantage. The proportion of Gaullists and Communists among those actually interviewed gives a more realistic reflection of their strength in the nation than a perfectly representative sample of the 1968 Assembly could have done.

The fifty interviews represent only half the original random sample. This poor completion rate means that in a statistical sense no valid generalizations can be made about the entire population (the National Assembly). Still, lengthy in-depth interviews were obtained with fifty Deputies and with numerous other French political leaders. The Deputies do appear representative of the upper political stratum in France, and they did provide a great deal of information about their political attitudes, motives, and behavior. Conclusions derived from this research rest on a solid empirical foundation.

Table 1-5

Representativeness of the Sample: Party Distribution Among All Deputies, Deputies in Sample, and Deputies Interviewed

Legislative Party Group[a]	Number and % of all Deputies from Metropolitan France in Group[b]	Number and % of all Sample Deputies in Group	Number and % of all Interviewed Deputies in Group
Non-Ins.	9 (1.9%)	3 (3%)	1 (2%)
RI app	3 (0.6%)	2 (2%)	1 (2%)
RI	58 (12.3%)	14 (14%)	9 (18%)
UDR app	20 (4.3%)	5 (5%)	3 (6%)
UDR	259 (55.1%)	47 (47%)	22 (44%)
PDM app	3 (0.6%)	0 (0%)	0 (0%)
PDM	28 (6.0%)	6 (6%)	3 (6%)
FGDS	57 (12.1%)	12 (12%)	5 (12%)
PC	33 (7.0%)	11 (11%)	6 (12%)
TOTAL	470 (99.9%)[c]	100 (100%)	50 (100%)

aFor explanation of abbreviations, see List of Abbreviations. Note that Deputies are shown as belonging to the legislative party group of which they were a member when interviewed. Some reshuffling has taken place since that time, and two of the above groups (FGDS and PDM) are now defunct.

bThese membership figures reflect party distribution in the Assembly during the month of May, 1969. They are taken from the *Liste des Députés, Mai 1969*, a pamphlet distributed by the administrative services of the National Assembly.

cDoes not add to 100% because of rounding.

The Key Finding: The Distribution
of Incentives Among French Deputies

It is now possible to show how incentive analysis and the findings in France bear directly on the original questions which stimulated this research. The research began in an effort to shed light on a long-standing argument in French politics: are French politicians ideologues or opportunists? It is now evident that a way to clarify this question is to frame it in incentive terms. The argument can be seen as a debate over the dominant incentive among French politicians. Those who support the ideological thesis would see these men as mission participants. Those who support the struggle-for-position thesis would see them as status participants.

By recasting the argument in this form, one can bring empirical evidence to bear on it. It becomes a question of learning what incentives actually exist among French politicians. My research was designed toward that end. Focusing on one particular set of politicians at one point in time, it was designed to uncover the distribution of incentives in that group. And since that group happens to be the national legislature, findings about it would presumably cast light on some other aspects of French politics.

The most significant findings, then, will bear on the distribution of incentives in the group. Are its members mostly mission or mostly status participants? The findings suggest that neither thesis is accurate; yet they also show why both theses could be advanced with conviction by intelligent men. Both mission *and* status particpants appear to be numerous in the National Assembly. Furthermore, program participants are also numerous there, along with a few obligation participants. These basic findings are summarized in Table 1-6 (see also Tables 3-1, 4-1, 5-1, 6-1, and 10-1). Although mission participants are most numerous among the respondents, they compose only thirty-eight percent of those interviewed. Program participants make up twenty-eight percent of those interviewed, status participants twenty percent, and obligation participants fourteen percent. It is clear that no particular incentive predominates among this group of French political leaders.

If these findings show anything, they suggest that politics in the Assembly, and in France as a whole, may be a good deal more complex than the proponents of these theses believe. These authors appear to have focused on a fraction of French political life and taken the part for the whole. The fact that mission participants do apparently exist in large numbers in France by no means indicates that all French politicians are "ideologues." In fact, it no longer seems possible to accept an interpretation of French politics in which political leaders are all assumed to be motivated in the same way. My findings suggest that the real complexity of French politics derives—in part, at least—from the intricate ways in which the four incentive types interact with, and conflict with, each other in the pursuit of their goals.

Table 1-6
Distribution of Incentive Types Among French Deputies

Incentive	Number of Deputies	% of Respondents	Legislative Party Group[a]	
Mission	19	38%	PC	6
			PDM	1
			UDR	9
			RI	2
			Non-Inscrit	1
Program	14	28%	FGDS	3
			UDR	4
			UDR app	1
			RI	6
Status	10	20%	FGDS	2
			PDM	2
			UDR	5
			UDR app	1
Obligation	7	14%	UDR	4
			UDR app	1
			RI	1
			RI app	1
TOTAL	50	100%		

[a]For explanation of abbreviations, see List of Abbreviations.

2 Portrait of Four Deputies

There was no "typical" interview with my respondents. I never knew what to expect as I entered each Deputy's office. Nevertheless, certain patterns did appear during these discussions. Deputies differed from each other in their central focus of interest, the basic concerns which held their attention during the interview. The following chapters portray these incentive differences in a systematic fashion. My aim in this chapter is to present a full picture of four individual Deputies who best represent the incentive types observed in France.

What follows are large portions of the interviews I conducted with four Deputies. Abstractions are often difficult to grasp without concrete examples. By giving an example of each incentive type, I hope to give some reality to the theoretical terms. I also hope to convey here some of the flavor and variety of modern French politics.

Each interview could not be presented in its entirety. Material judged extraneous or repetitive has been deleted. My aim is to present a clear and full picture of each incentive type.

Michel Dupont, a Mission Participant

Monsieur le député Michel Dupont is a long-time member of the Communist Party. A big, heavyset man, he looks like the dock-worker he had been in his youth. He appears gruff on the surface but is actually an extremely cordial man. I had no trouble getting an appointment to see M. Dupont. The interview took place in a dreary, drafty old building in the poor, ugly, industrial Northern city which M. Dupont represents.

M. Dupont had been a Communist Deputy for over twenty years. Because of his long experience, I decided to change the usual introductory questions and begin with his legislative orientations. I was also eager to avoid a beginning question about how he had entered politics, since other Communist Deputies had seized on this opening query to affirm their dedication to Communism as the motivating factor behind their entry into politics. Such replies might simply reflect the party line rather than an underlying motivation. The different interview opening, however, produced similar results with M. Dupont. His answers to the first questions clearly focus on dedication to a political movement and the ideological rationale for adherence to this movement—the identifying characteristic of the mission participant.

Q: You've been a Deputy for many years, so I'd like to ask you first, what in your opinion is the role of the Deputy in France today?

Dupont: When you say the "role of the Deputy," that means only one thing to me: the role of the *Communist* Deputy. Now this role has several aspects. First the Deputy is the representative of the most advanced faction of the working class. Thus, his job is to use the Assembly as a tribune where our ideas, the voice of our movement, can be heard by all. In this, he should use the press, television, and other means of communication to get the widest possible publicity for our cause.

Second, our position in the Assembly allows us to propose legislation which illustrates the main aspects of our political position. We can draft in legislative form the fundamental reforms which we would institute if we were in power. Of course, there's no hope that they will be accepted now, but at least we can prepare these proposals and let people know what we would do in the future.

Third, we must concern ourselves with the defense of the most immediate demands of the workers. For example, we long proposed that workers be given a fifth week of paid vacation a year. Some of our proposals have even been accepted by the Assembly, such as this one was.

Fourth, as Deputies we are able to put formal questions to the Government. These questions can be either written or oral. In these questions we can present the collective, national demands of our movement.

Fifth, there is our role in the major debates on the budget. These debates give us the opportunity to show our total opposition to the present Government and to state the major lines of our own position.

In our work we are always in contact with various groups and organizations—especially those which represent the workers, such as the unions. We get suggestions from them and then try to implement them. For instance, we've been working with some members of the national chemical industry, and they have helped us devise our plan for nationalization of that sector of the economy. In the same way we have worked with bank-workers' unions to develop our project of nationalizing all the country's banks.

Q: Do you feel that your efforts have some effect? Would you say you have some influence on the Government's policies?

Dupont: Yes! I think we are having more and more influence. Some of our proposals have actually been adopted. We are not, of course, effective on the main lines of our policy proposals, but we have an effective influence on secondary matters.

We cannot, however, modify the basic political stance of the Government. There we can only be critical—and our base in the legislature allows us to be very hard critics. But some of our good ideas have been taken up by the Government. The Government has picked up our ideas on modifying some of the tax laws. But when it feels that some of our proposals are important, it has its own legislative supporters write the law so they can get credit for it.

Q: Do you vote for those laws which originated from your group but were actually proposed by the Gaullists?

Dupont: Yes, we'll vote for them. We vote for any good proposal. We don't practice a systematic opposition. For instance, we voted for the amnesty laws [which pardoned political opponents of the Government's Algerian policy]. We abstained on the 1968 orientation-law concerning reform of national education. We thought some of its proposals were good, but we disagreed with others. But to show you how we can be quite effective, let me give you an example. We fought the introduction of the value-added tax. We fought it violently. We were against it long before the small businessmen [who had lately been agitating against this tax]. They didn't fight this tax at first, but look at them now! And during the 1969 Presidential campaign Pompidou took our position in this tax. [A gross exaggeration.] So this shows our effectiveness. We've helped to bring public opinion around to our point of view. The businessmen at first didn't realize what this law would do to them. We saw it from the beginning. Now there is a great movement against the value-added tax, which we opposed from the start. *We* did not vote for this law, and we have helped people to see its pernicious effects. It shows we are there for something.

You have to understand us in terms of the overall impact of our action. When our adversaries end up by taking our position, then you know we have a real influence. You mustn't look merely at what happens on the day of a debate or a vote. Our influence goes well beyond that.

[It is worth noting here that Dupont's reference to specific policies is not indicative of a program incentive. He refers to particular policies only in the context of his broader theme—the important political and social influence of his party. These policies interest him primarily because they illustrate the strength of his movement. He lacks the program participant's deep interest in policy problems per se. Although he refers briefly to this law or that party position, he never delves deeply into the subject matter of a desired policy, telling exactly how it would work or what its real effects would be. Compare his shallow policy references to those of the program Deputy in this chapter (Jean-Claude Schweitzer) discussing regional development policy in elaborate detail.]

Q: It's often claimed that the Government tries to keep opposition Deputies from getting the funds they want for their districts . . .?

Dupont: Yes, it's true; they do try to block our efforts. But their attempts are counteracted by our constant battle against them. The power of our impact overcomes their effort to stop us. We keep on acting, we keep on following up our dossiers, we keep applying pressure on the administrators and never give up. So the attempts to work against us are overcome by the power of our actions.

Q: I'd like to change topics now and ask you a few personal questions. For instance, could you tell me how you first became interested in politics?

Dupont: Yes, yes, I can tell you about that. It goes back a long way. At the age of seventeen or eighteen I was a rebel. I revolted against our bourgeois society and all the evil of that system. My revolt took final shape when I joined the Communist Party at the age of nineteen in 1934.

As a youth I worked at a variety of jobs. I started working at the age of fifteen and kicked around quite a bit. For a while I was errand-boy for an insurance company, but when the boss found out I'd joined the Communist Party he kicked me out. I did all kinds of things. I was a mechanic, a dock worker, even a civil servant. But I was fired from that job after taking part in a strike in 1938. When the War came I spent the whole time working for the Party in the Underground. My job was to gather and deliver arms for the Resistance. The Germans captured me once, but I escaped. I spent the entire War period in this underground work. By the end of the War I had become head of [a regional Communist military organization]. Then in 1946 the Party asked me to run for the Assembly, and I've been serving as Deputy since that time.

Q: Would you say that you have retained your original ideas about society and the Communist Party during this whole period?

Dupont: Yes, definitely! You have to understand that I am a *militant.* I'm a fighter. I have found that the workers' movement does some good and some bad things, but still it's *my* life, it's *my* movement. Our theory is good, although sometimes it's badly applied. On the whole, I've found that it's harder to put into practice than I had originally thought. You have to rely on men, and men don't always live up to your expectations.

Things haven't always been done right. We've condemned the USSR for its bad policies—especially, for its Stalinist period. [Again, quite an exaggeration.] But our *theory* remains good. I've just realized how much harder it is to apply than I had once thought. The relations among men are conditioned by the form of society, by the existing forms of exploitation. But men can't change overnight, even when the existing social forms are changed. It takes longer to change men.

When you are twenty years old, you create illustions for yourself. You think you will alter men from one day to the next. You think you can pass from one system to another overnight. But it's hard to change the consciousness of human beings. Men remain the same, with their defects and their dispositions. You can only change them slowly. I didn't know that when I was twenty.

Since then I've seen that it's a hard, difficult task before us. It's utopic to think that you upset a world just like that. The previous civilization took centuries to arrive at some kind of equilibrium. You had the wars of religion, the period of colonization, the imperialist wars, mass exploitation of the workers. A world is not created without much pain. But we will create our socialist society with much less agony.

When you see what bourgeois society has done over the past two centuries, the pain and suffering it has inflicted on the world, you can't make any comparison between its faults and those of the USSR. The accusations of the capitalist nations against Russia remind me of the La Fontaine fable, in which the animals gather to learn who committed the sin that brought on the plague. All the strongest animals who have committed the grossest crimes absolve themselves, but they put to death the poor donkey who merely ate a little of the farmer's grass. The Soviet Union is the relatively innocent donkey confronted by the rapacious but accusing capitalist nations. When you see the horrors wrought by centuries of Christian civilization and bourgeois society, it's difficult to see how they can accuse anyone else of any crimes at all.

Think, for instance, of the French with their seven years of colonial warfare in Indochina and their years of imperialist rule in Algeria, or the United States in Vietnam, the Dominican Republic, Latin America. The French alone killed thousands of Arabs, many, many more than the number of Czechs killed by Russians. [Dupont expands quite a bit on this theme, then concludes:] Yes, we condemn the USSR for Czechoslovakia, for its Stalinist failures. As Talleyrand said, "It is worse than a crime—it is a blunder." But let us not close our eyes to all the evil that other countries have done, and let us not forget that this evil is due directly to the capitalist systems they have developed.

[Dupont is unusual among mission participants in admitting at least some slight faults in his movement and evincing some doubts about the likelihood of that movement's imminent success. His many decades in the Party appear to have induced a certain degree of realism about the political world. Nevertheless, his total dedication to the Communist Party cannot be doubted, nor his view of it as the best imaginable force for transforming a corrupt society. It is also clear that, like other mission participants, Dupont unquestioningly believes in the ultimate triumph of his movement. For him the time span for this victory is simply a little longer than it is for others.]

Q: In closing, I would like to ask you a question about your personal satisfactions in politics. I know it's a difficult life and it takes up a great deal of one's time. Why have you decided to spend so much of your life in the political world? What personal satisfactions have you found in politics?

Dupont: By vocation I'm a militant. You have to understand what kind of man I am. I educated myself through my own reading. I live very simply; three-quarters of my pay goes to the party. My wife and I live just like the workers. She is a seamstress and works hard at it. In the summer we go camping. We militants have the little personal joys that all men share. We're ordinary human beings: we like to laugh, to joke, to look at a pretty woman, to eat a good meal.

But—and this is crucial—I cannot conceive of life without this *struggle*. I believe that this society with its private forms is outmoded. This private exploitation of the underprivileged can no longer be tolerated. I must struggle to create the conditions for changing that society. It may take a long time, but my children may see this new society, if I don't. So I continue my struggle to change the world. And one of the most passion-filled aspects of this struggle is my day-to-day work for the interests of the common man in my district.

Q: You have talked about this change to a socialist society. Do you feel that this change can take place under peaceful conditions?

Dupont: Yes, I believe it can. Now it's not true that everywhere there can be a peaceful transition to socialism. In Latin America, for instance, I very much fear that the heavy weight of U.S. imperialism will inevitably lead to violent transformations. But in the highly industrialized nations, there can be a peaceful passage to the new society. Still, this can only come about with the development by the working masses of the consciousness of their condition. Our movement plays a crucial role in this development. Our active presence, our combined actions, will weigh heavily in assuring a final, successful outcome. The whole force of our movement will help create the conditions for the eventual passage to socialism.

Q: How would you describe your personal relations with members of the other political groups at the Assembly?

Dupont: All of us in the Communist Party have relations with the other Deputies which can be called *courteous*. Beyond that, these relations vary according to the nature of the men involved. They will differ depending on whether the man is more or less open as a person. I myself am very open. I have no trouble at all getting along with the other members.

Q: How are your relations with the Socialists?

Dupont: That depends on the period and the political circumstances. Our relations *now* with the Socialists are very bad. We aren't getting along very well at the present. . . .

[As Dupont shows here, he is one of the more open Communist Deputies. None of the other five I talked with stressed the ease with which they got along with members of other parties. In fact, they specifically mentioned that it was *not* easy to get along with them. Even Dupont shows in his final remarks about Socialists that political differences do influence his personal rapport with other Deputies. Like most mission participants, he lets his political commitments color (at least to some extent) his personal relations with others.

The hour-long interview ended at this point. A telephone call interrupted Dupont's comments about the Socialists, and he indicated that our conversation would have to terminate. We shook hands cordially, and I left.]

Jean-Claude Schweitzer,
a Program Participant

M. Schweitzer appears at first sight as the embodiment of the *député moyen*. A voluble, hearty man, he could easily pass for the cartoonist's caricature of the backslapping, slightly stupid, provincial Deputy. A few minutes talk with M. Schweitzer, however, reveals an intelligence and a lively interest in the world around him one would not at first suspect.

M. Schweitzer lives in one of the poor, remote, but beautiful border regions of France. A Gaullist, he represents a varied group of constituents. His district comprises part of a large city, several small towns, and a good deal of sparsely-inhabited rural area. M. Schweitzer himself lives in one of the small towns. The interview took place in his provincial office, which is a renovated former garage sitting behind his middle-class home on a quiet side street.

My conversation with M. Schweitzer could have begun no other way than by a program-oriented question. In the opening pleasantries I had mentioned the fact that I had never before seen his part of France. He seized this opportunity to enlighten me about some of the characteristics of his region. Before I could even broach a first question, he had already told me much about "the hard-working character" of the local citizenry, the "poor quality of the soil," the type of products manufactured in the area, some regional history, etc.

M. Schweitzer's obvious interest in these matters led me naturally to begin the interview with a question about local problems. Throughout the long conversation which followed, his focus rarely strayed from regional problems and the policies which might alleviate those problems.

> *Q:* You've already given me some understanding of your district. I wonder if you could tell me what are some of the main problems you find here?
>
> *Schweitzer:* Well, our principal problem in relation to the rest of the country is that we are *far* from the rest of the country. We are far from the major centers of consumption and industry, and this area consequently gets neglected. What we need is large-scale development of this region. We need to create jobs, stimulate industrial enterprises, so that we can keep our young people here instead of watching them go elsewhere to find work. We have a host of young people here we need to help. In fact, [jokingly] if you know an American company that's looking for a nice place to settle, why not tell them to come here?
>
> *Q:* What can you as a Deputy do to encourage this regional development?
>
> *Schweitzer:* There are several directions in which one can work. For instance, I've worked to get our cities to create industrial zones. When they do this, they can get state subsidies to help attract industries. I helped get a small one of five hectares built here in my town. At X [nearby large city] they have one of twenty hectares. You can't build these zones everywhere, unfortunately, because it's too expensive. But we have to do it where we can, so that we can tempt industries to come into this area. The only way we can get our youth to stay here is to provide jobs for them.

There are other things that can be done. The State gives subsidies to help localities buy land for these industrial zones. I've helped some of our towns get this money.

Then there are state awards to businessmen for training, or retraining, their working force. These awards help the businessman to adapt to new conditions and to train local workers. This means that a businessman relocating here can move in with a minimum of expense incurred by this change. Then the State has helped us set up public technical schools so that we can train young people for work in modern industries. I try to help people become aware of these various ways to modernize the region and encourage them to make use of these opportunities.

The hardest part of all is probably changing people's opinions, and it's here that I make the greatest effort. The people here need to learn about modern business methods, they should want to learn the new technical skills. They are fully capable of hard work, and they do work hard. But they must learn to change the way they work in order to keep up with the rest of the country.

One of our biggest problems is the poor transportation system here. We need a better transportation network to tie us in with the rest of France, with the major centers of consumption. There just aren't enough highways, not enough trains. If you want to go to Paris, for instance, it takes over four hours, when you should be able to do it in two or two and a half. It takes much too long to send trucks carrying our goods into Switzerland or up to Holland. We just aren't connected in a satisfactory way with either the national or the European markets.

All of these problems are linked. We aren't an industrial area, so we don't have good roads to tie in with the rest of the country. And because we don't have good roads, we can't attract new industries and even those products we do make or grow can't be transported efficiently to broader markets. This means that there's much that has to be done, there are many fronts on which one has to work.

We are basically an agricultural area. But unfortunately, because of former land laws and customs farm property here is divided into small individual plots, which can't be worked efficiently. We can't use the big tractors and farm machinery because we have too many peasants working small pieces of land. We need to encourage *remembrements* [property mergers] as quickly as possible. By encouraging farmers to merge their lands, we will produce more efficient and more prosperous farms. But of course in doing this, we open new problems. We have to find homes to settle the old farmers who can no longer make a go of it. And we especially have to find jobs for the many young people who will no longer be needed on the big, new farmlands. And this brings us back to our attempts to lure new industries into the area so as to keep the young people here.

Q: You've said that changing people's attitudes was one of the most difficult aspects of modernization. Would you say these attitudes have been changing recently?

Schweitzer: This is a real difficulty, but yes, I would say that attitudes have started to change—especially since the war. People have started demanding new factories in their towns. They are realizing that they have to become part of the modern world. For instance, they have started school-bus pick-ups around here. School-busses make regular rounds every day picking up students from the rural areas and bringing them into the schools of our towns and cities. This is important, since it allows peasant children to go to good schools and get a decent education which their parents never had.

Q: Would you say you are succeeding in your efforts to build up the area?

Schweitzer: We are making a start, but we have a long way to go. We need more industrial zones, better schools, new highways, more vocational training centers. And the state isn't doing enough yet to help us. So our problems are far from solved. We have to keep on fighting.

One of our biggest problems is all the old people in the area. They've worked on their farms all their lives and have remained poor. They work on the land every day and life is miserable for them. Now their sons see how much trouble their fathers have had, and they refuse to put up with it. Many will leave the farms, and those that stay demand bigger farms so that they can make a decent living. Here's where it's important to encourage property mergers.

[M. Schweitzer went on at this point to explain just how small most local farms are, the kind of crops in the region, and their value on the national market. Finally, I was able to shift the topic of conversation to other matters.]

Q: Could I change subjects now and ask how you first came to be involved in politics?

Schweitzer: Yes. First of all, I have to explain that a Deputy must be known. This depends to some extent on the electoral system. [Here he explains carefully past and present voting systems in France.] In general, then, the Deputy represents 100,000 people and they like to know *who* they are voting for. This is especially true in provincial areas. In Paris, it's different. There people just vote Communist or Gaullist without knowing the man they're voting for. But here, in this area you have to be known.

Now politics is not my vocation. I had a local factory here, specializing in the manufacture of pharmaceutical products, and I had 100 men working under me. Now the people here, if they find a man who, in their view, has some merit, they like to put him on the town council. The Mayor of this town asked me to be on his list of candidates running for the council. We won, and I eventually became his *adjoint* [first assistant].

[At this point M. Schweitzer begins a long digression explaining to me how the administrative system of France operates, the different political-administrative divisions, relations between the local governments, the national administration, regional and departmental units. The purpose here was apparently to give me an understanding of how his local position related to the national system of government and how the country in general was administered. M. Schweitzer finally returns to the subject of my question:]

In 1962 the Deputy from this area had voted several times against de Gaulle, and this region is solidly Gaullist. So he lost many supporters and had little chance for reelection. The Gaullist who was running against him in the legislative election was looking around for a *suppléant* [alternate]. People said to him, "Why not choose M. Schweitzer?" So he turned to me. I had no idea at the time that I would become Deputy. [Schweitzer became Deputy when, four years later, this man, elected to the Assembly in 1962, accepted a ministerial position. The Minister later ran for the Assembly in another district, leaving Schweitzer in full control of this one.]

Q: Why did you enter politics as a Gaullist?

Schweitzer: Basically, I wanted to see France governed by men who were really capable. De Gaulle got us out of the Algerian War, he represents us well abroad, he has helped the people of France progress on the human level and national levels. But still, there have been some stupidities done under his régime. It's hard to govern any country.

Q: Are you close to the people? Are you well known here?

Schweitzer: Yes. I receive everyone constantly. I go about everywhere in the district. I go into homes, factories. These people never saw their Deputy before until I came along. When I was young, I remember our teacher telling us something I've never forgotten:

"Attention to details is the currency of success." This is something I always try to remember when dealing with people. I go out and see them, I greet them on the street, I talk with them and listen to their problems. People like this attention. They are open with me, and they remain faithful to me.

Q: Does one have to be in the present majority to get Government aid for one's district, as it sometimes claimed?

Schweitzer: I'll tell you what *we* say, we in the majority. When one is in the opposition, he gets *more* money for his district, more attention from the Government. *Our* voters are already supporting the Government and don't have to be wooed. [This is said half-joking.]

But on the whole, if a mayor or Deputy works hard, if dossiers are prepared well and sent to the proper agencies, if a good case can be made showing the need for money, it is approved, regardless of political factors. It used to be somewhat true perhaps in the past—you used to have to be in with the Government to get project funds. But that situation has been greatly altered since the war. People are more aware now of our social and economic problems and the need to combat them. The Mayors have to go ahead and ask the Deputy to help them, and I *will* help them, even when I know the Mayor is not of my political persuasion.

Often the Mayors have only themselves to blame for their inability to attract Government funds. They bring failure on themselves by not doing their job, by not working hard, by not preparing solid dossiers, by not coming to see the Deputy for help, *regardless of his political affiliation*.

[I next asked Schweitzer about his personal relations with the Minister for whom he had once been a *suppléant*. After expressing his generally favorable personal attitude. toward this man, he went on:]

Schweitzer: It does help to know a Minister. You can tell him things and know they will be heard by people who make decisions. For instance, just yesterday I wrote a letter to [the Minister] because I was annoyed that this *département* was not classified as a major milk-producing *département* [*département à vocation laitière*]. I was totally in disagreement with this decision. After all, our *département* is one of the leaders in total production of milk in France, so our omission from the list is absurd. I told [the Minister] to talk about this to his colleagues and tell them that, by any objective standards, the classification is a poor one. They should do something to change it. So you see, if you know a Minister, you can tell him things directly that may get quicker results than going through other channels.

Q: What do you have to do to be considered a good Deputy?

Schweitzer: You must be constantly present at the Assembly and you must *work*. You have to go to *all* meetings of your legislative committees. [Here he names all six standing committees, briefly tells what subject matter they cover, and tells which committee he himself belongs to.] Each Deputy is a member of one committee, and you have to work for it. You must not be afraid of asking to prepare a *rapport* on some subject which the committee is studying. This shows you are a hard-working and interested Deputy.

You must get along with others—and not merely those of your own group.

You should especially develop warm relations with those in your own committee. Within the committee you should minimize your political differences, listen to what each member has to say and evaluate his ideas, not his political position. In voting, of course, you often have political divisions, but I would prefer otherwise; I would prefer that each individual vote as he believes best. I don't really like the voting discipline imposed on us [by his own party, the UDR]. But on the other hand, this device does allow us to cover a lot of ground and get some things done. And if a particular bill turns out not to be perfect, we can always take up the matter again in the next session.

Q: Do you accept all the institutions of the Fifth Republic?

Schweitzer: No, not all. They are not all good. But on the whole they are excellent. I think they were over-influenced by de Gaulle's enormous stature. He was such an imposing figure that most Ministers didn't have the strength to stand up to him. They simply tried to please him instead. The Ministers were so happy to be favored by de Gaulle—by his appointing them to the Cabinet, receiving them occasionally—that they didn't want to bother him when things were going wrong. De Gaulle just wasn't told enough important *details* about policies. Only Debré, Giscard d'Estaing, Pompidou dared to do this. The other Ministers accepted things de Gaulle wanted without discussing them with him, then they made us all accept laws which we were often against. When we complained to the Ministers, they told us we had to accept them because they couldn't bother de Gaulle with these matters.

Something has changed now. There will be a modification and an improvement with Pompidou. It won't be easy for the President just to demand that something be done, without thorough consultation with Ministers and Deputies. De Gaulle was like a father; he had done so much for our country, for us, that it was hard to refuse him anything. We found it painful to be opposed to him. He was a great man, certainly. But now relations between the legislature and the Government will be more normal, there will be more flexibility.

[Schweitzer's answers to these last two questions show a thoughtful appraisal of existing institutions and a realistic evaluation of his party's leader. He is content to work within existing structures, although he has some criticisms to offer. His remarks about de Gaulle show neither the hero worship of the mission participant nor the scornful denigration of the status participant.]

Q: I'd like to close by asking you a general question about your personal view of politics. What are the basic satisfactions you gain from your political activity?

Schweitzer: I find it encouraging that I'm able to do some useful work for my district and its inhabitants. It's not worthwhile to be in politics simply to serve yourself. I lost everything when I decided to get into politics. I'm no longer in business, I've spent a lot of money. I thought about this a long time before I got into politics, but I do enjoy serving others and I'm encouraged to continue by what I've been able to accomplish so far.

Q: So you plan to remain in politics?

Schweitzer: You know, once you've gotten your teeth into it, it's hard to stop. You become *engagé*, committed to the fine people who have placed their confidence in you. In industry I might have had a better income, but that's not the kind of work I want.

Q: Have you had any disagreeable experiences in politics?

Schweitzer: I try to serve wholeheartedly, with real pleasure. I can't stand people who think only of themselves, who are ready to crush you if they get a chance, who work against you just to get somewhere. I find it disagreeable to have to work with such people.

Then there are the administrative encroachments on our local life. The national bureaucracy is trying to take over everything. We have to decolonize our local government. The admininistrators are supposed to provide services to the people, but they often do so in a cold, bureaucratic fashion and they often make people's lives more complicated. For instance, take the matter of the construction permit. [Gives long example of a local man who could not get permission to build a local apartment house because he had violated some minor regulation.] These petty administrative rules keep people from constructing useful and needed buildings.

[Schweitzer develops this theme of the civil servants' lack of contact with real problems of French citizens. To illustrate his point, he tells a long story about a local man who wanted to develop a large farm on some unused land which had recently come into possession of the national government. Although the man was highly qualified and ready to buy the land and put it to use, and although the Government had no plans for it, the individual was unable to obtain the rights to this property. He went from office to office, unable to find anyone who would make a decision on the case. Consequently, the land remains unused and the enterprising individual has left the area. For Schweitzer, this example illustrates the dangers of excessive bureaucracy whose spirit cramps private initiative.]

Q: How did you first get interested in politics? Was anyone in your family actively involved?

Schweitzer: I became interested in politics as a young man. My family was never in politics; I'm the first one. They did speak about politics at home, but that's all. I first became interested during the Popular Front days. I felt the need to make people equal, but I wanted to help raise them to the economic level of our businessmen, not pull everyone else down to the level of the poor. I agreed with the basic goals of the Popular Front; I wanted to help people improve their lives and I thought our business leaders showed too little social concern, but I disagreed with the tactics of street demonstrations, riots, and all that.

Then in 1938 I went to Germany and I was frightened by what I saw—an aggressiveness, an incredible driving spirit of work, while back in France people lazily played *belote* and talked village politics. Our country was sleeping! We absolutely must avoid this again in the future. What a war we went through! This must never be allowed to happen again.

[Throughout the interview M. Schweitzer tried to answer my questions in a way which would help me with my research. This orientation appeared clearly at the end of the interview. He talked freely with me on several new topics after I indicated that he had obligingly covered the subjects of major interest to me. We parted only after he remembered a luncheon appointment for which he was already thirty minutes late.]

Xavier Laurent, an Obligation Participant

Xavier Laurent had less experience in politics than almost any Deputy in my sample. A well-known writer and journalist, he was recruited by the Gaullists out of the blue to run for the Assembly in 1967. His name—well-known in his rural district—plus the Gaullist label brought him an electoral victory and re-election in 1968. Never active in politics before 1966, M. Laurent found himself a national legislator a few months later. Yet he has found few rewards in that position and, as his interview indicates, might have retired after one term had it not been for the May Events of 1968.

The interview took place at the National Assembly. M. Laurent replied calmly but without great interest to my questions. He appeared to regard the entire conversation only as a task it was incumbent upon him to perform. Nevertheless, he did reply dutifully to all my questions, and the entire interview lasted nearly an hour and a half.

Q: I know that you were elected for the first time in 1967. Were you active in politics before then?
Laurent: No, not at all.

Q: How did you come to be a candidate that year?
Laurent: I come from the X area. I lived there when I was young, I finished my studies there. Then I left and came to Paris, did various things, and finally started writing. Since I've written about my region, I've become fairly well known there, and besides I've kept up contact with many of my childhood friends. It was they who got in touch with me about becoming a candidate.

It happened in 1966 when preparations were being made for the 1967 legislative elections. There were some problems in the district where I had grown up. It appeared that the difficulty centered on the personality of the Gaullist Deputy, the incumbent, who was running for re-election. He apparently was beginning to show some hostility to Gaullism, beginning to move away from the party. The local activists were unhappy with this candidate and intended to campaign against him. The UDR leaders hoped to bring him back into the fold, but he remained adamantly rebellious. He wouldn't go along with the movement. My old friends knew that I was favorable to the Government, and they came to see me, asking me to run against the incumbent Deputy as the Gaullist candidate.

Q: Were there other candidates trying to obtain the UDR label?
Laurent: Yes. There were other candidates. A number of them were available.

Q: Were you favored by the leaders in Paris?
Laurent: The Paris leaders were at first hostile toward me.

Q: Then how did you become the candidate?

Laurent: The incumbent Deputy was very well entrenched. No one thought he could be beaten. He was the Mayor of Q [a big city] and a well-known lawyer. Everyone was sure he could not be beaten.

[Laurent here does not really reply to this question. Throughout the interview he showed little interest in questions about *political* situations, shows little sophistication in discussing them, and has to be prompted frequently before he bothers to discuss them at all.]

Q: What was your reaction when your friends asked you to run for the Assembly?

Laurent: I burst out laughing. I was on vacation, during the summer of 1966. I had gone to my home town, and my friends had come over to see me. It seemed impossible to me that I could be nominated by the Gaullists. "There are many political leaders who want this nomination," I told them. "I couldn't possibly obtain it." But they insisted, so I told them: "Come and see me when I have the nomination, and I'll give you an answer then."

After my vacation I returned to Paris and forgot all about this business. But it turned out that my friends had started writing letters and talking to many people. [He mentions various Gaullist leaders who had been contacted by his friends.] Then people in Paris started asking to see me, party leaders came around to talk to me, to size me up. I told them I wasn't very interested in politics, and I didn't want to run for office. Finally, Monsieur X [a high-ranking Gaullist leader] came to see me. I already knew him fairly well through social contacts. Well, Monsieur X asked me: "Do you think things have been getting better in France for the past eight or nine years?" Naturally, I said, "Yes." Then he asked: "Have things been getting better for you personally since 1958?" I said again, "Yes." Then he said, "Well, up to now you have been getting all of the benefits of our action. Now it's time to take on some of the responsibilities." I said, "Ah, I hadn't thought of it like that. But now that you put it that way...." I agreed to run. I really had no choice.

Q: Why were people so anxious to have you as candidate?

Laurent: I was generally well-known in the region. My writings had earned me some publicity. Also, I had a good knowledge of some of the problems of the area, having worked in real estate for several years when I was younger.

Q: Were you interested in politics before 1966?

Laurent: Never. Oh, I talked a bit about politics. I had certain political ideas. But I had nothing whatsoever to do with politics, nothing at all. It's true that in some conversations I had defended the Government's policies; occasionally at a dinner or a *soirée* I would express my views. But that was all.

Q: Was your family ever interested in politics?
Laurent: No, not at all. Neither my own family nor that of my wife. They had absolutely nothing to do with politics.

Q: When you finally became a candidate, how did you like the campaign? What did you think of it?
Laurent: I must admit that it was all new to me. The first political meeting I ever went to was also the occasion of my first political speech. I had never even attended a political meeting before.

Q: Did you have any trouble speaking? Do you like doing this?
Laurent: It wasn't the first time I had spoken before a group. I had given lectures, even courses before many students—150, 200. So I was used to public speaking. But I must admit that a political meeting is quite a different thing from a class lecture.

Q: Did you enjoy speaking at these meetings?
Laurent: I don't see how anyone could find it enjoyable. I don't think you can influence the audience. Everyone comes with his mind already made up. They are already for or against. They come either to applaud or to shout you down. Very rare are those who come with a real desire to gain information. Very few people decide how they will vote *after* hearing the speakers; they have already decided.

Q: So what is the purpose of these meetings?
Laurent: If you want my opinion, they don't have much purpose.

Q: Then why do people have these meetings?
Laurent: Well, look. You're expected to go to all the little communes. When you go, there may be one or two percent of the people come to hear you. So you don't gain much. But the candidate has to come. If you don't, people will say, "Why didn't so-and-so come to visit us?" And then they will vote against you. The people are like that. It's a tradition, that's all.

Q: What did you think of the idea that you might become Deputy?
Laurent: I wasn't very excited about it. I thought I would be in the lead

at the end of the first round of voting, but thought I had little chance to win on the second round. I thought my only possibility of winning was if my opponent made an error in voter psychology. This is precisely what happened, so that the election was close, but I did much better than I had thought, and won on the second round.

Q: What was the error your opponent made?

Laurent: My sole opponent at the second round was the outgoing Deputy, this former Gaullist, who had meanwhile become a Centrist. At the end of the first round he allied himself with the *Fédération* [Socialists and Radicals] to win their support. In fact, he actually joined the *Fédération.* At that point I cried, "Thief!" I said, "What kind of candidate is this? First, he was a Gaullist, then a Centrist, now a Fédération member. All that's left for him to do is join the Communists, and then he will have been part of the entire spectrum. What kind of candidate is this?" This psychological error on his part helped me win a victory I had not thought possible.

Q: During the election did you have many contacts with the voters in your district?

Laurent: Very few. I didn't get much help in this part of the job. Gaullists weren't very well organized in my region, and we didn't have regular lists of supporters, and that sort of thing.

Q: Is the party better organized now?

Laurent: After I was elected, I first had to learn my trade. I had little chance to organize the local party. But since June [1968] I have been actively working toward this end. I've found party representatives in every commune, I meet with them once or twice a month.

Q: You did this because you thought it necessary to strengthen the movement. . . ?

Laurent: Yes. I was going to do it anyway. I think it's important for a legislator to have contacts with all his constituents. But these contacts can't always be direct. You must have permanent representatives to help you—first, to let you know what the voters want, what they are thinking. Also, to help counteract the hostile press. I come from a region with a hostile press, and it is necessary to explain the Government's policies and ways of thinking to the people.

I see my constituents a good deal. I always try to find ways to serve all of my district. I am known as a Deputy who works.

Q: And what does this work consist of?

Laurent: I try to fulfill my responsibilities to my constituents, to those who are victims of the government bureaucracy, who don't know their own rights. I try to attract the attention of government leaders toward such-and-such measure which might facilitate the solution of problems in my district. I have been concerned, for instance, with problems of employment, of education.

Q: Could you describe this work that you do at the Assembly?

Laurent: In the legislature I am on the Q Committee, and I have been *rapporteur* [translated loosely: "floor manager"] on proposed laws involving the organization of primary schools. I've also been *rapporteur* on a bill to encourage cancer research. It was my own idea.

Q: Where is this bill now?

Laurent: In committee somewhere [waves his hand to indicate the entire Assembly building].

Q: Do you think the bill will succeed?

Laurent: It must succeed. We have greater and greater need for a breakthrough in this area. More people die of cancer every year. We must get public support for research to find a cure for this disease.

Q: How did you get interested in this subject?

Laurent: All by myself. I read about the problem in the papers, and I thought something needed to be done.

[The conversation makes it clear that Laurent's work at the Assembly grows out of his belief that Deputies *ought* to work hard and *ought* to find ways to benefit and serve the voters. From this motivation grows his work on legislation, not from an intrinsic interest in solving problems, as for the program participant. Laurent clearly does not have a burning interest in any particular bill. Only after several probing questions does he begin to discuss matters of programmatic substance.

Additional probing questions brought Laurent to discuss another bill on which he had worked—a bill to limit private real estate sales of historical buildings or areas. The subject was directly related to Laurent's earlier work in real estate and he discussed it with some detailed knowledge—but again only after lengthy probing. After these questions about his substantive work as Deputy, the conversation took this turn:]

Q: They say that every legislature has its own parliamentary customs. What are the customs you have noticed at the National Assembly?

Laurent: It's hard to say. My trouble is that I am not at all a political man. I've noticed that many of the Deputies are much more concerned about what happens within the Assembly than with what goes on outside it. There is too much interest in internal maneuvering and not enough in outside affairs.

Q: Would you say this was true of all the parties?
Laurent: Yes, it doesn't make any difference which party you talk of.
[Laurent here, as elsewhere, shows his dislike for politics and his belief that most men in politics, including those in his own party, are selfishly out for themselves.]

Q: What exactly are these internal practices?
Laurent: They often involve personal squabbles. To some extent they are habits of many of the Deputies who entered politics under the Fourth Republic. It's less true now, but before the election of 1968 I always had the feeling that the Assembly was regarded by most of the Deputies as a club. For many it was more a game than a real mission. Consequently, getting things done was a secondary concern. And there was another reason perhaps: too many Deputies had numerous other activities: mayor or some other political position. And they continue their professional life as well. They weren't able to spend enough of their time in their role as Deputy.

Q: One thing that interests me is what attracts men to politics. What satisfactions have you found through your political activity?
Laurent: In 1967 I knew nothing about politics, and I must admit that I haven't had any satisfactions since then. I've been very active, I've done many things, but I haven't found any satisfactions. I've had many satisfactions in my life, in my business, in my hobbies. But I haven't found a single satisfaction at the Assembly.

Q: It seems strange to me that a man who found no satisfactions would continue to remain a Deputy. For instance, you ran again in 1968...?
Laurent: You would have had to live the events of May, 1968, to understand. We had really revolutionary conditions then. The future of the whole country was at stake. I had the impression that my actions would have results for the whole country's future. I'll give you an idea of how important this was. My wife in 1967 had a totally different view: she was wholly opposed to my running and we even talked about divorce. [He smiles.] But in 1968 she told me that I had no choice; I *had* to run as candidate. She told me: "You have to think about the living conditions in this country, about the future of our children." That's the way things were.

As a Deputy I'm making much less money than I was. My income has been reduced by at least one-third. From a personal point of view, I could never be as popular in politics as I have been in private life. In any case I'm not in politics for popularity—this isn't important to me. When you've written material that's been read by thousands of people, how much more personal attention can you get by going into politics? I'll never be in a position to give a political speech before the number of people who have read my words.

So how could I say I'd found any satisfactions? Unless it's a certain idea to which I'm attached: fulfilling my responsibilities to the people of my district and to my country.

Q: Do you think you will run again—say, in four years?
Laurent: That's hard to say. Here I work sixteen hours a day. I'm always working on my business as Deputy. One can't predict what one will do that far ahead. But there are many drawbacks—for instance, the aggravations, the intrigues, in one's own party, the constant in-fighting. Sometimes I say to myself that it's time for me just to get up and leave.

[Laurent's statements indicate dislike of politics, suspiciousness of other men's motives, and a belief that he is doing a necessary but thankless job—all important characteristics of the obligation participant. The interview ended with Laurent's expression of his Gaullist philosophy, and his indication that he supports Gaullism as much for its style of governing as for its substantive accomplishments:]

Q: One final question: You've mentioned your attachment to the Gaullist movement. What would you say attracted you to Gaullism?
Laurent: I have given some talks on political economy, and I always call the attention of my students to the fact that in the industrial world political cleavages cannot be allowed to attain the diversity they have in an agricultural country. Previously, when France was mostly rural the changes in Government didn't do any harm. People just went about their business, as usual. But now when you have a much more complex economy, with a five-year Plan, for example, the cleavages and the crises of former times are no longer conceivable. They can't be allowed in an industrial country because they upset everything. Now, for instance, when a one percent change in the discount rate can cause enormous disturbances, you just can't have that kind of politics.

[Throughout the interview Laurent maintained his air of reserve. He did not find the experience enjoyable, nor did he show any interest in me or my project, even though he was willing to give ninety minutes of his time to help me. We parted on the same formal terms on which we had met.]

Alexandre Philippon, a Status Participant

In one important respect M. Philippon differed from the other status Deputies. He was more open than the others, more willing to talk frankly about his ambitions and the tactics he has used in pursuing them. Speaking delightedly and almost exclusively about his political career, M. Philippon even appeared somewhat naive. Other status Deputies at least tried to conceal their motivation for politics—through short interviews, rudeness, and refusal to answer questions about personal satisfactions. M. Philippon tried to conceal nothing. He was chosen for presentation because he provides the clearest example of the status participant's interest in personal advancement and the techniques of position-getting, but one should bear in mind that he does lack one important characteristic of the status type: the rude interview behavior, the tendency toward formalism, and the slick cover-up.

Even more than most status participants, Philippon expressed unmitigated sarcasm when discussing nearly all other individuals. He reveled in pointing out the foibles of other members of the human race. This orientation was all the more surprising to me as I had expected something quite different. M. Philippon is a long-time Socialist (although still in his early forties), a supporter of Gaston Defferre and various reform movements within his party, an educated man who has written in *Le Monde* on ways to improve the functioning of the National Assembly. Before our conversation I had been expecting a program participant. I had also been hoping to learn something about the reforms then being proposed for the National Assembly. Philippon's interview makes clear that these subjects held little intrinsic interest for him. He never brought them up without prompting from me, and when he did discuss them, he did so from a personal, tactical point of view. (How will these reforms affect me? Why haven't others accepted *my* reform proposals?) I conclude that this Deputy's writings have been a strategic ploy, designed simply to make a national name for himself.

M. Philippon has long been a Socialist and has held numerous positions. He is presently Deputy from a rural, mountainous area—one of the classic strongholds of Socialism in France. Throughout the interview his attention centered on his own career. I found it difficult to switch the conversation to other topics, as it became clear from the very first question that this man would eagerly talk at length and with zeal about his personal exploits in politics.

> *Q:* To begin, I'd like to ask how you came to be involved in public life?
> *Philippon:* I first became interested in politics when I was quite young.

I was only eleven years old, and they were having a legislative election. My father took me to a public debate between two of the candidates. I was literally overwhelmed by it! The excitement, the crowds, the speeches! To me they resembled two noble gladiators dueling, fighting to the death, before the cheering throngs. I can still see the scene today, it was so vivid. From that moment I knew that was what I wanted to do. I knew that I'd have to get up there myself on that stage, get into that life. From then on, I always knew I'd have to become a Deputy some day.

I didn't, however, get into politics immediately as a young man. I was just starting out in life; I had to finish my studies, get a job, get married, have a family. Finally, by 1953 I had gained a decent position [as a high-ranking civil servant], and I knew it was time to start getting myself entrenched [*implanté*] in politics.

To get anywhere, I knew I'd have to follow the *cursus honorum*. I'd have to become a Mayor, become solidly entrenched at the local level, then work my way up to Deputy. So I started looking around to see where I could begin. I had two possibilities. I could run for local office in the Paris suburb where I lived, but I decided against that. Life is too unstable in the Paris area: It's always fluctuating, people move in and out, the character of the district changes, and you're never certain how long you will last there. I decided to go to the home town of my wife [in a mountainous, rural area of France] where we had some social ties. I knew it would be harder for me there where I wasn't really known, but I decided to go ahead anyway. After a difficult campaign I was elected Mayor of Q in 1953.

Q: You said you were impressed by this incident of the political debate. What in particular struck you about it?

Philippon: The spectacle of it. When I was a boy and saw those two men debating, I was struck by the way they dominated the crowd. Since then, I've come to know what a crowd is. I always find an intense satisfaction when I'm before an audience. In the first fifteen minutes you don't know if you're going to be eaten up or if you'll bend them. But after fifteen minutes you feel them relax and give before you. You hold them in the grip of your hand. You can play with them at will. You've succeeded in mastering them.

Q: How did you learn to speak before a group?

Philippon: It's something I picked up as part of my professional training. When I was taking university courses in administration, we were taught to speak. We had to be able to take any subject and give a speech on it for varying lengths of time—ten minutes, forty-five minutes, an hour etc. I practiced at this. Then I started to give lectures. At first they would be before small groups in Paris suburbs or in nearby towns. Then the groups became bigger, and I began to be taken seriously. In 1953 I gave many political speeches, I gave a great many talks. In 1955 I ran in the *canton* elections [for *départemental* office]. I knew I had no chance to win, but I needed to make myself known. I needed to make a splash in my district. I held twenty-seven political meetings. This is unheard of in a cantonal election. It had never been done before. And I only lost by eighty votes. I made an error at the last minute, a tactical mistake. I went to talk in the town that was the fief of my adversary—to fight him in his lair. This was a bad tactic. People don't like this sort of thing. It just isn't done. I've learned since not to do this; we all make errors from time to time. But my overall strategy was good, because I was becoming known around my area, so that by 1958 I had no trouble at all getting the nomination.

Q: Why not in 1956?

Philippon: That was too short a time. I hadn't been active in my area long enough. And besides we had an incumbent Socialist Deputy. I went to see him and agreed to help him. I worked for him in the 1956 election. He sent me to all the most difficult areas of the district. I did what I could, but he was beaten. As soon as I learned the election results, I thought right away: "The next time *I* will be the one to run." His defeat opened up new perspectives for me. Of course, I hadn't planned it that way. I had worked for his election, but that's how it happened.

Q: This man did not run again in 1958?

Philippon: No. I had things going my way by that time. I was the only one left who could be a good candidate. And my having been on the staff of a former Prime Minister helped my position. There was an old Socialist Senator from the area who had some hopes, but in the end he threw in the sponge; he didn't even try to beat me.

Q: What was your position in the local party?

Philippon: I was supported in the different sections. I had made myself known. And my youth helped a great deal. It was very useful to me. It was a trump card that finally carried the hand.

Q: How did you come to join the Socialist Party?

Philippon: I wasn't much of a Socialist in my youth. I leaned more toward the center, toward liberal ideas. But in 1948 I was assigned to the staff of [a Socialist Minister]. That helped bring me into the party. I had studied law and political science, and I felt the New Deal was a sensible development. I saw the need for a directed economy. But I place myself to the Right of the party. I don't believe in nationalizations. I want a directed economy as in the Scandinavian countries: progressive but not collectivistic. I feel this way by temperament. I don't like to be told what to do. So I was brought into the party by this way of thinking and especially by my experience on the Minister's staff.

[Philippon's "dedication" to socialist principles hardly appears strong. He relates his entry into the party primarily to the close ties with one of its leaders which brought him his first political office.]

Q: Have you been very active in working for the party?
Philippon: I stopped working for it very quickly. I started taking university courses, I was working hard in my job. But by the mid-1950s I thought my position with the State was in bad shape. I had been working on colonial problems, but the empire was decaying, disappearing. I needed to change my orientations, find something else to do. So I went back to party work in 1954-55.

Q: How were you able to win election to the Assembly in 1958 during the Gaullist tidal wave that year?
Philippon: It wasn't so hard. It was a very rough campaign, but it wasn't too difficult for me to win. The incumbent Deputy was a Communist, so you can imagine his problems! I appeared to be a new man, someone not too closely connected to the Fourth Republic. Yet I had good relations with Guy Mollet [Socialist leader] who was then serving in the de Gaulle Government. So I had good connections with men of the Fourth Republic, yet looked like a new man who would fit in with the trend of the Fifth Republic.

Voters in the district normally divided about one-third Communist, one-third Socialist and one-third to the Right. But although there was a moderate in the race that year, he didn't count for much. My problem was to beat the Communist. In 1956 he got over half of the votes in the area, but he was supported then by a coalition of fellow travelers—so-called socialists and radicals. The situation was very different in 1958. I thought I would do well, but I surpassed my expectations. I got more votes than the Communist on the first round and was easily elected on the second.

Q: Who do you align with in elections?

Phillippon: This has changed over the years. At first I was elected with the help of the Right; now it's with the help of the Left. My main goal in the first round of an election is to reduce the Communist vote as much as possible. That way I come in ahead of the Communist on the first round and get their support on the second. These days, rightist candidates are getting much more help from the Government, and this gives me a lot of trouble. I need to steal votes from the Right in order to come in ahead of the Communist on the first round. I have to compete with the Gaullists to get enough votes on the first round to stay in the race. [Socialists and Communists often agree to support in the second round of voting whichever of their candidates has the larger vote on the first round—in order to prevent Gaullist victories.] But many voters are turning to the Gaullists these days. Too many voted for de Gaulle in the last election [June 1968].

Q: Has the *Fédération* [short-lived alliance of Socialists, Radicals and other Left forces] helped increase your support in the district?

Philippon: The *Fédération* has brought me about 1500-2000 additional votes from leftist anarchist types [said with sarcasm] but it has lost me all the Radicals in the district. They have already passed over into the Gaullist camp. The leftists all vote for me, but the moderate elements that I need are turning toward the Right. But luckily things are looking bad for the Gaullists now [March 1969]. People are complaining about everything these days: prices, jobs, taxes. What did they expect? I told them what would happen if they re-elected the Gaullists in 1968. They didn't know any better.

Q: Outside of the party, do you have friends or local supporters who help you during elections?

Philippon: Yes, but their help was lacking this last time [1968]. In the past I've always visited certain leaders in each locality, sat down with them at little dinners and asked for their help in the election. This time there was no one who wanted to see me. One of my contacts told me that things were looking very bad. The peasants actually thought the Revolution had come again. They were sure heads were being chopped off in Paris. They thought the workers would come marching down and take all their money and land away from them. It was ridiculous. You can't imagine how frightened they were. And I got no help at all from local leaders. The voters swung straight to the Right. They almost elected a Gaullist against me, and my opponent was a man who didn't know a thing, not a thing! It shows how blinded they were by the events of May.

[Digression here to describe the incompetence and stupidity of his main electoral opponent in 1968.]

Q: Did you get much support from your party leaders?

Philippon: None at all. What our party leaders are doing is a complete joke. It amuses me to see the leaders of our movement play at being revolutionaries—brandishing their slogans, shaking their fists, all that nonsense. It's a complete charade. Do they think they're going to seize power? Don't make me laugh! There's no one around who can do it. The Communists don't want it; our leaders couldn't do it. The students? It's a joke; it's not serious.

The Gaullists are trying to cement their position in my area, and they are using the bureaucracy to help them; the prefects distribute favors wherever possible to Gaullist supporters. The *administration* is up to its ears in politics; it does all it can to help the UDR. The Prefect, for instance, opens all the Government files, all its dossiers, to the Gaullist candidate in this area. The Prefect will give him any help he needs. But this Prefect isn't so bad. The one we had three years ago was unbelievable. He went around to all the *cantons* in an effort to work against me, distributing favors and promises as he went. When he learned that I go to all the communes, he vowed he would go to each one also. So I even had to start going to each hamlet to stay ahead of him. You see how it is!

When de Gaulle says he wants decentralization, what he really means is he wants to spread Gaullist power out more evenly throughout the country. He wants to concentrate power in the hands of the Gaullist Prefects and take it away from elected opponents. Our Prefect watches the way each commune votes. When a commune comes to him for approval of some project, he asks them why they voted "wrong" in the last elections. He puts pressure on these "bad" communes to change their votes, and he rewards the "good" ones.

And the way the State throws money away is shameful. It gives away money to its little friends, its supporters. It builds an airport in the middle of nowhere instead of using it for good projects. But this will some day turn against them. Government waste and extravagance. That was the theme of my 1967 campaign. People are becoming aware of this fact. Luckily, I'm a Mayor and I'm also President of our *Conseil Général* [the very weak legislative body in each *département*]. This gives me access to at least some funds, so I have some money of my own to distribute to keep my supporters.

Q: Do you enjoy electoral campaigns?

Philippon: Yes! I adore the campaigns. I go everywhere in the district. I talk in the smallest communes. I establish headquarters in all the larger towns. I've succeeded in winning the rural people over to my side through my efforts. There's no doubt that campaigns are hard, but you have to like them if you want to get somewhere in politics. [Philippon goes on at some length. His attitude toward the voters is patronizing, at times scornful. He describes incidents involving his constituents which "sophisticated" observers (like he and I) can smile at. In telling how he talks to farmers in his district, he says with a laugh that you must always start by asking them about their pigs, and only slowly bring the conversation around to politics. Another incident is described this way:]

Philippon: Some of the things that people bring to me are incredible. Two neighbors both came to see me over some lawsuit concerning their property. One actually tried to get me to bribe the judge. Can you believe it? I hope the judge condemns them both.

Q: I've read a couple of things you've written about reforming the legislature, and I'd like to ask you what you think the chances are that your ideas will be adopted?

Philippon: The reaction to my ideas was one of conservatism. People told me I would never get any results from what I had written. They said it was interesting but that nothing will ever come of it. I got named to a National Assembly committee to investigate reform possibilities, and we've met ten times already. Some proposals have been made which aren't bad, but the hard-line Gaullists have already indicated they will scuttle any real changes in the present set-up. They don't want *any* changes. The Government is happy the way things are now. The present Assembly is weak. It lacks specialization. Deputies aren't specialists, so they have no way to control the Government. We should increase the number of committees, but the Government won't allow this, so we've gotten nowhere.

[Philippon's claim that Deputies need to specialize is never backed up by any apparent interest on his part in particular legislative subjects. The following question and answer indicate a very low level of interest in legislative work:]

Q: What aspects of your work in the Assembly have been of most interest to you?

Philippon: At first I turned to work on problems of our political institutions. And I also spent some time on colonial matters, since I had had some experience in that area. But I soon found that I wasn't able to accomplish anything in my committee, so I gave that up and joined the Committee on Foreign Affairs—de Gaulle's "special domain" [said with biting sarcasm]. But nothing happens on that committee. It has the least power of any. It's run by his son-in-law, and de Gaulle does whatever he wants in foreign affairs anyway. I went to its meetings just for amusement. At first I talked up, I showed some interest, but it was all for nothing. So I've decided it's not worth it to fight any more. What good does this committee work do?

Q: How do Deputies get along with each other in general?

Philippon: I'm on good terms with everyone, but it's difficult. It's hard to get along with the Gaullists, even though we are courteous with each other. The strained relations in the Assembly result from one basic problem: the Gaullists are not really democrats, they aren't for a democratic system. They will do anything to stay in power.

Q: How do you get along with members of your own party?

Philippon: I was violently criticized for my stand during the last election. Our party leaders were too extremist, and I tried to prevent their taking the whole party further to the left. I tried to use my leverage within the Assembly party caucus against the national party organization, but with no results. I learned a lot at that time. I learned that customs are of no help at all against superior power. You either have power or you don't. If you don't have it, you lose. You have to have superior force or you get nowhere.

Q: Do you have the support of your local party organization?

Philippon: Yes. It's at the national level that I am opposed, fought. They don't like me because I got where I am with no help from the party. I did it all myself. And besides, I say what I think. I'm an individualist, I can't stand being bottled up, so they look on me as a political adversary.

Q: Would you yourself like to have a position of Governmental leadership?

Philippon: You know, we are in politics to *govern*. This is the function of the political man. If he doesn't want to govern, what is he doing in politics? He could go off and knit in a corner somewhere. Of course, I would like to get into a position of power. I've often said this—we Socialists shouldn't be afraid of power, and we shouldn't be afraid of seeking to gain it.

Q: Do you think you have a chance of getting into power some day?

Philippon: A lot depends on chance. Chance is an important variable in politics.

Q: To close, I'd like to ask you what personal satisfactions you have found in your political activities?

Philippon: Politics allows me to get to know the world. For instance, I've been in the Inter-Parliamentary Union for some years. My position there allows me to get to know the world, meet other men, gives me a chance to speak with leaders from many other countries. I've met [names important American and Russian leaders]. These things give me great joy. I wouldn't have these real satisfactions if I weren't in politics.

Q: Have you had any disagreeable experiences in politics?

Philippon: Yes! Probably the worst came during the last elections. The Gaullist who ran against me was a former friend of mine. I knew his family, I had helped them out in the past, I'd done his uncle a business favor. He came to me before the elections wanting my help to get into politics, and I was willing to help him. In fact, I was going to make him my *suppléant* [alternate]. I told him many secrets about the campaign. But then it turned out that for political reasons I couldn't make him my *suppléant* after all. I still wanted him to work for me, but four days later he announced that he was going to run against me as a Gaullist. I was out of the district at the time, but I was waiting to hear from him about a job I'd asked him to do for me. It was unbelievable, incredible. To do such a thing to me! I was very bitter about it. I can't forgive him that kind of dirty move. This is the kind of thing that can happen in politics.

[Philippon has to get to a meeting, and in any case I have asked most of my questions. We shake hands, and I leave his Assembly office.]

Four different Deputies have answered questions about their life and work in politics. Each has focused on topics which the others find dull or peripheral. By indicating their main concerns and interests, these men have revealed their different incentives for politics. It is now time to examine these incentives and their behavioral consequences in an analytical manner.

3 The Mission Participant

The mission participant seeks to serve a cause. He is a man intensely concerned with problems of purpose: the meaning of life, in general; the way to give meaning to his own life, in particular. One way in which he can resolve these problems is to attach himself to a militant movement which proclaims a trancendental doctrine. The doctrine provides not only an intellectual framework for viewing the world and society, but also a rationale for personal action.

The idea of the mission participant should be familiar to students of extremist movements, religious movements, totalitarian systems, and revolutions.[1] Incentive analysis suggests that these phenomena can be understood partly in terms of the mission incentive. They illustrate activities in which the mission participant is likely to engage, and they show how he is likely to behave when activated.

The need motivating the mission participant has many similarities to religious fervor. Individuals driven by this need may, therefore, gravitate to nonpolitical institutions. When their faith emphasizes a need to transform the material world, however, they may feel impelled into political action:

This anxiety to find meaning for one's existence . . . is commonly considered a religious need. It becomes an incentive for political participation when the transcendental mission has a secular political focus, such as the establishment of a real-world utopia. Marxism-Leninism affords the obvious illustration of such a secular religion; but other, less defined ideologies, such as Christian Socialism or Gaullism, may also have mission-incentive adherents.[2]

The *main identifying characteristic* of the mission participant directly reflects this religious need. In interviews it is expressed in his intense concern with purposive aspects of his movement: its formal goals, its doctrine and ideology, its "true meaning" in contemporary politics. He relates the meaning of his own life to the stated purposes and ideology of his movement.

> *Q:* Could you tell me how you happened to get involved in politics?
> *Deputy, PCF:* That question takes me back a long way. Well, it's like this. I was born in 1920, and when I reached working age we were in the middle of a great world crisis. In 1935 I was in a position where I was without work and without hope of finding work. There were unemployed people everywhere. I felt strongly that people simply could not allow such a situation to exist. It wasn't right, it could not

Table 3-1
Distribution of Mission Participants by Legislative Party Group

Party[a]	Number of Deputies	% of Mission Deputies
Non-Inscrit	1	5%
RI app	0	—
RI	2	11%
UDR app	1	5%
UDR	8	42%
PDM	1	5%
FGDS	0	—
PC	6	32%
TOTAL	19	100%

[a]For explanation of abbreviations, see List of Abbreviations.

be accepted. The society that allows such things to happen is rotten to the core.

In order to change that society, this man entered a local union and soon after joined the Communist Party.

Q: Why did you get into union activity?
R: It was the situation of the unemployed workers. The society that tolerates such things must be condemned, a better society must be built, and I wanted to work toward those goals.

He clearly sees his entry into politics as an initial step in his life's work toward a distant, all-encompassing but poorly-defined goal: "a better society."[3]

Like this Deputy, most other mission participants quickly situate themselves in relation to an ideal or a movement. Witness this exchange at the very beginning of an interview:

Q: I know you were first elected to public office when you ran for the Chamber of Deputies in 1936. How did you come to seek that post that year?
Deputy, PCF: I must first tell you that I'm an old Communist militant. I first joined the Socialist Party in 1918 even before the creation of the French Communist Party. I celebrated this year over fifty years of party membership, and I've held many of the different party posts over this time. . . .

Running for the legislature is not a discrete act. Rather, it is a logical sequence in a life dedicated to his party's cause.

Whenever possible, mission Deputies looked for doctrinal-ideological interpretations of specific questions and situations. A third Communist Deputy had mentioned that personal relations between Communists and Socialists in his district were not good. I asked him why, expecting to learn about some local clash of personalities or the particular political disagreements that separated these parties during the Presidential elections. Instead, this Deputy launched into a twenty-minute lecture on the history of European Socialism and Communism, beginning with Marx. He argued that there have always been "hard" and "soft" Marxists—Lenin and Bernstein, Guèsde and Jaurès, revolutionaries and revisionists—that followers of these two schools have always been at odds over how to change capitalism, and that they remain at odds today in their institutionalized forms, the Socialist and Communist Parties. It was this same disagreement, according to him, which provoked the local conflict between Socialist and Communist militants. It is remarkable that this man gives an historical-ideological explanation for a situation which a nonmission politician might have interpreted in terms of concrete, present-day differences.

Mission participants frequently resort to their ideology to explain or understand current political situations. This habit follows from their strong belief that their doctrine discloses all the important truths in the universe. Bertrand Russell summed up this attitude in 1920:

Bolshevism is not merely a political doctrine; it is also a religion, with elaborate dogmas and inspired scriptures. . . . A full-fledged Communist is not merely a man who believes that land and capital should be held in common, and their produce distributed as nearly equally as possible. He is a man who entertains a number of elaborate and dogmatic beliefs—such as philosophic materialism, for example—which may be true, but are not, to a scientific temper, capable of being known with any certainty. This habit, of militant certainty about objectively doubtful matters, is one from which, since the Renaissance, the world has been gradually emerging, into that temper of constructive and fruitful skepticism which constitutes the scientific outlook.[4]

It is this "militant certainty about objectively doubtful matters" which characterizes the mission participant and which he obtains from his belief in an all-encompassing doctrine.

Other mission Deputies differ little from the Communists in their dedication to a transcendent cause. When I asked a Centrist Deputy why he had become active in a Catholic farmers' union, he replied:

> *Deputy, PDM:* I had always seen my father involved in this work, and I became so taken up by these matters that I continued in his path. I

wanted to work like he did for the betterment of the life of the people. I wanted to see an amelioration of our society, a better and more just society. I wanted to help resolve some of the problems that our society faces and raise that society to a higher level. Look around you. You can see that life for many people here is abominable. We need to have a more just distribution of society's goods for all.

The mere expression of these vague sentiments does not by itself define the mission type. What distinguishes the mission participant from others is the persistence of his interest in doctrinal matters. In replying to my questions, mission Deputies continually turned the conversation to ideological issues. These men feel compelled to explain their ideology, often and vehemently.

Two examples may illustrate this compulsion to state an ideological position. I asked a Gaullist Deputy about his primary concerns at the Assembly. He began by telling about his work for handicapped children, a response I initially interpreted as indicating a program incentive. Soon switching the topic to foreign affairs, however, he launched into a tirade against opponents of Gaullist policy.

> *Deputy, UDR:* I'd long been interested in foreign affairs. You may remember that I said I supported General de Gaulle for three reasons, one of which was the way he saw relations among nations. I've been supporting his position in this matter since 1943, when I began to take an extremely hostile attitude toward the *politique des blocs*. I can tell you that Yalta absolutely infuriated me.
>
> *Q:* What bothers you about this *politique des blocs?*
>
> *R:* I feel that I have a humanist outlook on life, and this leads me to be totally opposed to the idea of one or two nations directing the affairs of all the other nations of the world. The idea of interference in the affairs of others angers me. I was always opposed to colonialization, and I'm one of the rare people in France who early advocated that France get rid of all her colonies around the world. But after a time I began to perceive that there are different kinds of colonialization. There is the colonialization of the nineteenth century, which simply means the physical presence of one nation in another. Then there is the more marked and efficient colonialization of Russia in regards to the countries of East Europe. But there is also an economic colonialization, which is just as effective and perhaps more insidious than the others.

This deputy is not content simply telling about laws he has worked on. Nor does he wish merely to express an opinion on a foreign policy issue. Rather, he wants to state an entire political philosophy about international affairs.

In the same way, a Communist Deputy seized a chance to refer to general ideological matters in responding to a specific question.

> *Q:* Can one have this change in French society which you talk about without violence?
>
> *Deputy, PCF:* That is precisely a question I am very concerned with. I've been reading up on that lately, and in fact I'm going to make a report before a *départemental* party meeting on that subject very soon. I am not alone in my view on this matter; many others agree with me. If you read Marx closely you see that when he uses the term "revolution" he *never* uses the word "violence" next to it. I defy anyone to find that word next to "revolution" in Marx's words. For Marx revolution meant a total change in society. For instance, the Orientation-Law on National Education [1968] was called revolutionary because it was a radical transformation of the educational system. Yet that law was passed peacefully in the Assembly. Such a transformation can be made without violence under our present conditions.

Some men might have answered this question in specific terms: the changes the PCF would institute and the likely response to such changes by the Army, shopkeepers, students, other parties, etc. Instead, he elevates the question to the realm of general ideas. It becomes, for him, "the problem of society and revolution." He can now happily answer the question by referring to the sacred tracts of his movement: writings of its long-dead philosopher-priest.

As one listens to the doctrinal statements of these men, one comes to wonder precisely what content their ideology has. Their general statements hardly seem able to provide a guide to action:

> *Deputy, UDR:* [Gaullism] means, first of all, the independence of France. And then—for *me,* I don't know what other Gaullists would say—the search for a new social humanism. Everything that centers on man's dignity. As de Gaulle says, the only worthwhile cause these days is the cause of man.... But this is not just fidelity to a man. I agree with de Gaulle's ideas; I'm not giving blind obedience to the man.... He represents devotion to a certain conception of man. It's a philosophy: against Fascism, for a worship of man.

One instantly feels how nebulous these ideals are. They provide no well-defined goals, only a hazy vision of a "better future society."

Yet the very generality of their ideas serves these men. They seem more interested in striving toward ultimate good than in reaching it. Thus, the breadth of their ideals impels them to constant action:

> *Deputy, PCF:* I cannot conceive of life without this *struggle*. I believe
> that this society with its private forms is outmoded. I must struggle
> to create the conditions for changing that society. My children may
> see this new society, if I don't. So I continue my struggle to change
> the world.

The tenacity with which these men affirm their faith underscores their desire
to give meaning to their life and actions. Constant contact with social reality in
all its complex and contradictory forms can lead men to question their original
motives for acting. A set ideology can help them overcome doubts about
purpose. It not only answers a host of philosophical questions: it also provides a
key for understanding a multiplicity of daily events and for resolving the
apparent contradictions between reality and the movement's stated positions.

All mission Deputies, significantly, were either Gaullists (12) or Communists
(6), except for one man who could best be described as a Christian Democrat.
All openly espoused the standard political tenets of their movements. A
willingness to consider new intellectual ideas was rarely in evidence. This passive
acceptance of revealed doctrine is a positive source of strength and stability for
parties dominated by mission followers. These men want to believe in a universal
ideology. A movement which changes its ideology frequently in response to
changing times provokes doubts, since an objectively true doctrine should have
little need for change. A party or religion which insists on the continuing truth
of its old doctrines retains the allegiance of mission participants within its ranks.

This reliance upon established ideas serves the party well, since mission
participants have a tendency to let doctrinal disputes become party splits and
church schisms. PCF leaders have prevented frequent or fundamental changes in
party ideology, thus choking off one of the causes of internal friction. The party
as a bureaucracy benefits from retention of the old ideology.[5]

Although Gaullists have remarkably similar ideas on many subjects, they are
obviously not as unified in their beliefs as are French Communists. Since there is
slim theoretical basis for a Gaullist "ideology," this fact is hardly surprising. The
movement can point to no set of writings as profound or as comprehensive as
those of Marxists. Yet Gaullist mission Deputies *believe* they have a real
ideology. This faith in the existence of an overriding set of ideas which explains
the purpose of life matters more than the intellectual quality of the ideas
themselves: "To others ... the mission participant's ideclogy may appear
threadbare, inconsistent, or even unintelligible. What really matters to him is his
belief that there exists an extensive, self-contained, intellectual superstructure
which gives meaning to his activity."[6]

The lack of a clearly enunciated, fully accepted doctrine, however, constitutes an ever-present danger for the Gaullist movement. Gaullists do not agree on
all the tenets of their ideology. Since doctrinal disputes often lead to organizational rupture among mission participants, some future event might generate

widely divergent interpretation by leading Gaullists and eventually cause irreparable divisions within the party.

These facts suggest, by the way, that leaders of movements which attract mission participants will be under constant pressure from their followers to provide a well-articulated ideology and to use that ideology to explain day-to-day political occurrences. Parties which have little need to formulate a set ideology (e.g., American parties) probably contain few mission participants.

Attitudinal Correlates of the Mission Incentive

1. Absence of the Expression of Satisfactions Which Define Other Incentive Types

a. Absence of the Program Incentive. Mission Deputies are not wholly lacking in concern for policy details—the main identifying characteristic of the program participant. Within their various organizations they are, after all, constantly engaged in daily work of a technical, detailed nature. These activities necessarily bring them into contact with major and minor problems of their society. When they discuss their own activities in interviews, they will not fail to mention how they dealt with some of these problems.

There is an important difference, however, between mission and program Deputies. Program Deputies are *mainly* interested in policy problems. These problems are only secondary matters for mission Deputies. They wish primarily to promote their cause and their organization. They have learned that within a highly institutionalized, modern country they cannot work for their party without some attention to the details of policy and administration which affect their society. But they explicitly state that specific program goals are only a means of promoting their party's cause, and they distinctly prefer direct work for their party than work on programs:

> *Q:* What specific projects have you worked on while Deputy?
>
> *Deputy, PCF:* You must realize that I am first of all a *political* person [*homme politique*]. It's true, I've been on many Assembly committees. I'm a specialist on American economic penetration in France. I've helped to get things for this district: low-income housing, a sports arena, hospitals, a pool. *But the important thing is the bigger struggle. My main work is on the Central Committee.* [Emphasis added.]

Clearly mission participants, unlike program participants, do not find their basic satisfactions in work on the concrete details of public policy.

b. Absence of the Status Incentive. In contrast to status participants, mission Deputies were horrified at the idea of using politics to serve personal interests. They vehemently denied any interest in obtaining positions or other formal political rewards.

> *Q:* Did you seek the party's nomination for the post of Deputy?
>
> *Deputy, PCF:* [Upset and indignant] No! I'm not a careerist! Others might act like that to save their career. I blush to think that I might have taken such an action. That doesn't interest me. What's important is to continue working for the workers, to help improve their lot. The party asked me to replace X, who was getting old. I didn't even want the nomination, since I was happy in the work I was doing.

Communist mission Deputies were especially anxious to see themselves as pure and dedicated.[7]

Gaullist mission Deputies were not as self-effacing. They appear to identify their own advancement with that of the Gaullist cause. That is, when they reach important positions, Gaullism itself has taken a step forward. This difference between Gaullists and Communists probably springs from the different history and structure of the two movements. Neither the RPF nor the UNR (now UDR) have been highly structured bodies. Beyond reliance on the popularity of General de Gaulle, success of the movement has depended on the leadership of a comparatively few, dedicated activists. It is natural that these activists should identify their own success with that of Gaullism.

Although Gaullists do not take pains to deny their interest in gaining particular positions, their manner of expressing this interest shows that they see positions primarily as additional platforms from which to promote their cause:

> *Q:* Why did you run for the Assembly in this [poor working-class] district?
>
> *Deputy, UDR:* It was a challenge! This district is one of the most working-class in the country. It had been in the hands of the Communist Party for thirty years. I wanted to show people that Gaullism could win here. I wanted to prove that Gaullists could establish themselves even in the most Left-wing areas, even in the most solid Communist fiefs.

One can hardly accuse this Deputy of cold, self-interested calculations. He took the great risk of losing an election solely to prove that Gaullism could appeal to all classes. Close to all Gaullist leaders, he could have had his pick of safe districts throughout the country. Something more than the love of office and the desire for personal prestige motivated his decision.

c. **Absence of the Obligation Incentive**. The mission Deputy has little interest in abstract questions of morality and duty. It is clear that he has moral concerns, but these concerns relate to the welfare of his movement. Morality reflects what is best for the cause. It is immoral to vilify in public a member (in good standing) of one's own party, but perfectly moral, and even commendable, to slander a party opponent. It is immoral to criticize party member A today, but perfectly moral to do so tomorrow (when he has been expelled from the party). For mission participants, normative attitudes depend on what is best for the party. They are thus secondary to the primary concern: promotion of the cause. Mission participants do not see morality as a set of personal, internal standards of right and wrong, as do obligation participants."

2. Attitude Toward Interview and Interviewer

Mission Deputies were talkative and expansive in the interview. They apparently saw this situation as a chance to reaffirm their own beliefs and possibly to make a convert. They seemed to enjoy the situation. I had the impression that they welcomed the chance to break their mundane round of daily activities to expostulate on the broad purpose of their work. One indicator of their responsiveness to the interview is the amount of time they granted me. Interviews with mission Deputies averaged an hour and a half, slightly above the average interview time.

3. Attitude Toward "Significant Others"

a. **Leaders in Higher Positions**. The mission Deputy has a deep faith in his movement's leaders. He sees in them the epitome of the human qualities he values. Gaullists were especially prone to glorify their leader:

> *Deputy, UDR:* During the war de Gaulle's speeches helped to give life to the population. They confirmed our will to continue and gave us hope. I was attracted to de Gaulle because he's a superior man, a fantastic man. His only fault, you might say, is that he sees the truth too soon. Others aren't always ready to accept the truth right away. But a man like that can't be judged. It's not for someone like me to judge him, after all he's done.

> *Deputy, UDR:* De Gaulle still has an energy that is incredible! Did you see him on television while he visited Brittany this weekend? [Very

excited.] He's still a man of immense activity. He has an incredible force, a strength of spirit, a global vision that is fantastic. Watch him on television before all those crowds. Did you see him constantly on the go for three days, getting no rest, talking, moving around, meeting people! And despite his global vision, he has a grasp of the little, daily events as well as anyone. But of course most of the time he lets others worry about these problems.[8]

Another Gaullist illustrates the mission participant's intellectual and emotional dependence on his leaders:

Q: What first attracted you to Gaullism?

Deputy, UDR: I became politically aware toward the end of the 1930s when I was in school. That period was the darkest era imaginable for France. Governments falling every day, the country facing grave dangers with no leadership! I looked around and saw nothing but chaos and incapable politicians. I asked myself, "Why did I have the misfortune of being born in this century?" There was simply no noble cause in which a dedicated young man could work for the good of his country.

Then I heard the call of June 18, 1940, by General de Gaulle and a great sense of relief broke over me! Here at last was a dedicated man who was pointing the way, who provided a cause into which Frenchmen could throw themselves with fervor and good conscience. De Gaulle awoke in me a sense of dedication to my country and my beliefs which has never left me since that day.

One cannot exaggerate the importance for mission participants of this idea that a great leader *calls* on dedicated followers to support him. De Gaulle's first radio speech to the French people is always referred to as *l'appel du 18 juin 1940* (the call of June 18th, 1940). In many of de Gaulle's famous television broadcasts he *called* the French people to aid him. One writer has gone as far as to make *l'appel* the central aspect of Gaullism.[9]

The survival of Gaullism may depend partly on the ability of its mission adherents to transfer their faith in de Gaulle into loyalty to his successors (and upon the successors' ability to "prove" that they are faithful to Gaullist doctrine). From interview comments of mission Gaullists this transfer of allegiance appeared to be taking place as early as April, 1969.

Q: What was your reaction to de Gaulle's resignation?

Deputy, UDR: It was a hard blow, no doubt about it. [Silence. Then speaks up strongly.] But it won't stop us! We still have the largest mass of the voters. After all, Pompidou got forty-four percent of the vote with *seven* candidates in the running. It would be a disaster, a catastrophe if Poher won. He's a weakling, he could provide no leadership. Now Pompidou is a strong man. He would provide stability and a strong, dynamic Government. Look at the difference between Poher and Pompidou on television. One is a leader; the other is soft, a nothing. What a difference! How could anyone who sees them both vote for Poher?

The above quotation illustrates another aspect of the mission participant's view of leaders. They heap obloquy on opposing leaders. Opposing leaders possess qualities that are opposite to those of one's own. In this case Pompidou is strong, Poher is weak. Other Gaullists pointed to the treachery of opponents' leaders compared to the honesty of their own or the opportunism of other leaders compared to the statesmanlike conduct of theirs. Communists stress the "fact" that opponents' leaders serve the reactionary classes, while their own leaders serve the working masses.

It should be noted that, among mission Deputies, Communists put less stress than others on the perfections on living leaders. This phenomenon undoubtedly derives from criticism of the "cult of personality" since Stalin's death, as well as from the simple fact that no one powerful figure has dominated the PCF since the death of Maurice Thorez. Communist Deputies tend, instead, to glorify the party itself. It appears that they have transferred their desire to glorify a leader into glorification of their collective leadership. Students of totalitarian movements are, of course, familiar with this phenomenon:

[Totalitarian parties] become the object of genuine worship. The Party is personified (with a capital letter: a typical sign of the process of "sacralization"), as the all-powerful, infallible, protective, transcendent Party; the Party is elevated to the dignity of an end in itself, instead of remaining in the realm of means and techniques. Thus, participation gains a truly religious nature. Some have wanted to call Communism "a secular religion:" the term applies equally to Fascism and to all totalitarian parties. And the religious character does not derive solely from their structure—very close to that of a Church—or from their totalitarianism (by nature a religion is totalitarian, since it constitutes a global explanatory system): it rests even more on the truly sacred nature of the ties of solidarity.[10]

Although mission-motivated Communist Deputies put little stress on the qualities of their living leaders, their reverence for past, defunct leaders was clear. Nearly all, for example, referred to Marx as if his words were the embodiment of truth. This phenomenon is too well known to merit elaboration here. As Bertrand Russell noted in 1920: "[Bolshevism is] a religion, with elaborate dogmas and inspired scriptures. When Lenin wishes to prove some proposition, he does so, if possible, by quoting texts from Marx and Engels."[11]

Communist mission Deputies also showed reverence for other leaders from their party's past history.

> *Q:* What qualities did you most admire in Thorez?
>
> *Deputy, PCF:* Everything! Everything! Thorez had all the best qualities. He was an open spirit, always interested in learning and always open to new ideas. He was a real fighter. He never gave up in struggling for the interests of the oppressed classes. He was a man who was humble with the people. He never gave himself airs. He always knew how to receive people of the lowest stations and to show his respect for them. He had an incredible intellectual interest. In his last years he taught himself Latin, just because he was always interested in language and had always wanted to learn it. He was generous, brilliant. And he was never discouraged, no matter how dark things might seem for the cause.

Note that the "intellectual" and "brilliant" qualities of the leader allow him to devine and interpret doctrine in situations where lesser mortals are confused. This attitude is a psychological mechanism which allows the mission participant to escape from the ambiguity of most real-world situations. ("I may be uncertain, but our leader knows the correct line to take, and I will follow his lead.")

The leader does not, of course, have complete freedom of ideological interpretation. He cannot stray too far from his mission followers' image of what the basic doctrine says. Pompidou, for instance, must continue to appear like a faithful implementer of de Gaulle's ideas or risk mass defection from mission Gaullists. Leaders are always in some sense prisoners of what their followers expect of them.

b. Other Political Activists. Mission participants see themselves as part of a large organization of united co-believers. All in the movement work together closely, remain loyal to each other, and struggle for broad common goals. The familiar Communist term "comrade" symbolizes the way these men see each other. The well-known tendency among Communists to refer to "the Party" as the source of strength and wisdom symbolizes the value they place on their common efforts. These men want very much to feel part of a united powerful group working together for the highest ideals. This desire suggests why *dévotée* parties everywhere invariably develop the theme of "brotherhood" or "comradeship" as a central norm for personal relations among party activists.

This same attitude prevails, with some nuances, among the Gaullists. In speaking of party members in their own district, Gaullist Deputies glowingly praise the men who work with and support them, stressing the close rapport between them and their followers. In referring to the national party, however, they often stress the theme of unity in diversity. Probably because Gaullism does not possess as unified a structure or as articulated an ideology as Communism, many mission Gaullists took care to point out that "one finds everything" in Gaullism. By this they meant all ideological positions—from extreme Right to extreme Left. These same Deputies hastened to stress that these "old-fashioned differences of opinion" have been submerged in Gaullist thought, which provides new dynamic ideas on which all agree. In these expressions one feels a definite fear that this present unity may not be a lasting one. This fear leads to vehement assertions that Gaullist unity is real—even after de Gaulle:

Q: Some people say the UDR may now break up with de Gaulle's departure from politics.

Deputy, UDR: [Very upset.] How can they say that? Gaullism is not one man! It's an idea—an ideal—about how our institutions should work. You don't abandon your ideas. The UDR is *more united than ever*. Experience alone proves this fact. We were the *only ones* in France to remain together and true to our ideas during the Presidential election. My opponents—I won't say anything to criticize them. They have the right to exist. They are honest men. I can only state the facts: every opposition party splintered after de Gaulle's departure. The Center was deeply divided, some for and some against de Gaulle. The Independent Republicans joined us only after some deliberation. The non-Communist Left gave utter proof if its divisions: the FGDS no longer exists. Yet we, the majority, got together and obtained the biggest support we've ever had. This should demonstrate the continued strength of Gaullism without de Gaulle.

The *will* to unity shared by many Gaullists has surely helped to give real cohesion to the Gaullist movement.

This passion for close relations with others in the cause takes its extreme expression in the sentiment that unity is most often found in battle. The metaphor of war is common. Both Communists and Gaullists tell how they have struggled and suffered together against common enemies, thus forging an unbreakable party unity.

Q: What is the future of Gaullism now [after de Gaulle's resignation] ?

Deputy, UDR: Those who said we'd fall apart have been shown to be absolutely wrong. They didn't take into account the unity of our movement. *After years of battle together, after struggling and fighting together, we have a spirit of unity.* We're not going to split apart at the first adverse moment. [Emphasis added.]

This theme of never-ending struggle against enemies is, of course, common in the literature on groups which seem likely to contain mission participants.[1][2]

Political actors outside the party can only be enemies for mission participants, since their actions undermine the only worthy political cause. Hostility toward outsiders is intense:

> *Deputy, PCF: We* are not in politics for personal reasons, but to work for the public good. We're not like the other politicians. They seek money, often. They accumulate positions and keep their private jobs, so as to gain personal advantages.

> *Deputy, UDR:* There was a factory in X which was going to shut down. The Communist Mayor was doing nothing about it. In fact, he was happy to see it shutting down, because that would mean several dozens of workers unemployed. So there would have been more discontent, which would help him.

> *Deputy, PCF:* The difference in the way Gaullists and Communists work in their districts is in the people they see. *We* see the great mass of the people—the workers, the little shop-keepers, all the little people. The Gaullists see different kinds of people—primarily the bourgeoisie and the factory-owners.

> *Deputy, UDR:* It's not possible! You can't allow a group (i.e., Communists] to exist that takes its orders from another country, that is ready to destroy us all, that wants to impose a dictatorship, that wants to take away all our liberties. They have only one goal: total power.

Why do mission participants see other politicians in this light? Religiously dedicated to their own ideals, these men apparently have difficulty understanding why other political actors refuse to join their movement. They seem to postulate only two possible motives: selfish ambition or total opposition to their cause. The first motive is by definition the exact opposite of selfless dedication, and the mission type therefore feels nothing but contempt for men of this nature.

The second motive corresponds to his own, but it involves dedication to the "wrong" cause. Therefore, these men must be fought with every weapon at hand. If the mission participant sells "opportunistic" politicians short, he grossly exaggerates the strength and unity of purpose of his mission enemies. He sees them as more clever and more ruthlessly dedicated to his own destruction than they in fact are. The existence of this enemy gives him a concrete object to fear and to fight. He can blame the setbacks of his own group on the visible enemy and believe that destruction of this enemy will automatically signal the attainment of his goals.

These attitudes lead to a misperception of the power and determination of one's opponents. Both Communists and Gaullists believe that they are the main opponents on the French political scene; each group believes the other is steadfastly determined to annihilate it. Each sees the other as the incarnation of evil.

By providing an objective enemy to fight, these attitudes insure the internal unity of each of these movements. In addition, they have proved to be useful in electoral campaigns. Gaullists have always run in elections on an anti-Communist platform: only *they* can save France from totalitarian rule. Communists picture themselves as the only true working-class party, leading the workers' fight against the Gaullist party of Big Banks and Capitalist Monopolies. These electoral tactics have not only bolstered the emotional needs of both Gaullists and Communists, but have also served their causes well. They have in addition, however, sustained a deep schism in French society which contributes to the shakiness of French political institutions.

c. Voters. The mission Deputy likes to see himself as part of a mighty movement which most voters enthusiastically support. Certain that they are following a true doctrine, these activists cannot admit that most ordinary citizens are not zealously devoted to the cause. Both Gaullists and Communists believe that "the great masses of the people" support them. Only a fraction of "discredited" or "unreliable" elements support their opponents.

Gaullists, for example, repeatedly assured me of their nationwide backing. Only "a few die-hard Centrists," "the small fractions of the disunited non-Communist Left," and the "totalitarian Communists" opposed Gaullism. Communists claimed that they represented "the people," while the Gaullists stood only for some small "reactionary elements." These attitudes are illustrated in the following remarks by a Gaullist and a Communist:

> *Deputy, UDR:* I am very proud of being an elected official. That is, of having the confidence of tens of thousands of people. It's very important, and it's a support for the sometimes very difficult job that must be accomplished.

> *Deputy, PCF:* In this district we have really close contacts with the people. We're all united in the same struggle. The people are behind us in complete harmony with the Party.

These large faithful masses demonstrate the validity of the doctrine to which these men have devoted their lives.

These men must, of course, reconcile their feelings with the ostensible fact that their parties do not have even majority support in the nation. They usually do this by projection. Feeling that their party represents the truth, they believe that most people's "real" sympathies must lie with their party. Not all the people vote for this party because they are duped or misled by the party's opponents. Thus, Gaullists claimed they could best serve the workers, but Communist propaganda and control of the unions kept the workers from realizing their own best interests. Communists claimed that Gaullist control of radio and television "confused" the voters and prevented "democratic" election outcomes.

These explanations are mechanisms which allow mission participants to explain why a divine, unquestionable truth is not accepted by everyone. If they could not explain why their doctrine is rejected by many, they might begin to question it themselves. Their explanations reinforce a psychologically necessary conviction that they are embarked on a mission of transcendental truth.

4. Conception of One's Role in the Legislature

The mission Deputy sees the National Assembly simply as one structure, among many, in which he can support his cause. It is not even the central institution for this purpose. Gaullists see control of the executive branch as most important for their goals. Communists stress that the major way to promote their cause lies in "organizing the masses"—presumably through the PCF and the CGT (France's largest labor union).

Gaullists and Communists both admitted, however, that the Assembly could be of use for their purposes. The Gaullists recognized the importance of a solid Assembly majority to back the Gaullist Government at all times. For them the legislature is a body which should support their control of the executive branch. Communists held that one of their important functions in the Assembly was to use that body as a springboard for national attention. Since speeches in the Assembly make news, Communists felt that these speeches should be made with an eye to the national publicity they could gain for the PCF.

It seems safe to conclude that the primary function these men assign to their work in the legislature is a political one: support for the national movement to which they belong.

5. Attitude Toward One's Own Party

Mission Deputies see their party as a tight-knit group of fellow believers. One might predict that this attitude would strongly affect the structure which mission Deputies impose on their political organizations. Internal party democracy, for instance, implying free and open discussion of party goals is unnecessary if those goals are seen as evident in the party ideology. Furthermore, those who see the party as a militant fighting organization would stress the need for rigid discipline in the ranks. One would therefore expect parties containing large numbers of mission participants to show less internal democracy and to impose greater discipline on party members than do other parties. My data suggests that the UDR and the PCF contain larger numbers of mission participants than other French parties, and these two parties do indeed seem less democratic and more disciplined than other parties represented in the Assembly.[13]

6. General Orientation Toward Politics

One of the most significant findings is that mission participants love conflict in politics. They feel most exalted in intense life-or-death struggles for their cause. These struggles apparently confirm their belief in the purposefulness of their actions. They proclaim with joy the closeness they find with their fellow comrades while fighting a common enemy. Given their political backgrounds, these attitudes are not surprising. At least twelve of these nineteen men served in some way in the French Resistance; the other seven entered French politics in the 1945-48 period. These periods were remarkably well suited for developing the idea of struggle *against* a common enemy, *for* a glorified ideal, *with* dedicated compatriots.

Typical of this attitude is the delight with which a Gaullist Deputy described a political battle during recent elections:

> *Q:* What has been your most enjoyable political experience?
> *Deputy, UDR:* Oh, just about everything. I'd say especially the electoral campaigns. During the campaigns you leave aside all the ordinary everyday problems, all the everyday restraints. You forget all that and engage completely in a real struggle. It's like a sporting event, with your teams of militants. You bring together all the militants that you haven't had time to see lately, those faithful who have been a little neglected, and you reunite them. You bring together all those people of the same point of view, you meet others every day of your own point of view. Or else you fight the people who aren't on your side. You get your team together to combat the others.

Another Gaullist Deputy reflected the same attitude when he remarked:

> *Deputy, UDR:* I don't really like making a speech on very abstract technical problems. I don't like to rise and give a complicated speech

at the Assembly. On the other hand, I do love to speak at public meetings. I even look forward with enthusiasm to the questions people put to me there.

Q: Aren't you afraid of the questions your opponents might raise at these meetings?

R: No, on the contrary, I welcome them. That adds more zest to the meeting and gives me more interest. *It seems to fire me up and make me more eager to dispute them.* [Emphasis added.]

Direct confrontation with acknowledged opponents provides exciting moments in the lives of many mission Deputies.

These men, then love to perform under fire. If danger threatens their movement, they summon up deep inner reserves to meet the threat:

Q: Didn't the resignation of General de Gaulle make you think about leaving public life yourself?

Deputy, UDR: Absolutely not! I had exactly the opposite reaction! His departure gave me *more* desire to continue, to keep up the fight. It's that much more important now. Before, while he was here, there was no danger. Now there's a real need to keep active. In fact, if I hadn't been active before, I would become active now. I would enter politics now to help defend my ideas.

This response would surprise no one who followed the Gaullist Presidential campaign during May and June, 1969. It was typical of the Gaullist faithful throughout France. The moment of gravest threat to the movement proved the moment of the movement's greatest unity and activity.

The Communists, too, feel this reinforcement of ties with the PCF during threatening periods. After one Communist Deputy had described an incredible period of suffering in his life (imprisonment, underground hideouts, near-starvation, etc.), I asked if he had grown discouraged or begun to question his reasons for supporting a revolutionary organization. He replied:

Deputy, PCF: Discouraged? Never! In the worst of times less than ever. These moments give you the exaltation to keep going! In the midst of struggle you can't give up. Then it's most important *and most enjoyable to continue.* [Emphasis added.]

The mission participant wants to witness for his faith, and his opportunity to do so is best when sin is most widespread. In other words, the mission participant will be most active when the world about him looks darkest: it will then have the greatest need for his saving mission.

These insights into the attitudes of mission participants may help to shed light on the well-known tendency for extremists to feed on each other. The political struggle seems most useful and enjoyable to these men when danger and adversity are highest. When are danger and adversity likely to seem high? Primarily, when a very visible opponent with a strong power base is single-mindedly working for your own destruction. This opponent provides a clear objective against which to fight, as well as a rationale for explaining why one's own cause has not yet triumphed.

Leaders of mission movements therefore find it in their interest to play up the power of other mission movements, so as to give their own followers a concrete evil against which to fight. The resulting intensification of political conflict may attract additional mission participants into politics, which in turn raises the political temperature still higher. The result is an ever-increasing spiral of new participants and increased conflict which may eventually result in anarchy, a civil war, or military intervention. A process of this sort seems to have occurred in the last years of the Weimar Republic—with well-known disastrous results.

During the early years of the Fourth Republic, Gaullists and Communists found it easier to fight each other than the Republic itself.[14] The Fourth Republic was a nebulous entity, which could only with difficulty be seen as a single-minded, purposive opponent. But Communists and Gaullists were highly visible and could easily be made the epitome of evil ("the Communist totalitarian menace," "Right-wing militarist adventurers"). By picturing the other side as its principal opponent, each organization could inspire its followers to increased efforts, while posing as the only dynamic force wishing to protect the nation's real interests. These tactics were able to mobilize activists and the general public when the threats from both sides seemed very real, as they did in the 1947-48 period. Most observers agree that the vigorous actions taken by the then Socialist Minister of the Interior Jules Moch against followers of both the PCF and the Gaullist RPF, coupled with the long Queuille stay at the Presidency of the Council in 1948-49, ended the initial threat of these two groups to the Fourth Republic. Moch's actions and Queuille's stability simply gave the lie to both sides' claims that the other side posed an immediate threat of taking over absolute power.

Both sides then turned to castigating the Fourth Republic itself. In keeping with their interests they tried to picture it as their main opponent and a threat to their existence. For the Communists it became "the puppet of American imperialism," for the Gaullists, "the instrument of little, self-serving men and divisive factions." The Gaullist tactics were especially valuable. One finds that even today Gaullists continue to spread this one-dimensional image of the Fourth Republic. At every opportunity, especially during elections, they characterize their non-Communist opponents as "men of the Fourth Republic," who wish to restore "a weak, divisive style of governing in order to serve their own petty ambitions." Both Gaullists and Communists have found electoral payoffs in painting their opponents as determined and base enemies of the true national interests.

Conclusion

The personality of the mission type impels him inexorably into conflict with other political activists. When large numbers of mission types of *opposing* movements exist in a nation, the probability of intense conflict becomes high. The mission activist does not want to resolve conflict or solve problems. He wants to promote his beliefs and to defeat all other politicians. Since these other men naturally oppose him, he comes to see them as symbols of evil. This attitude helps to justify any action which may defend the cause and defeat the opponents.

When many mission participants are actively opposing each other, violent and spiraling political conflict seems inevitable. The chance for conflict incites new mission participants to enter the fray: they enjoy the conflict and they see a "need" for their action to "save a rotten world." Thus, while pursuing high ideals, mission participants may help to bring about situations in which those ideals have less chance of realization than if they had never entered politics.

4 The Program Participant

The program participant enjoys learning about his environment, manipulating it, solving problems in it. He needs to feel that he is effectively dealing with real situations external to his own personality. Hence, he gains satisfaction from involvement in problem-solving activity. When he enters politics, his main satisfactions derive from working on policies which affect social reality.

This participant has been described, in part, by other social scientists. Smith, Bruner, and White call this orientation to politics "object appraisal."[1] Fenton says activists of this type have an "issue-orientation" to politics.[2] Sorauf speaks of a "policy-making incentive"[3] and Browning of "policy-influencing behavior."[4] One of the legislative roles observed by Wahlke, et al., was that of "inventor," a role adopted by the legislator who "is interested in solving the current problems of his state...."[5] Numerous autobiographies of former political leaders reveal the concern for solving problems and influencing public policies that is characteristic of this participant.[6] Perhaps the most comprehensive description to date of the program-motivated political leader can be found in Barber's portrayal of a type he calls the "Lawmaker."[7] Of legislators with this orientation Barber writes:

... their satisfactions come from the active manipulation of the [legislative] process, rather than passive reception of benefits. In other words, Lawmakers more than other members stress adaptation to the role, rather than the status, of legislator. They invest intellectual and emotional energy in coping with the elements of the environment most relevant to the tasks which define this role.... Lawmakers show a pressure for completion, for following through and finishing legislative tasks.... They are especially pleased when they themselves take some effective part in a successful action.[8]

Payne first described and labeled this incentive in his study of Colombia.[9] Since that time program participants have been observed in Connecticut, the Dominican Republic, Brazil, and France.[10] It would appear that at least a few program participants will be found in most political settings. It is equally clear that the ratio of this type to others varies considerably from setting to setting and has important consequences for political behavior.[11]

The *main identifying characteristic* of the program participant is the strong interest he expresses during interviews in working on public policies and in overseeing the application of those policies. This interest usually manifests itself in three different ways: (1) he talks at length about laws, public programs, and

Table 4-1
Distribution of Program Participants by Legislative Party Group

Party[a]	Number of Deputies	% of Program Deputies
Non-Inscrit	0	–
RI app	0	–
RI	6	43%
UDR app	1	7%
UDR	4	29%
PDM	0	–
FGDS	3	21%
PC	0	–
TOTAL	14	100%

[a]For explanation of abbreviations, see List of Abbreviations.

social problems; (2) he spontaneously and enthusiastically refers to his own efforts to shape public policy; and (3) he enjoys discussing the concrete details of policies and policy-making.

1. *Lengthy discussion of public programs.* Men will usually seize an opportunity to talk about their favorite subject. When the interviewer asks a program-oriented question, the man who talks for fifteen minutes on this topic and issues related to it clearly reveals his programmatic interests. Asked about their work in the Assembly, some status Deputies made laconic replies such as "I work on the budget"—period. Compare this uninspiring and conversation-blocking response to that of a program Deputy after a similar, program-oriented question:

> *Q:* You said just now that your work as Mayor was a tough job. What exactly has this work consisted of?
>
> *Deputy, UDR:* Well, it consists primarily of obtaining public facilities for a small town whose economic growth has long been retarded. It's difficult to explain to an American. You can't know what it's like where I come from. When I became Mayor, there were only two new buildings in town, and they hadn't even been completed. Now there are 350 new housing units, thanks to the efforts I've made.
>
> When I came there, they didn't even have running water; in fact, hardly *any* drinking water. I helped to set up an entire water system. They didn't have a single secondary school in the town. Now I've seen that a high school has been built for the local children.
>
> Then there's also the problem of flood control. They used to have terrible floods every year. The land was being wasted. For over

100 years nothing had been done about it. I worked to see that the water was channeled, that dams were built, to prevent this waste of land. So, you see, I've been concerned with modifying the rural areas nearby, as well as the town itself. But it's pitiful what few means we have. It's just a small town, and there's not enough money.

Program participants do not, as do other participants, mention public policies casually or in an offhand manner. Focusing directly on these issues, they tell the interviewer a good deal about them and about their own role in influencing the outcomes.

This orientation can clearly be seen in the response of another program Deputy to a different program-oriented question:

> *Q:* What aspect of your work in your committee interests you most?
> *Deputy, UDR:* . . . I've been especially active on a project for reforming the social security system.
> *Q:* What kind of reform would this be?
> *R:* It would make a standard system for *all* French citizens, eliminating the multiplicity of different laws and measures we now have. I've been working with my colleague, X, on a test to elucidate the exact means for financing this new reform. At present, labor-intensive industries finance the greater part of the system. This is a handicap. It's all right in a period of full employment, but it does not provide enough money in times of underemployment. So we propose a different means of financing the system. It would be based on the value-added tax paid by industry. This would make for a more just system. . . .

He went on to explain at length just what the system would entail. This man is obviously wrapped up in his work and anxious to talk about it.

2. *Spontaneous enthusiasm for programmatic work.* It is difficult to prevent the program participant from talking about programs. He brings them up with little or no prompting from the interviewer. One Deputy (Jean-Claude Schweitzer; see Chapter 2) began to tell me about the problems of his region before I could ask my first question. At several points in the interview he seized on unlikely topics to turn the subject back to policy matters. For instance, I asked about his relations with a Minister from his *département*. Rather than discuss his political dealings with this man, he described an incident in which his friendship with the Minister helped him have an impact on Government policy relating to milk production.

This eagerness to discuss his ongoing policy activities reveals the respondent's underlying incentive for his work. One Socialist Deputy was not content with merely telling me what he was doing in his town. He wanted to show me the results of his efforts. Already late for a wedding he had to perform, he would not let me leave his village without giving me a half-hour tour. On almost every street he pointed to some new building or piece of work he had helped sponsor, often stopping to tell me about it in detail.

> *Deputy, FGDS (Socialist):* Over there you see the addition to the school. Enrollment has jumped fifty percent in this town in the last ten years, so we simply needed more space for the children. . . . Those are some low-income housing units we've put up for the old people of the village. . . . This street we're driving on used to be a dirt road three years ago. I finally succeeded in getting it paved last year. . . . Here's the main factory in town. This street is narrow, and there's no other place to park a car, so you can hardly get through when the men are at work. I plan to have that abandoned house over there torn down and set up a parking lot for the workers. We can't go on like this. . . . Here's a playing field for the children. It used to be an overgrown, empty lot, so we converted it for the young people's use. They play soccer here on weekends and after school. . . . [And so on. . . .]

This unsolicited tour indicated clearly the enjoyment this man derives from active involvement in local policy-making.[12]

3. *Interest in concrete details of policy.* Concerned with effectively influencing public policies, the program participant naturally shows great interest in specific aspects of policy-making. Concrete policy details are not side matters for him, as they are for other participants. Exactly where a new road will run; the actual number of gallons a dam will hold; the type of apartment house to be built in his city—these matters are of central interest to him because they indicate precisely how, in the real world, problems can be solved. Participants who do not share a program incentive find these topics boring or petty.

In their concentration on programmatic details program Deputies often neglect "larger" issues of ideology and government policy. They often become so absorbed in telling precisely how they have influenced particular programs that one never does learn where they stand on an ideological spectrum. The focus is on matters of substance, not of style.

This emphasis on concrete issues is illustrated in the lengthy remarks of one program Deputy (Jean-Claude Schweitzer; see Chapter 2) concerning his work in promoting regional development. Many Deputies told me they were "interested" in this problem, but then said no other word on the subject. This man could hardly speak of anything else. And his conversation is sprinkled with concrete points and examples: the exact size of industrial zones; their advantages and disadvantages; state subsidies for relocating businesses, training workers, and setting up technical schools; the highway system in his region; ways of consolidating small plots of land; the use of modern agricultural machinery. His eagerness to explain these specific substantive matters indicates his program motivation.[13]

Attitudinal Correlates of the Program Incentive

1. Absence of the Expression of Satisfactions Which Define Other Incentive Types

a. Absence of the Mission Incentive. The main identifying characteristic of the mission incentive is the participant's emphasis on devotion to his cause and its ideology. Program Deputies laid no stress on dedication to a movement, nor did they show abiding interest in ideological matters. In contrast to mission Deputies, the commitment of program Deputies to their parties is not an all-absorbing passion. They can describe their party in matter-of-fact, even casual, terms:

> *Deputy, RI:* We're all very individualistic. You might say we have a pleasant anarchy in the group. Luckily, we don't try to impose voting discipline on ourselves. We have a *cameraderie*, but not a very good organization.

> *Q:* Did you have the support of a party when you first ran for the Assembly?
> *Deputy, UDR:* Parties had no importance. They're not important at all. All that's important is to have local support. I've never run under a party label. I never use a label in my campaigns. We don't have parties here the way you do in the United States. Sure, we have some groupings, some organizations, and maybe now some of the parties are getting a little more strength. But it's totally different. Someday perhaps it will come; someday we may have parties like you do. But not now.

Program participants do not see their party as the dedicated band of marching militants perceived by mission types.

Program Deputies also showed no interest in ideological issues. They rarely volunteered to discuss the politico-philosophical tenets of their belief systems—even when questioned directly about it:

> *Q:* What attracted you to Gaullism?
> *Deputy, UDR:* Basically, I wanted to see France governed by men who

were really capable. De Gaulle got us out of the Algerian War, he represents us well abroad, he's helped France progress on the human and national levels. But still, there have been some stupidities committed under his régime. It's hard to govern any country.

A mission Gaullist would have seized on this question to explain "the true meaning of the Gaullist philosophy." This program Gaullist is more pragmatic (and incidentally, shows no trace of the blind hero-worship of mission Gaullists).

b. Absence of the Status Incentive. Program Deputies were not preoccupied with obtaining offices or marks of prestige—the identifying characteristics of the status participant. They did not indicate, as do status participants, that they saw their life in terms of a ladder of positions they must scale. They would even stress their own humble background, or their discomfort at the marks of status accorded them as Deputy:

> *Q:* Have you ever thought you would like to be a Minister?
> *Deputy, FGDS (Socialist):* Never. I'm too old now anyway, but I've honestly never thought of it. When I was thirty-five, I had absolutely no idea I could ever become a Deputy. It still seems strange to me. You see, I come from the working class, from *very* humble origins, and it's hard to get used to my new position.

> *Deputy, RI:* I go to various meetings around my district; I show up at fairs, road shows, student award ceremonies. And it bothered me at first that they always put me in the front rows, that they would always introduce me to the people as "*Monsieur le Député,*" and ask me to say a few words. I wasn't used to this kind of treatment. It seemed strange to me. Now I've grown used to it. I accept the idea that the Deputy is considered something of a local figure and is supposed to make little speeches whenever he shows up at these gatherings.

The status participant, eager for signs of deference from others, would never make such modest remarks about himself or his background.

The lack of enthusiasm for status-related topics indicates the lack of this incentive:

> *Q:* How did you come to be elected committee chairman?
> *Deputy, UDR:* I don't know. It's hard to say. Because I was an old hand there, that's all.

This man appeared embarrassed at a question relating to personal promotion.

When I persisted, he changed the subject from how he obtained the post to what he did in the position.

When program Deputies did discuss the tactics of position-getting, they were able to stand back and analyze the factors which helped them win or lose public office—without the status participant's high elation at winning and anxious fear at losing. Like Barber's "Lawmaker," the program Deputy appears "to be unusually objective. He is much less prone to distort reality for defensive or need-fulfilling purposes."[14]

c. **Absence of the Obligation Incentive.** Obligation Deputies participate in politics to relieve feelings of guilt about their nonparticipation. While in politics, they are especially concerned with morally proper behavior and with exhibiting their own personal purity. I found no such concerns among program Deputies. Neither in their description of their entry into politics nor in their discussion of their present work did I feel any inner moral drives impelling program Deputies to participate. Throughout the interviews they stressed policy goals and manipulation of the policy process as their main focus of interest. Their attention centers on problems and results, not on principles and moral behavior.

*2. Attitude Toward Interview and
   Interviewer*

Program Deputies appeared genuinely interested in helping me understand what I wanted to know. Their interview behavior contrasted with that of other respondents. Unlike mission Deputies who used the interview to expound their ideology, program Deputies stuck to the point of the questions. They were open and friendly during the conversation, while obligation Deputies were formal, status Deputies uncooperative. Program Deputies granted an average of one hundred minutes for each interview—somewhat more than mission Deputies (ninety minutes) and obligation Deputies (eighty-five minutes), and nearly twice as much as status Deputies (fifty-five minutes).

These men, in short, respond positively to the interview situation and try to be useful to the interviewer. In this regard they again appear very similar to Barber's "Lawmakers," who show "a generalized ability to pay heed to the work at hand, whether it be politics or something very different. For example, in the interview situation, Lawmakers appeared unusually interested and cooperative, attentive to the questions, thoughtful in reply."[15]

3. Attitude Toward "Significant Others"

a. **Leaders in Higher Positions.** Mission and obligation Deputies endow their leaders with superhuman qualities. Status Deputies tear them down to less than human size. Program Deputies neither glorify leaders nor denigrate them. They try to evaluate them objectively, often giving them the benefit of the doubt, but evincing no signs of hero worship.

> *Q:* How do you see the régime in the future—that is, without a leader as strong as de Gaulle?
>
> *Deputy, UDR:* I think there's no problem at all. All countries have had, at one moment or another, a man. Look at England. England had Churchill, who was a very extraordinary man, and then after him she's just had a certain number of ordinary Prime Ministers. In short, England has continued on its path with the policies she wanted, but it hasn't raised any problems. You can have from time to time an exceptional man. Adenauer was an exceptional man, but German politics has continued perfectly well without him. You have also had in the United States some exceptional men, but not all American Presidents have been exceptional, and American political life has continued. I think there is absolutely no problem at all.

Although this man has great respect for de Gaulle, he is able to see him—and leaders in general—in a more sensible, matter-of-fact light than mission Gaullists, who feared that France would fall apart without the great leader.

Without worshipping leaders, program Deputies usually do respect them. They admire their ability to gain the voters' trust and especially their intellectual qualities, their ability to understand the nation's problems. One Independent told me: "Giscard is brilliant. He can take the most complex problems, analyze them and state solutions in simple language." A Socialist declared: "I admire the intellectual rigor of Guy Mollet." And a Radical said of Edouard Herriot: "He was a remarkable man, a man of immense culture." As one expects, program Deputies are willing to trust those men who, they feel, understand social problems and provide intelligent policies to tackle them.

Program Deputies, not inclined to glorify their leaders, are also not inclined to denigrate the leaders of others. When leaders have little significance for one's personal stability, one does not see opposing leaders as personal threats. I saw this clearly in interviewing two different Gaullists between the first and second round of the Presidential election of 1969. One, a mission participant, denounced candidate Poher with a viciousness born of total hatred. The other, a program participant, evaluated him calmly as a person and a politician in a particular political situation. In doing so, he made the most rationally telling criticism of Poher's attempt to become President: he could not govern France with an overwhelmingly Gaullist Assembly; stalemate would result and Poher would soon be forced to dissolve the legislature and call for new elections. For this reason, the program Deputy explained carefully, a member of the UDR could not look with equanimity upon Poher's election.

b. Other Political Activists. The program Deputy respects other politicians and is eager to cooperate with them in the formulation of public policy. Each of these Deputies made positive comments about most other political actors mentioned in the interview, including some far removed from them on the political spectrum:

> *Deputy, FGDS (Socialist):* I consider myself the representative of everyone. I have friendly relations everywhere in this district. You see, I'm not sectarian. I'm a straightforward man, and I treat everyone the same. I have very good relations, for instance, with several UDR Mayors and with two Communists. But I have no trouble getting along with all the others.

> *Deputy, UDR:* I have quite cordial relations with Deputies of the Left. I have excellent relations, for example, with X [a Socialist Deputy], or with Y [a Communist Deputy], who's in my committee. Our personal relations are fine. There's a difference between the parliamentary group's position and personal relations between members of the Assembly. As a member of a group you take a political position; but outside of that group each person is an individual and you treat them as such.

These comments are striking since the three other incentive types in France went out of their way to criticize their political opponents.

Occasionally, program Deputies are critical of other politicians. They become annoyed, for instance, when they feel that others are not carrying their full share of the legislative work load. They also criticize other politicians for closed-mindedness. Program participants value open discussion and pragmatic approaches to social problems. They find it unpleasant to interact with politicians totally committed to one viewpoint. They describe this attitude with the pejorative adjective *sectaire*. Independents usually told me that Gaullist *sectarisme* was the main factor separating them from the UDR. I asked a program Independent if he felt his point of view would be given greater weight in the new Pompidou Government. He replied:

> *Deputy, RI:* I don't know. I'm not sure. There are some Gaullists who don't understand anything. They don't seem to have understood the significance of the May Events or the Referendum. There are two kinds of Gaullists: those that are more open and the sectarian ones [*les sectaires*], those who think that only they have the truth.
> *Q:* Which ones will come out on top?
> *R:* There will be some real battles. It's uncertain yet, but we'll see in the near future.

Significantly, program Socialist Deputies took the same attitude toward their Communist electoral allies. They stressed that Communist sectarian leaders hoped to engulf the Left and control all its forces.

Program Deputies, who wish to share in policy-making, know that they must be open to other politicians and their ideas if they wish others to consider seriously their own policy proposals. They lay great stress on personal independence, cooperativeness, and give-and-take relations with others. Sectarian politicians try to impose their own views without consulting others. It is hardly surprising that program participants resist these attempts to cut them out of the policy process.

c. Voters. The program Deputy sees voters in two different ways. On the one hand, he sees his constituents in realistic political terms; on the other hand, he sees them as individual people whom he likes and enjoys helping. This ability to distinguish between political and personal characteristics of his constituents sets the program Deputy off from the other three types of French legislator.

Unlike mission Deputies, who exaggerate the support their movement receives, and unlike status and obligation Deputies, who see elections as praise or condemnation of their own personality, program Deputies try to analyze local politics objectively. I heard several different descriptions of local political forces from politicians who came from different parties and regions, yet each description seemed to fit what I took to be the political situation in the particular district. This variety differed from accounts other types gave me. Status Deputies, for instance, almost always stressed their own personal appeal in explaining election victories, mission Deputies the appeal of their movements.

When the program Deputy considers his constituents as people—not as voters—his frame of reference changes. He sees them as individual citizens whom he will help if he can. He appears to enjoy contacts with his electorate:

> *Deputy, RI:* In your activities for constituents your own life becomes enriched. You feel that you are really helping to get people out of jams. You get a real satisfaction from helping them. Helping people with their many daily problems gives you a very human sense of satisfaction.

> *2d Deputy, RI:* You are enriched by human contacts. You get to know the problems of the people in your district. In coming to understand these problems and in helping these people, you yourself gain human stature.

> *3d Deputy, RI:* I'm a profoundly social being. I'm very interested in people. I like to see them rise just a little higher than they are, and I can help them do this.

As far as I could tell, these statements were made in all sincerity. Program Deputies have respect for, and interest in, their own constituents.

4. Conception of One's Role in the Legislature

Program Deputies see the Assembly as a policy-making body. They see their main task as the formulation of laws, and stress the importance of committees in lawmaking.

> *Q:* What aspect of your work as legislator has interested you most since your election?
>
> *Deputy, RI:* I was especially involved this past session in two major debates on areas I knew well: education and union rights. I followed with extreme interest the entire course of these debates. I'm on the X Committee, and I worked on the proposed laws in these areas which came up before the Committee. I followed every detail of these debates in both the Committee and in public sessions. I studied the very numerous amendments presented and didn't miss a minute of any meeting.[16]

All program Deputies took this view. Most emphasized the importance of their committee work and specialized knowledge.

> *Q:* What aspect of your work as legislator has interested you most since your election?
>
> *2d Deputy RI:* For many years I've specialized on problems of national defense. I'm a committee *rapporteur* on the French Navy's yearly budget. I have to study these problems year-round. It also means that I have to get about a great deal: I've traveled throughout France, and I've been abroad inspecting military bases, arms factories and the like. . . . We meet with Navy officials frequently, several times a week at some periods. Hardly a week goes by when I don't come to Paris to work on committee problems.
>
> *Q:* What specific problems have you worked on?
>
> *R:* There are two basic areas the committee handles: Title 3, which deals with military administration [*fonctionnement*], and Title 5, the area of *matériels*. I work mostly on Title 3 problems. I've studied all the texts which concern administration of the military service. For instance, we've recently been talking about shortening the term of military service. . . .

Some Program Deputies chafe under the present institutional arrangements which favor a weak Assembly. They would like to have more power to influence legislation than they now have.

> *Q:* In your work do you think you have been able to modify any of the Government's policies?
>
> *Deputy, RI:* That's exactly where we make reproaches to the Government. We don't think they've taken sufficiently into account the observations of us legislators. They just don't listen to us enough.

> *Deputy, FGDS (Socialist):* In order to study the legislative texts and the various bills, you have to have facts which are simply not handed to you by the Government. You need independent facts and sources to make your own judgments, and it's hard to get them. Even the administrative aides furnished the committee and the Assembly are suspect, because they are controlled by the majority.

Program Deputies—even those in the opposition—do not, however, advocate sweeping institutional changes. They manage to find issues on which they can exert influence within the legislature. Most stated that specialized knowledge is the way to achieve this influence.

> *Deputy, FGDS (Socialist):* If you work on one problem fully and objectively, people pay attention. Those on the Minister's staff take notice of your arguments. I'm optimistic on this subject: if you do your work well, it will have an influence.

The belief that hard work and specialized knowledge will lead to specific policy influence is central to the program Deputy, and only partial doubt is cast on his belief when he operates in what appears to an outsider as a highly centralized, executive-centered system in which, supposedly, legislators have no power.[17]

In discussing the legislature, program Deputies distinguish themselves from all others by emphasizing "rules of the game." Although they do not use this term, they clearly support informal norms which insure cooperative interaction and policy-making opportunities. They stress *expertise* and *hard work*, as already shown. A third norm is that of *courtesy*. Deputies must, they believe, avoid personal recriminations which poison the atmosphere and hinder legislative work.

> *Deputy, UDR app:* We try to do a constructive job. And almost all the Deputies get along well together. We have many contacts with each other, and we work well together.

> *Deputy, FGDS (Radical):* We have excellent relations with each other at the Assembly. It's a milieu that is not in any way closed. Even during the electoral campaigns, when you are competing against each other, you maintain a courtesy, a *camaraderie*. I'd say that our relations are much more intimate than they were previously—more close.
>
> *Q:* Than in the Fourth Republic?
>
> *R:* Yes, they are closer now. We used to have violent conflicts then.

This desire to cooperate with other Deputies leads to a fourth norm: *depersonalization of conflict.* Unlike other Deputies, these men distinguish the individual from his political position.

> *Deputy, UDR:* There's a difference between the group's position and your personal relations with members of that group. When the group takes a position, that's a political act. But individually each person in the group should be treated as a fellow human being.

> *Q:* Do people in your committee get along, even if they come from different parties?
>
> *2d Deputy, UDR:* Sure. We get along fine with the Communists, for example.
>
> *Q:* There are no personal conflicts?
>
> *R:* Never. Of course, they will tell us that they can't vote for a particular law, but it's always for political reasons only.

These Deputies help to defuse conflict by concentrating on issues rather than on personalities. Status or mission Deputies usually see those who stand between them and their goals as despicable individuals. They then impose these personal antagonisms onto political struggles, intensifying the conflict.

In supporting norms which tone down conflict and promote effective work, program Deputies constitute a class by themselves in the Assembly. None of the other respondents support those basic legislative rules of the game which are simply taken for granted in American politics.

5. Attitude Toward One's Own Party

My initial expectation was that program Deputies would have favorable attitudes toward their parties, seeing them as necessary tools by which men can work together to achieve common goals. The findings do not wholly bear out this expectation. In trying to understand the program Deputy's view, one must know the history of French political parties. The French have usually had many antagonistic parties; some have been weak and fragmented, others centralized and rigidly ideological; parties have usually been unable to provide stable government; and they are seen in a critical light by voters and political leaders.[18] These facts, along with my own research findings, suggest that status and mission politicians have played important roles in French political parties.

These participants have probably helped to create political parties with different aims and methods of operation than those which appeal to program participants. When program participants find themselves in organizations where many men squabble bitterly over positions of prestige and others seek to gain control of the organization to impose their own ideology on it, they are unlikely to see those organizations as effective structures for promoting their own programmatic goals.

In addition, the present structure of French government and the overwhelming strength of Gaullists since 1958 have, in fact, prevented most French parties from playing important policy roles for some years. For these historical, institutional, and political reasons, program Deputies outside the UDR do not see their party as an effective organization for influencing policy. This view seems realistic within the French context.

Program Deputies do, nevertheless, feel an attachment to their party. They trust and respect other men and like to cooperate with them. This positive attitude toward others probably extends in time to the organization in which the bulk of their interactions with other men takes place. Indeed, their ability to develop close personal relations with others may provide the cement that holds their parties together during periods of internal friction and political defeat.

Program Deputies *within* the UDR *do* see their party as an effective organization for achieving policy goals. These men asserted that their majority status and voting discipline allowed them to be effective legislators. By working within the party caucus at the Assembly to promote their own policy preferences, they can have a real impact on legislation, since a victory in the caucus usually assures them of eventual victory in the Assembly. Their own experience therefore leads these men to see this major party as a useful instrument for involvement in policy formulation.

6. General Orientation Toward Politics

Program Deputies love politics. They enjoy all aspects of it—as anyone who talks to them quickly realizes. They like to build bridges, write amendments to agricultural bills, help constituents establish pension rights, and construct promising tickets for coming elections.

> *Deputy, RI:* It's a fascinating occupation. You lead an incredibly active life. You examine all the problems of society. You see everything.

> It's something you couldn't do anywhere else in life. You work on the national level, even the international level. It's a work which interests me enormously, even though it's hard, especially on one's family, one's children. It imposes strict obligations on you. But it's an interesting life. When I consider the variety and importance of the subjects I deal with. . . .

These men would find it painful to withdraw from politics. In discussing their satisfactions, most stressed their programmatic successes and the enjoyment that comes from involvement in policy-making:

> *Q:* What single experience could you describe for me that gave you a great deal of satisfaction?
>
> *Deputy, UDR:* How can I answer that? I don't know. Look, I've been especially interested in my work as Mayor. In my town, when I go for a walk and I see everywhere buildings and homes which were put up because of my efforts, I feel a nice little sense of pleasure. To build a house, to see it grow out of nothing, take shape and become a house—and I don't know about how it is in your country, but here it takes a long time, a very long time, to build a house—that gives me a real satisfaction.

Some of these men do experience frustrating moments in politics. Most claimed they had had no disagreeable experiences, but three or four did expound on this theme. They disliked situations in which they found themselves excluded from the policy process:

> *Deputy, RI:* I find it disagreeable when we can't do anything at the Assembly: when discussions are cut short by the majority; when *votes bloqués*[19] are used to prevent changes in programs and to back up Government decisions which don't even meet the wishes of those in the majority. It's very frustrating. And it's hard for us to accept.

They also mentioned another experience they found disagreeable: personal conflict with highly antagonistic individuals.

> *Deputy, UDR:* I try to serve wholeheartedly, with real pleasure. I can't stand people who think only of themselves, who are ready to crush you if they get a chance, who work against you just to get somewhere themselves.

Politics loses its savor when they are unable to work on programs or when their time is spent in personal struggles against men who wish to denigrate them.

The few program Deputies who mentioned disagreeable aspects to politics did go on to state, however, that these moments were offset by the great variety of satisfactions they found in their work. None of these men is likely to withdraw voluntarily from politics. This conclusion closely resembles that reached by Barber concerning the "Lawmaker": "All things considered, the most probable sequel to the Lawmaker's initial legislative experience is a lifetime of political involvement. . . ."[20]

Conclusion

Program Deputies gain satisfactions from working on and influencing public policies. In their districts they work to improve social and economic conditions. As legislators, they become experts on particular subjects, then work to gain support for their policy proposals. They are open and cooperative with other legislators, trying to prevent political conflicts from souring personal relations among men who must work with each other every day. Although they feel strong ties to their respective parties, they do not allow partisan attachments or leadership ties to dominate their lives and political choices. Program participants probably provide an important element of stability in any political system. They almost certainly play creative and constructive roles in their nation's legislative body.

5 The Obligation Participant

The obligation participant is a man concerned with morality and morally correct behavior. Questions of "ought" and "should" loom large for this individual. He believes that men must act in a manner consistent with their moral principles. His drive to be consistent with his beliefs occasionally leads him into politics. This entry into politics usually occurs when his own internal belief that the "good citizen" "ought" to participate in politics is confronted by a particular external event which makes it clear to him that he must participate in politics or be untrue to his own principles.

While these men remain active in politics, they are likely to put special emphasis on the need for "men of principle" who follow "proper standards of conduct." The word "amateur" is the best known term to denote this participant.[1] Other terms used to describe this type are: "purist," "Reluctant," and "moralizer."[2] A variety of studies, then, and several autobiographies, make it appear that a number of men get into politics because they feel it is their duty to act in accordance with their beliefs about participation.[3] Incentive analysis suggests that all these men can be seen as a particular type of politician. They participate to fulfill a moral obligation.

The *main identifying characteristic* of the obligation participant is his focus in interviews upon moral principles and behavior consistent with them. Personal integrity and purity of motives are central concerns.

Obligation participants are most likely to reveal themselves in reacting to questions about how they entered politics and obtained their past or present political positions. They wish to make clear that these political actions, which might be interpreted as self-interested, were in fact dictated solely by their sense of duty. All seven obligation Deputies assured me that they had no political ambitions, they did not like "politics," they despised professional politicians, and they entered politics only because imperative circumstances or respected friends compelled them (in a moral sense) to accept this citizenship obligation.

There appear to be two basic patterns to their entry into politics. They become active when they perceive their nation or society is threatened, or when acquaintances in politics persuade them that they "owe" their fellow citizens service in the public arena.[4]

Three of these men felt obliged to enter politics at moments of national danger to save *la patrie* or *la république*. For instance, one entered the Resistance movement in World War II in the service of General de Gaulle. He later became active at other moments of unrest in French history after hearing

97

Table 5-1
Distribution of Obligation Participants by Legislative Party Group

Party[a]	Number of Deputies	% of Obligation Deputies
Non-Inscrit	0	–
RI app	1	14%
RI	1	14%
UDR app	1	14%
UDR	4	57%
PDM	0	–
FGDS	0	–
PC	0	–
TOTAL	7	99%[b]

[a]For explanation of abbreviations, see List of Abbreviations.
[b]Does not add to 100% because of rounding.

de Gaulle's pleas for help from "patriots" and "good French citizens." Two obligation participants were greatly influenced by the events of May, 1968. Their reaction appeared similar to that of the hundreds of thousands of Frenchmen who filled the Champs-Elysées on May 30, 1968, after an emotional television appeal by de Gaulle. They expressed shock at the recent student riots and worker strikes; horror at the possibility of a revolution or civil war; and desire to show their support of the Government during a moment of national crisis. Both men felt obliged to shoulder the burden of public office at that time. Neither had been very active in politics before May, 1968, yet each found himself Deputy a month later.

It is worth describing in detail one of these men's reactions to the "May Events," since it shows how these men explain their entry into politics. This individual claims he had had almost no contact with the political world before May 30, 1968, yet he was elected Deputy thirty days later. According to him, the situation in his city during May was very tense. "The workers controlled the streets for several days and felt they could take power into their hands." As an interested citizen, he became extremely upset that nothing was being done about the situation. He felt the local authorities should take drastic action to reassert their control. Finally, he heard de Gaulle's speech on May 30 and nearly exploded with relief. He took it as a signal for action from loyal French citizens.

For the next twenty-four hours this man single-handedly set about organizing a mass demonstration of Government supporters in his city: no mean task in a city lacking telephone service and gas for cars. After feverish efforts and with the help of trusted friends he was able to lead on June 1 a mass demonstration of Government backers, in which twice as many people participated as had participated in any workers' rally. This act, according to him, showed the "revolutionary forces" that they in fact did not have the upper hand and could not seize power without a bitter struggle. From that moment the atmosphere in his city changed and life soon returned to normal. This man then became so much a local symbol of loyal support for the Government that the UDR urged him to accept its nomination in the June legislative elections. He was swept into office on the Gaullist tidal-wave.

Before late May, 1968, this individual was a political unknown. What led him, almost alone, to lead citizen opposition to the revolutionary currents of that month?

> *Deputy, UDR:* I *had* to do it, because those who should have done it simply didn't! I waited for a while, and I began to see how the people who are responsible disappear from the scene during grave moments. When the professionals don't do their job, the amateurs have to take over.

It was a public duty, and when no one else stepped forward to do it, this man assumed the obligation to act.[5]

Four obligation Deputies did not decide to seek political positions precisely at moments of crisis; rather, they entered at times when it was made clear to them that their services were badly needed and that the time was right for them to perform their civic duty. Each claims he was persuaded to run for the National Assembly by political friends who convinced him that his fellow citizens truly needed him in that office. For instance, one Deputy, who claimed he had always disliked politics, said he had been pressed to run for the Assembly in 1962, even though he had never been politically active before that date.

> *Deputy, RI:* I was head of a local farmers association at the time, and the farmers federation told me I absolutely had to run. *I had no choice.* I didn't want to. I would just as soon have remained president of the local branch. [Emphasis added.]

Obligation participants frequently illustrate their concern for principle by stating that they *have* to act in certain ways. Implied in these statements is the idea that they must act in a particular fashion in order to live up to their own standards of right and wrong.[6]

This feeling that one must accept one's responsibilities is clear in comments of another obligation Deputy who had to be persuaded to run for the Assembly. This man (Xavier Laurent; see Chapter 2) was not active in politics in 1966 but was known to be sympathetic to Gaullism. Powerful friends in his district began urging him to run for the Assembly in the 1967 election. At first he did not take them seriously, then simply refused to run. Finally a high-ranking Gaullist leader contacted him.

> *Deputy, UDR:* Well, Monsieur X asked me: "Do you think things have been getting better in France for the past eight or nine years?" Naturally, I said, "Yes." Then he asked: "Have things been getting better for you personally?" I said again, "Yes." Then he said, "Well, up to now you have been getting all of the benefits of our action. Now it's time to take on some of the responsibilities." I said, "Ah, I hadn't thought of it like that. But now that you put it that way. . . ."

He agreed to run.

At another point in the interview this Deputy illustrates the case of the man moved to political action by the need to aid his country. He too was profoundly moved by the events of May, 1968. Elected Deputy in March, 1967, he assured me that he had found little satisfaction in that role. I naturally asked why he had bothered to run for reelection in June, 1968.

> *Deputy, UDR:* You would have had to live the events of May, 1968, to understand. We had really revolutionary conditions then. The future of the whole country was at stake. I had the impression that my actions would have results for the whole country's future. I'll give you an idea of how important this was. My wife in 1967 had a totally different view; she was wholly opposed to my running and we even talked about divorce. [He smiles.] But in 1968 she told me that I had no choice; I *had* to run as a candidate. She told me, "You have to think about the living conditions in this country, about the future of our children." That's the way things were.

This man, like the one previously cited, felt the same necessity to serve his country at a dangerous time.

Obligation participants reveal their concern for moral behavior not merely when they speak of entering politics and obtaining positions, but at numerous other points in the interview. Their emphasis on moral behavior often leads them to be more interested in the way things are done—the style of decision-making—than in what is done in terms of government policies. One Deputy stressed the style of decision-making when he stated he was unhappy with the way de Gaulle had handled the Algerian problem, even though he had agreed with de Gaulle's actual policy.

> *Deputy, UDR:* I wasn't necessarily against Algerian independence. But I was against his *manner* of doing it: making the Army think it was fighting for a French Algeria while all the time it was actually being used to promote an Algeria free of French influence. [Emphasis his.]

This man's interest in the correct way of acting led him to withdraw his support from de Gaulle in the 1958-62 period.

Style concerns are also evident in the following exchange:

> Q: What separates you from orthodox Gaullists?
>
> Deputy, UDR app: It's our separate backgrounds. In the Resistance orthodox Gaullists became attached to de Gaulle as a person. It's their *style*—their strong attachment to one man—that separates us from them. We have a different *style*. My own beliefs are what one would call Christian. I believe in respect for man, personal responsibility, devotion to others and hard work. [Emphasis added.]

Another Deputy told how moral principles influenced his attitude toward the substantive matters involved in his committee work at the Assembly on veterans' benefits. He stated that veterans deserve more assistance from the State than other citizens.

> Deputy, UDR: It's more a problem of principle than of the exact amount allocated. You have to consider the moral claims of veterans to state aid. They *should of right* be helped, and more than other citizens, because they have a moral claim to the nation's gratitude. [Emphasis his.]

A fourth Deputy stressed another principle which, he felt, ought to govern political behavior: the idea that some roles should be incompatible with politics altogether.

> Deputy, RI: I was never in politics before 1962. And since I was the president of [a local farmer's union], it was simply not right for me to be involved in politics.

Throughout the interviews these men responded to questions about politics with answers reflecting their moral and normative concerns.[7]

These interviews suggest that similar family backgrounds shaped their orientation toward politics. The families of each of these men saw politics as a dirty business. They were not, however, typically apathetic citizens. They encouraged in their sons an interest in "public affairs" and a belief that the patriotic citizen must sacrifice himself for the "national interest" at critical moments. Their attitude could be summed up in this way: politics as an activity is suspect; one enters the political arena only to perform some important service to one's country or one's fellow citizens.

This attitude may help explain why the obligation participant often appears to be an "amateur" in politics. These Deputies were raised to believe that participation in public life could be respectable—and even necessary—whereas "politics" as a career could not. These Deputies see "politicians" as out to serve their own narrow interests and do not enjoy prolonged contact with such men. None could be called a professional politician. Not one of the seven has ever held a position within a political party. Six of these Deputies together averaged less than one year of experience in any public office before election to the Assembly! Yet all claimed they had "always" or "for a long time" been interested in "public life." They give the general appearance of interested citizens who follow closely, but do not usually participate in, politics.

Attitudinal Correlates of the Obligation Incentive

1. Absence of the Expression of Satisfactions Which Define Other Incentive Types

a. Absence of the Mission Incentive. Little in these interviews suggests devotion to a cause or movement. The two Independents were—as the name implies—unattached to any movement and little interested in questions about the broad meaning of their political activity. The other five Deputies were undoubtedly attracted to various aspects of Gaullism, but only in the way "strong party identifiers" in the U.S. might be attracted to the Democratic or Republican parties. That is, they accept major tenets of Gaullism, but they have not devoted years of their life to advocating those tenets and backing political organizations that support them. Of the five Gaullists, three had simply never played a role in any political grouping. The other two had sporadically volunteered their services to the Gaullist cause, usually during elections, although neither had held any party positions.

b. Absence of the Program Incentive. The interviews make it clear that these men do not derive great satisfactions from working on public programs. Although they will talk about policy problems when asked, they clearly think this kind of work is something they ought to do as Deputies, not something they enjoy doing. They lack the problem-solving and environment-shaping orientation of program Deputies. None spontaneously talked at length about policies he had helped influence.

The following exchange is typical of unsuccessful attempts to induce obligation Deputies to talk about program interests.

> *Deputy, RI:* Supporters of X [a national figure] talked to me in 1966 and asked me to run for the Assembly in this district.
> *Q:* What was your reaction?

R: I wanted to think about it. I waited about two months before deciding to run. I wanted to be sure I could support X's program.

Q: What was this program?

R: The objectives of the program stressed freedom and independence, while accepting the present majority as a necessary fact in French politics.

Q: What precisely attracted you about this program?

R: Nothing in particular. I liked it as a whole.

Q: What was X's goal at that time?

R: He wanted to modify the Government's power. He hoped to open up a dialogue with it, to encourage more participation by the Deputies, more openness with them. [Emphases added.]

Italicized above are the three questions which would have allowed this man—had he desired—to talk about roads, schools, bridges, tax policies, etc. The brevity and generality of his responses indicate the lack of any real programmatic motivation.

c. **Absence of the Status Incentive.** These men could not be mistaken for status participants. They did not seek office and often had to be urged to get into politics. Furthermore, they often played down their own personal status. One told me, "I'm just a small-town lawyer." Another said: "I replaced a wealthy farmer as Deputy. He had thousands of hectares of land, whereas I've just got a small farm of fifty hectares." A third Deputy's comments were even more striking. In early June, 1968, he received a telephone call from Pompidou asking him to run for the Assembly. Status politicians would have been elated. What was this man's reaction? "I thought it was a bad decision on his part. I didn't think I would make a good candidate."

2. *Attitude Toward Interview*
   and Interviewer

Obligation Deputies viewed the interview as a duty but not a particularly enjoyable activity. I had no trouble getting to see these men, and they gave me, on the average, nearly as much time as did the average Deputy in the sample. Yet they appeared to have little intrinsic interest in my questions and showed no enthusiasm for any of the subjects discussed. At times they seemed nervous and uneasy, especially when questions centered on their motives and satisfactions. It would appear that the focused interview causes some anxiety for obligation participants—introspective men concerned about the purity of their own motives. They may fear that a close examination of their rationale for acting will reveal some moral inconsistency on their part.

3. Attitude Toward "Significant Others"

a. Leaders in Higher Positions. The obligation participant views most men in politics, including leaders, as "mere politicians." Assuming they are "out for themselves" and do not have his own high motives for political participation, he is rather scornful of them—sometimes even bitter or malicious. He does, however, hold a few leaders in great respect. These are the men who, for him, symbolize virtue and integrity.

Unlike status Deputies, then, obligation Deputies do have good words for some men in leadership positions. Gaullist UDR Deputies, for instance, saw in de Gaulle the incarnation of virtue. He is a man who stands by his principles and does what he says he will do: thus, the epitome of moral rectitude. If he says he will save France in World War II, provide governmental stability in the Fifth Republic, and insure economic progress—he does (these men assert). This belief that one finds only one or a few men of real moral integrity in politics is, apparently, characteristic of obligation participants.[8]

b. Other Political Activists. The obligation Deputy judges others from his own moral perspective. In this judgment most politicians are found wanting. They seem narrowly self-centered and unconcerned about "the public interest."

Criticisms centered primarily on the way these men act. Thus, one Gaullist hated the Centrists because "they go first to one side and then to the other;" because "one never knows where they really stand;" and because "they are men who always straddle the fence, so you can't have any respect for them."

Another Gaullist criticized his election opponent for much the same reason: he was so "unprincipled" as to court voters of the Center, the Center-Left, and even the Communists. An Independent criticized the Deputy he had recently beaten because "he had done nothing at all in his first term of office." Obligation Deputies are shocked at the selfish behavior of others in politics.

Status and mission Deputies also show this tendency to denigrate other politicians. Yet there are differences. Status Deputies simply distrust all other men. Mission Deputies distrust all men not in their own party but feel close to those within it. Obligation Deputies also distinguish between "good" and "bad" political leaders, but do not see all leaders in their own party as "good." They single out for approval only the small number of men who, they believe, hold pure motives for politics. These men may or may not belong to their own party, and they certainly do not include everyone in it. I heard biting comments from all obligation Deputies about others in their own party. One summed up this attitude of trust for a few men in politics and scorn for most:

> *Deputy, UDR app:* At the Assembly you do find men of high quality. But you also find others: personally ambitious, out for themselves, self-centered. You have to watch out for these men.

Suspicion of others probably hinders effective work by obligation Deputies. I witnessed one incident which suggests this possibility. I was talking with a Gaullist at the Assembly when an obligation Deputy, whom I had already interviewed, burst into our room, nodded to me, turned to the person with whom I was talking, and launched into an indignant criticism of some recent Government action. After ten or fifteen minutes in which the other man tried to persuade him of the justice of the Government's point of view, the obligation Deputy left unhappily. The man with whom I had been talking then turned to me and asked, "Do you have people as rude as that in the United States?" This person was obviously annoyed at the way X had interrupted our conversation, as well as by his criticisms of the Government. Having allowed himself to give vent to his moral outrage, X may now find in his influential colleague a less than cooperative legislator when he wants help with a bill of some importance to him.

The obligation participant's distrust of others and his inability to restrain his moral indignation lead him to work by himself or alienate those around him. He thus makes it more difficult to work effectively for policies he says he wants. Unable to compromise with other politicians of their own persuasion, for instance, Goldwater and McCarthy "purists" tore their own parties apart and thus assured the election of men with policy views diametrically opposed to their own.

c. **Voters**. According to obligation Deputies, their constituents are an important reason for the sacrifices they have made by entering the unprincipled world of politics. These men say they are working to bring "social justice" to the people in their district (or to all Frenchmen). Taking seriously their ties to the voters, they spend much time working in their district to help individual citizens or alleviate local problems. "I know all the problems of the people in my district, because I live in my district like a fish in water," an Independent Deputy declared. Their attitude appears similar to that of Barber's "Reluctant," who "sees himself as duty bound to be of service to others, particularly his small-town constituents. This need to serve comes from the inside, grows out of a deeply ingrained sense of civic duty."[9]

Interestingly, it is not clear that these men enjoy this work on behalf of their fellow citizens. Several talked about the sacrifices they make in order to carry out this work, and some felt that the voters did not appreciate enough what they did for them. Nevertheless, they felt that this work had to be done and that it was their duty to go ahead and do it.

4. Conception of One's Role in the Legislature

Obligation Deputies view the National Assembly in much the same way as might a politically interested citizen from Laurence Wylie's French village of "Peyrane."[10] On the one hand, they have absorbed the civics-books clichés. The legislature is the body which makes laws, resolves national problems, and supports the Government, while the Deputy's job is to represent his constituents and work for "good" legislation. On the other hand, they have absorbed many of the prevailing French attitudes of cynicism and distrust regarding national political leaders.

Thus, all seven Deputies stressed the normative view of the Assembly as an effective law-making body, while criticizing most legislators for corrupting its "true purpose." One told me, ". . . many of the Deputies are more concerned with what happens inside the Assembly than outside it;" a second criticized the Deputies as "professional politicians;" and a third said he disliked the "ambition and intrigue" that prevailed in the Assembly. Despite these negative comments about others, all seven stressed that they themselves were trying to be "good Deputies" and contribute to the Assembly's work on legislation. (In practice, however, they are the least active members of the Assembly. See Chapter 7.)

Since these men are all Gaullists or close to the Gaullists, they accept as norms for the conduct of public affairs many Gaullist political positions. Primarily, they believe the Assembly should be subordinated to the Executive. All are suspicious of giving the Assembly too much power, because they fear that it will become dominated by "the politicians of the Fourth Republic," who will weaken the executive branch as they did before 1958. They accept the idea of a strong Government because this is something a modern nation ought to have. One Deputy explained why France must no longer permit weak Governments:

> *Deputy, UDR:* Previously, when France was mostly rural, the changes in Government didn't do any harm. People just went about their business as usual. But now, when you have a much more complex economy, with a five-year Plan, for example, the cleavages and the crises of former times are no longer conceivable. They can't be allowed in an industrial country because they upset everything.

Obligation Deputies believe an important part of their legislative role is to back the present (Gaullist) Assembly majority and thereby prevent a governmental crisis.

5. Attitude Toward One's Own Party

The party as a political organization has little significance for obligation Deputies. They have not been party activists. They do not see the party either as a united group of crusaders or as an alliance of men cooperating to promote common interests and policies.

Q: What do you Deputies in the RI Group have in common?

Deputy, RI: Well, we're all liberals. We have the same ideas, but we all like our freedom. We try to follow the lead of the group leaders, but we don't have to if we disagree. We have freedom to vote our consciences. [N.B. The UDR imposes voting discipline on its members.]

Obligation Deputies in the Gaullist camp took a similar attitude, downplaying the importance of their party:

Deputy, UDR: I have my own supporters, but I don't set up any political structures. These aren't useful in modern times. We already have too many means of information. People don't need political structures that might in time become heavy, conservative, in need of change. In my district the party is just a group of men who meet once in a great while to talk things over, to renew acquaintances, and to be ready to mobilize the people rapidly, when necessary.

Obligation Gaullists have not developed a strong emotional tie to the UDR. None could be termed a devoted party worker—judging from both interview comments and political career data.

This inability to develop strong party loyalty appears consistent with the obligation participant's orientation to politics. His focus is upon the moral behavior of individual men. He judges other people according to the rectitude of their conduct. Groups as a whole cannot be judged as either moral or immoral. One can only judge the behavior of the individual person. It is true that obligation participants may perceive some groups as containing more "men of principle" than others, and they will gravitate toward those groups when they enter politics. Even after joining a particular party, however, they will continue to scrutinize the conduct of those around them since their focus is upon the personal integrity of themselves and others. Their support for their party will fluctuate over time and will depend on their own perceptions of the moral quality of those in command at any given moment. Since most party leaders most of the time do not project an aura of perfect integrity, obligation participants will rarely exhibit deep attachment to any political party.

6. General Orientation Toward
   Politics

These Deputies do not like politics. For them the political world centers on personal, group, and party struggles for position and power, and it is these struggles and the manipulative aspects of them which they abhor.

Q: Have you ever wished to be a Minister?

Deputy, RI: No, never! I don't want anything to do with such matters. ... I could never stand to have a position which required manipulating other people, giving orders. I never even wanted to be on the *Counseil Général.*[11] I wanted to avoid all that business, to avoid all political maneuvers.

Obligation Deputies equate politics with ambition, intrigue, and manipulation of others for private ends. Since they believe the political arena contains few men of high moral standards like themselves, they do not enjoy their political activities:

Q: What satisfactions have your found through your political activity?

Deputy, RI: Satisfactions? I've found very few. It's a duty, a job someone had to do. I happened to be the one who took it on.

Deputy, UDR: I have no taste for politics. I never have. I prefer to fish or climb mountains. I have no ambition at all. ... I'm not sure I'll stay in the Assembly. I have absolutely no desire to become Minister. In politics you need to have ambition; I have none. I have no taste for intrigue—though I understand those who do.[12]

It is clear that these men see political activity as a sacrifice. They are not doing something they want to do. They are simply performing a duty for their country and their fellow citizens:

Q: What satisfactions have you found through your political activity?

Deputy, UDR: In 1967 I knew nothing about politics, and I must admit that I haven't had any satisfactions since then. I've been very active, I've done many things, but I haven't found any satisfactions. I've had many satisfactions in my life, in my business, in my hobbies. But I haven't found a single satisfaction at the Assembly. ... So how could I say I'd found any satisfactions? Unless it's a certain idea to which I'm attached: fulfilling my responsibilities to the people of my district and to my country.

This attitude may explain why few obligation participants are found in politics at the national level. Most men do not continue to engage in a voluntary activity unless they enjoy it, and most men do not enjoy the act of carrying out a necessary duty. Your sense of obligation might carry you momentarily into politics, but it will not impel you to a lifelong political career.

Probably for these reasons, obligation Deputies were the least numerous group in the sample and, as a group, had the fewest years of political experience in their background. Obligation participants rarely reach the top levels in politics. And if they do reach these levels, it is because they have risen quickly before their moral fervor faded.

Conclusion

The obligation participant seeks to live up to his beliefs about how men should act. When his beliefs imply political participation (a widespread norm of "the good citizen" in many nations), he feels guilty if he does not act on them. His impetus for participation thus springs from an impulse toward moral consistency.

In politics he is most interested in the way things are done, the *style* of decision-making. This interest follows from his concern for proper behavior. He is minimally interested in the ends of policy-making: public programs. He does not enjoy working with other politicians, believing (rightfully) that most are not in politics to express moral concerns. Although he may accept a particular leader as the embodiment of virtue, he scorns most leaders as opportunists. He has a highly negative opinion of politics as a form of activity. He sees it as an arena where men often compromise their principles while maneuvering ruthlessly to gain narrow personal rewards.

The satisfactions the obligation participant gains in politics relate to his belief that he is doing an important duty and his hope that others recognize the morally high standards which underlie his action. In general, however, he is likely to feel unappreciated and to see himself as a moral man in an immoral world. Eventually, he is likely to flee the sordid world of politics. If he cannot reform it, at least he can keep himself pure by withdrawing.

6

The Status Participant

The status participant seeks social prestige. He constantly tries to enhance his stature in the eyes of his fellow men—driven, perhaps, by a secret fear of inferiority. His life is a long personal struggle for the marks of respect and social status. Politics is merely one of the avenues which this man may take to satisfy his need.

The rewards of the status participant derive from recognition by others—in particular, that conglomerate set of others known as "society":

Status is the condition of being considered higher, above, or superior with respect to other members of society in a general, widely recognized sense. It is unspecific and anonymous; it adheres to appearance and position, not to the substance or detailed content of the appearance. The doorman tips his hat for the full professor because the professor has status; whether the professor has advanced or hindered the growth of knowledge in his discipline the doorman does not know, and need not know, to accord him status.

In a sense, then, status is accorded by strangers, by society.[1]

Since the focus of the status participant is upon societal evaluations, he will attempt to gain social positions which automatically confer status. The occupation of medical doctor carries more prestige than any other in the United States.[2] Therefore, a young American with a status drive might well decide to become a physician. Similarly, a status-motivated individual in almost any country might decide to enter politics, since nearly everywhere high public offices confer status upon those who hold them.[3]

The satisfactions of this participant derive from social recognition, not from any inward sense of personal accomplishment. The focus is entirely on positions and appearances. The satisfactions of the status participant in politics come from the holding of high political positions, not from anything he might do in those positions or from anything intrinsic to political activity itself—e.g., the enjoyment of the game or friendly interaction with others. As Payne puts it: "[Status motivation] produces ... an emphasis upon 'credit-getting' or fame. The important thing is not to achieve but to be credited with achieving, whether one has or not."[4]

The idea of the status incentive was first enunciated in Payne's study of Colombia.[5] Much of this work is a systematic description of the ways status participants interact with each other in one political setting. Barber's "Advertiser" clearly holds a status incentive. "His primary focus of attention is not on

111

the softer rewards of good fellowship but on the use he can make of political office for his own advancement."[6] Some status participants have also been observed by Woshinsky in Connecticut and in France and by Payne in the Dominican Republic.[7] In these three settings and in Barber's study, they compose ten to twenty percent of the samples. Given the status-bearing nature of high office in most countries, it appears that at least a few men with status drives will be attracted into politics everywhere.[8] (The percentage should vary considerably over time and from place to place. The conditions which lead to the entry into politics of the various incentive types is a subject which calls for much additional study.[9])

The *main identifying characteristic* of the status participant is his focus on political positions, the techniques for gaining those positions, the outward signs of social prestige connected with the positions, and career plans based on rising to higher positions. This participant is "the young man in a hurry." The concern with success—"making it"—is apt to be strongest among the young.[10] Barber found that his "Advertiser" was "a person in a hurry, seeking, partly through politics, to reach a position of power and security. His attention is occupied by calculations of his place on the ladder of success."[11] This individual "takes a hard-headed, calculating stance toward his legislative office," and betrays a "surface attitude of cynical self-advancement."[12] This habit of cold calculations about one's career, of describing particular actions or positions as steps upward on the ladder of success, identifies the status participant. Like Berg in *War and Peace*, he measures his life not by years but by promotions.

French status Deputies see life through this focus of calculated self-advancement:

Table 6-1
Distribution of Status Participants by Legislative Party Group

Party[a]	Number of Deputies	% of Status Deputies
Non-Inscrit	0	—
RI app	0	—
RI	0	—
UDR app	1	10%
UDR	5	50%
PDM	2	20%
FGDS	2	20%
PC	0	—
TOTAL	10	100%

[a]For explanation of abbreviations, see List of Abbreviations.

> *Deputy, UDR:* When I was a young member of the Prefectural Corps, a Minister I knew asked me to join his staff, and I accepted right away. It was a step forward for me. I knew it would add to my professional development. I thought that, after all, it would be nice to have a fine stay in Paris. It couldn't do anything but help me. But I still thought I'd go back to my prefectural career. I wasn't yet thinking about being a Deputy. Accepting this job couldn't hurt me and would probably help me rise faster in my career. I was still young, only twenty-five, and it would be a good thing for me.

The concern here is with social advancement in general. When this man found advancement coming rapidly in the political sphere, he remained in politics. Only six years after his appointment to the Minister's staff, he was elected Deputy.

Life, for the status-motivated individual, involves a series of decisions timed to boost his social standing as quickly as possible:

> *Deputy, UDR:* I got into politics in a classic fashion. I had gone to the Ecole Normale Supérieure [one of France's most prestigious academic institutions] and engaged in research and teaching. But I soon found I had no vocation for university work. I decided that I'd probably like politics, so I started getting involved and found I was wild about it. Once I knew that, I worked to get myself attached to the staff of Minister X, through a friend I knew. I was his legislative liaison for three years. Then I became the second in command on the staff of Minister Y. Finally, I was able to get the nomination for Deputy in 1968 and was elected.

This focus on offices and positions per se, with no substantive explanation for the interest in politics, identifies the status participant.

> *Q:* I'd like to ask how you came to be involved in public life?
> *Deputy, PDM:* Very young! I was very young when I first decided to become a Deputy. I decided to become Deputy when I was only twenty. I don't even know why. I'd always wanted this—by inclination, I'd say.

When I tried to probe deeper into his reasons for entering politics, this man kept replying: "I just wanted to become Deputy." The desire to hold high public office alone motivated his political activity.[13]

Status participants plan early in life to reach high political positions:

> *Q:* To begin, I'd like to ask how you came to be involved in public life?
>
> *Deputy, FGDS (Socialist):* I first became interested in politics when I was quite young. I was only eleven years old, and they were having a legislative election. My father took me to a public debate between two of the candidates. I was literally overwhelmed by it! The excitement, the crowds, the speeches! To me they resembled two noble gladiators dueling, fighting to the death, before the cheering throngs. I can still see the scene today, it was so vivid. From that moment I knew that was what I wanted to do. I knew that I'd have to get up there myself on that stage, get into that life. From then on, I always knew I'd have to become a Deputy some day.

For this man the desire to become Deputy was related to no cause, no moral impulsion, no program, but solely to the idea of personal glory and attention.

The concern for status is also seen in a tendency toward self-praise. Several status Deputies told of situations in which they had won approbation from others or widespread publicity. One—a former Minister—told me three times that the reforms he had instituted while in office were more significant than any in that Ministry since the time of Napoleon. Another told me twice that he was one of the few "well-qualified" candidates for the Assembly: "There are few really good candidates these days, so I had no trouble at all getting the nomination." A third flattered himself by telling how much prestige he obtained by his first political position. While still a law student, he was appointed to a Minister's staff on the recommendation of his renowned professor.

> *Deputy, UDR:* Imagine my surprise when one day I saw a chauffeur in a big car stop before my house. The chauffeur brought me a letter signed by the Minister asking me to come directly back to the Ministry to see him. I was only twenty-three, and I was overwhelmed at the honor being given me. This made me very happy.
>
> *Q:* What was your reaction at being asked to join the Minister's staff?
>
> *R:* I was very flattered. I was only twenty-three and was proud that I would be considered for such a position.

This man relished telling about the personal marks of deference which he received in this incident: a chauffeur calling for him, an important appointment coming to him, and a mark of success at an early age.

Life is not all satisfaction, however, for the status participant. Several Deputies worried out loud about their past career decisions.

> *Deputy, UDR:* I didn't really get involved in public life before 1958, because under the Fourth Republic, within those institutions, I didn't think political activity was worth the sacrifice of my profes-

sional life [as a lawyer]. It's well known that you have to sacrifice your private life if you decide to become a Deputy, and I was very much interested, naturally, in my professional affairs.

Q: I've noticed that political activity in France imposes many personal difficulties and takes up a great deal of time. I wonder why people engage in it? What are the personal satisfactions that you yourself find in politics?

R: Yes, that's a good question. It's certainly true that parliamentary life offers many frustrations. It's difficult. For instance, in terms of professional life, *you lose a great deal.* I won't deny that *my position professionally was infinitely superior before* I entered politics than it is now. [Emphases added.]

Anxious about his professional status, this man weighed carefully his decision to embark in politics. He suggests now that he might have gained more status by concentrating on his law practice. His frustrations and dissatisfactions in politics clearly derive from a nagging fear that he might have been more "successful" had he not entered politics.

This feeling of frustration and anxiety is common in this type. "Ambition poses a heavy burden for the [status participant]. When he begins to doubt that he is moving fast enough, that he is on the right occupational ladder, that others are not surpassing him, that the goal is possible of attainment—he feels anxious."[14]

Attitudinal Correlates of the Status Incentive

1. Absence of the Expression Satisfactions Which Define Other Incentive Types

a. Absence of the Mission Incentive. The status Deputy does not see himself in politics to serve a cause. None of these men talked about ideology or party doctrine. None saw himself as a longtime supporter of a particular movement. When these men did join a party, it was at a time when the party's fortunes were clearly rising.

Q: How were you attracted to Gaullism?

Deputy, UDR: [Looks surprised at question] Why, you have to understand that I had to become a Gaullist, since I held a position on a Minister's staff. If you want to get into the Government, you have to be Gaullist, since we have a Gaullist Government. Since I wished to remain in power and later become a Deputy, there was no question about what party I'd join.

Status Deputies know how to jump on the bandwagon of a successful party. Significantly, all six of the status Gaullists began sustained political activity only after 1958; nine of the twelve mission Gaullists were working for their party before that turning point in its history.

b. Absence of the Program Incentive. Status Deputies showed no desire to influence public programs. Five of these men did not mention a single piece of legislation or a single local project on which they had worked. The others did so offhandedly or after probing questions by me. One of these Deputies was a former Minister and held an important post on the legislative committee directly concerned with his former Ministry. I had expected to learn a great deal from him about public policy in this area. Yet, when I questioned him about his present legislative work, he seemed offended at being reminded that he was no longer Minister and petulantly answered that he no longer had real means to influence Government actions.

Other status Deputies appeared bored by questions about policy-making. Most simply would not allow themselves to be drawn into a discussion of specific, programmatic details. The following typical and frustrating exchange illustrates their lack of interest in such matters:

> *Q:* What has been your primary work at the Assembly?
> *Deputy, UDR app:* I'm especially concerned with economic and financial problems. That's what I've spoken about a good deal—economic and financial problems.
> *Q:* Specifically, what problems in these areas have interested you?
> *R:* Those I mentioned. Financial and economic problems. The budget. I've also been concerned about amnesties for former French Algerians. And I've been interested in housing problems, too.

After telling me that he was "interested" in almost all the socioeconomic and political problems in France (the budget, finances, and the economy), this Deputy sat back as if he were satisfied with his answer to my question, obviously ready to go on to other topics. He never mentioned a specific economic program on which he had worked. Throughout the interview he kept insisting on his "nonpolitical, technocratic" interest in financial matters. Yet, it seems safe to say that he revealed his true interests when he launched into an enthusiastic description of the many positions which he had attained because of his supposed economic expertise: special *rapporteur* to represent his committee before the Assembly, European Parliament delegate, "and then, best of all, I was named to the French Delegation at the United Nations."

One tenet of prevailing Gaullist (and conservative) ideology holds that men truly working for the national interest should be "technocrats," busily engaged in solving economic problems, rather than "politicians," serving narrow, partisan or personal interests. These ideas provide an excellent cloak for the status Deputy. The above quotation illustrates the belief that one can prove one's worth simply by stating that one is interested in solving technical problems. Another Deputy took this same line.

> Q: What are your major interests in the Assembly?
> Deputy, PDM: Problems of the economy and national finances. I'm on the Finance Committee. [Silence. Volunteers nothing more.]
> Q: What problems have you spoken on during this session?
> R: All the problems concerning economic and financial matters.

Additional questions could not induce this man to elaborate on these statements. A person really concerned with these problems would be willing and eager to talk at length about specific details on which he himself had worked. This man's brief replies show his utter indifference to concrete problems in the area of his ostensible interests.[15]

Other Deputies expressed even less focused program concerns than the two already cited.

> Q: What problems have especially interested you at the Assembly?
> Deputy, UDR: [Long silence.] Well, I've been interested in participation in the work of laws, in the formulation, in the making of laws. But there hasn't really been anything in the last year that has attracted my attention, nothing that has really excited me.

> Q: What problems have especially interested you at the Assembly?
> 2nd Deputy, UDR: I'm interested in working on the laws. Nothing in particular, just the formulation of the laws.

> Q: What problems have especially interested you at the Assembly?
> 3rd Deputy, UDR: What I enjoy are the general discussions of the major political questions. I've spoken in the big debates on all major policy problems.

These men seem bored by the details of policy-making. In fact, they seem to have no policy preferences at all.

The last-cited Deputy, for example, never told me what positions he took in his "numerous speeches" on major policies:

> Q: So you speak frequently . . . ?
> R: What interests me is being able to bring something to the discussion of major national questions, to help define general policies. A Deputy, after all, is political. His job is to define, give direction to, general policies.

Q: So you've spoken on many subjects . . . ?

R: I've intervened in all the important debates this session—the university, the construction permit, regionalization, union rights in the factory.

This Deputy was interested in telling me about his speeches, but not about what he said in them. His comments remind one of what Barber wrote about the "Advertiser": "The important thing, to him, is that *he* is speaking, not that the issue is being clarified."[16]

This same orientation is evident in the autobiography of William Jennings Bryan, a probable status participant.[17] Bryan's love of speaking is evident throughout this work, as well as his lack of detailed knowledge of public policies. In a chapter entitled, "The Lure of the College Prize," he writes: "I felt the lure of prizes from the start and took part in every contest for which I was eligible. A prize always stirred me to activity. . . ."[18] In this chapter he tells exactly what prizes he won in oratorical contests and how he went about winning them (the gestures he used, the voice modulations, etc.). His anxiety about winning prizes was so great that decades later he can recount in detail a dream he had about winning a prize, a dream which made an "indelible impression" upon his mind.[19] Yet the reader never learns what Bryan said in his prize-winning speeches on such topics as "Justice," "Labor," and "Pauperism, Its Causes and Remedies." As with status Deputies, the focus is on what one gains from the activity, not on what the activity is about.

c. Absence of the Obligation Incentive. No status Deputy showed any interest in morally and normatively correct conduct. They generally assumed that all men are out for themselves, but seemed to accept this as "normal" human behavior, not something to become morally outraged about. A Gaullist told me: "Sure, there are men of bad faith in politics. But no more than elsewhere. You find them all over, not just in politics." This bears a strong resemblance to a statement by one of Barber's "Advertisers": "Once again, I'm an egotist, like you and everyone else. You like to be in the public eye, you're a big shot—that has its advantage."[20]

These men do not stress their own moral purity. They do not disclaim political ambitions, nor feel it necessary to apologize for being in politics. Finally, they do not stress political activity as an obligation for the good citizen or the true patriot. Because they show no concern for morality and proper behavior, they cannot be said to hold an obligation incentive.

2. Attitude Toward Interview
and Interviewer

Of the incentive types observed in France, the status participant was particularly rude and uncooperative. He dislikes the dependent (therefore status-reducing) role of interviewee. To avoid this role, he will refuse to give interviews, refuse to be helpful if he does give an interview, and constantly act to remind the interviewer of his own inferior status.

Status Deputies were more likely than others to put off seeing me, to cancel appointments, to break off interviews and force me to return. During interviews they tried to show that they were busy and important men. By trying to carry on other business during the interview, they indicated that my own petty questions were a waste of their precious time. Several responded absentmindedly to queries while opening, reading, and sorting out enormous piles of letters. *No other Deputies behaved in this way.* Such action is impolite. Other participants do not have the need to feel superficially important which leads status participants to behave in this manner.

Status Deputies adopted another tactic to frustrate the interviewer. They did not talk very much. They often answered probing questions with one-sentence statements, showing irritation when I attempted to follow up the subject. Their short, brusque answers showed they were eager to be rid of me, again implying they had more important things to do. The time they granted for the interviews provides an objective indicator of their lack of desire to talk. The average interview with all fifty Deputies lasted nearly an hour and a half—and the average interview with each of the other three incentive types lasted slightly more or slightly less than this average. The average interview with status Deputies lasted fifty-five minutes! This fact provides striking evidence of their unusual interview behavior.[21]

3. Attitude Toward "Significant Others"

One important characteristic of the status Deputy is his *aloneness.* A man who seeks status is competing with all other men, since status is a personal attribute that is difficult to share. As Payne puts it:

[One] implication of status motivation is its corrosive effect on friendly personal relations. The desire to appear "higher" and not "lower" impels the individual into competitive personal relationships. He resents those who are above him, such as legislative leaders, and attempts to dispel the impression of submission by acting independently and even obstreperously toward them. With his equals, he is constantly jousting for a position of superiority, of respect. It is only with the abject supplicants that he feels comfortable because they are visible proof of his status. Even here the interaction is not a friendly one since it depends on the constant confirmation of the superior-inferior relationship.[22]

a. **Leaders in Higher Positions.** Status Deputies talked little about political leaders, who appeared to have no significance for their personal needs. I heard little praise for leaders from any of these men. Eight of the ten status Deputies had nothing good to say about a single French political leader, while two Gaullists did briefly show respect for de Gaulle—a man so far above themselves in stature that they could not conceivably feel diminished by the comparison.

These men do not feel personal attachments to their own leaders. This lack of affective ties is all the more striking when one learns that seven of these ten Deputies began politics under the direct tutelage of important political figures. Status Deputies apparently attach themselves to leaders in calculated attempts to help their own career. They exhibit, however, no personal attachment to these leaders after they themselves have "arrived."[23]

b. Other Political Activists. Status participants see themselves in competition with other politicians for the limited number of higher offices. The fear that others might gain one of the prestigious offices they seek leads them to distrust those around them. As one status Deputy put it: "You must never trust any other person at any time." Sprinkled throughout the interviews were other comments of this nature:

> *Deputy, UDR:* Today in France all the parties lack good candidates, candidates of real stature.

> *Deputy, FGDS (Socialist):* What our party leaders are doing is a complete joke. It amuses me to see the leaders of our movement play at being revolutionaries—brandishing their slogans, shaking their fists, all that nonsense. It's a complete charade.

> *Deputy, FGDS (second Socialist):* You find nothing but troubles in politics, moral deceits; people don't understand you. You try to do things, and they accuse you of wrongdoing.

> *Deputy, PDM:* I'm disappointed at the behavior of politicians—people who are favorable to you when you help them, but who forget later. They don't remember what you did for them and won't help you out when you need it.

The status participant's intense personal struggle against all others induces in him a negative and cynical attitude toward men in general—even toward those in his own party.[24]

c. Voters. This negative view of men also applies to the voters. In a sense status participants begrudge the voters their direct dependence on them. They retaliate for this unwanted dependence by adopting a patronizing attitude toward their electorate.

In numerous biting or jesting comments status Deputies revealed their scorn and disdain for constituents. A Gaullist Deputy complained that "the job of the Deputy has become nothing but that of a glorified social worker—helping the people with all their little personal problems." This same man told me he saw no reason to continue holding public meetings during election campaigns: "The only voters who come are the village drunk and the regulars from the local bar."

A Socialist told me the voters from his district had no idea what they were doing in the 1968 election.

> *Deputy, FGDS (Socialist):* They almost elected a Gaullist against me, and my opponent was a man who didn't know a thing, not a thing! It shows how blinded they were by the events of May.

This individual enjoyed recounting with sarcasm the absurd reasons voters find for coming to see him:

> *R:* Two neighbors both came to see me over some lawsuit concerning their property. One actually tried to get me to bribe the judge. Can you believe it? I hope the judge condemns them both.

Another Gaullist told me that he was obliged to go into his district from time to time, receive the people, listen to their problems and thereby "play at being the average Deputy." A third Gaullist told me:

> *Deputy, UDR:* It's not always the real problems that interest people. That's one of the problems in a democracy. I think democracy is the least evil system of government—but only the least evil. The people are not interested in real problems or solutions.

The undertone of fear and distrust of the voter was present throughout the interviews with these men.[25]

They do realize, however, that their political future depends on their ability to win the confidence of their constituents. They therefore adopt a manipulative attitude toward them:

> *Q:* You say you receive constituents in your home every week?
> *Deputy, UDR:* Yes. I'm in my district every week, and it makes a better impression on people if you do this. They like to be received at the home of a Deputy. I also receive many Mayors and local personalities there. They appreciate this. It goes over better than meeting with them in some dreary town hall.

Exhibiting this same spirit of calculated manipulation, many status Deputies stressed the hold over voters which their speaking ability gives them. Yet they constantly fear desertion by these same voters:

> *Deputy, PDM:* I think the situation in X is very good for me now. I've just carried off two big victories: The "Non" at the Referendum and

the victory for Poher in my city. These elections were important for me. They constituted tests, sample polls, so to speak. They show that the voters of X follow me and back me. In the future they will follow me too. I don't think I'll have difficulties. Of course, you never know, but I think I'm in good shape now.

This Deputy interprets two national elections solely in terms of his own local popularity. His happiness at victory, mixed with a few remaining doubts about his local strength, shows that he sees voters primarily in terms of the political prestige their support brings him.

4. Conception of One's Role
in the Legislature

His sense of life as a continual jockeying for position shapes the status Deputy's view of the legislature. He sees the Assembly not as a place where men work together on social and economic problems, but as a national center for the promotion of ambitions.

> *Deputy, UDR:* What are the parliamentary customs? They are no different here than in any other country, I imagine. There's what I call a certain parliamentary deformation that is always inevitable in a legislature. The feeling of clans and intrigues and ambitions reigns. There's a certain tendency to exaggerate things. Deputies are more volatile than other people.

What is interesting is that this man clearly disliked political maneuvering in the Assembly, but he saw it everywhere. In fact, status Deputies expressed distaste for "the political intrigues" which they saw as rampant in the Assembly.

> *Deputy, UDR app:* Some of the Deputies are constantly scheming about the make-up of the next Government. Some are always haunting the corridors, whispering together. That's not for me.

He then claimed that he goes to the Assembly "only to deliver my speeches" and never "hangs around the corridors" afterward.

Another Deputy clearly indicated that he saw personal relations at the Assembly as a Byzantine maze of manipulation and calculation:

> *Deputy, PDM:* There are thousands of "rules of the game." I can't even begin to describe them. The uninitiated could never understand. If you haven't lived in this house for years, it's impossible. It has its

own elaborate procedures and ways of acting. You have to know all about the psychology of other men, the things to do and not to do. Some men have been here for three or four years and haven't yet understood a thing.

Status participants, themselves constantly calculating, manipulating and worrying about outcomes, are likely to imagine many more "rules" for gaining "success" than there actually are in a given situation. For them the Assembly is a tense, competitive arena where each man vies with all others for public attention and political position.

Status Deputies would apparently agree with Nathan Leites: the Assembly is a place of a thousand intrigues fostered by men struggling desperately for Ministerial positions.[26] By no means, however, would they regard it as a "game." Politics, for the status participant, is not a frivolous endeavor. It is a personal struggle for self-promotion. In all his actions the status Deputy feels that his own prestige is at stake. When he engages in tactical political maneuvers, he craves attention and respect as a reward for his action. This action does not spring from a need for intellectual stimulation, from a desire to test his own political skills against those of others, or from simple delight in complex gaming activity.

In short, political interactions are not ends in themselves for the status Deputy—as they are for the game participant.[27] Politics is rather a means to the desired end: status. The means themselves are not enjoyed. In fact, they are feared, since during the tense moments of a political power struggle, outcomes are uncertain, and this uncertainty frightens the status participant. The stakes are very high for him, and the uncertainty—the possibility that he may suffer a status loss—is hard to bear. Thus, contrary to what one might expect, these men do not enjoy intrigue in politics. They engage in it only because they believe this is an essential element in the winning of high office.

In contrast to their dislike for "behind the scenes" politics, all status Deputies stressed their enjoyment of public speaking, especially before the Assembly. In giving a good speech, one automatically gains publicity and probably prestige. One's fate depends on one's own oratorical powers, not on the machinations of other men. Thus, status participants overwhelmingly prefer this activity to ordinary political dealings. This attitude was best expressed by an old French politician, a status participant whom I interviewed before beginning the formal interviews with Deputies:

> *Q:* You spoke about "arriving." What must a Deputy do in order to "arrive" in politics?
>
> *Former Deputy, Radical:* In the past you had to give a good speech which was appreciated by the party leaders. They came to hear the youngest Deputies and gave grades, so to speak. They wanted to see if you were a man of the future.

Q: How does one become a Minister in France?

R: In the past you had to know how to speak well. You had to be eloquent.

Q: When you were young, what aspects of politics especially appealed to you?

R: I was always interested in the spoken word. The spoken word and the ability to express yourself have always seemed to me very important. *To be able to speak well is one of the most essential qualities of the politician.* [Emphasis added.]

5. Attitude Toward One's Own Party

Apparently because status Deputies feel no personal allegiance to other men in general, they feel no strong ties to a particular group of men—their own party. None of these Deputies showed any personal interest in his party, none pointed to worthy social goals his party pursued, and few attributed their own political success to their party. The political party seemed to play no salient role in their lives.

Six of these Deputies told me specifically they were not involved in party work. The four others implied that their work for the party contributed greatly to the party's success, while bringing them little in return. One man railed against the "intrigues and struggles for position" that characterize party politics. Another declared: "I'm a Gaullist, but not a very fervent Gaullist." And a third described the agitation he had caused in his party by fighting the party apparatus "composed of unimaginative bureaucrats."

These men apparently see the political party as a possible restraint on their own freedom rather than as a cohesive group of men working toward common goals. This fear of their own party follows from their desire to avoid being coerced by others. By emphasizing the weakness of ties to their party and by stressing their own independence, status participants try to avoid giving others the impression that they are obedient followers—a role which automatically (for them) implies low status.

6. General Orientation to Politics

Some men fall in love with politics. The status participant is not one of these. Ambivalence is an apt word to describe his feelings. He enjoys politics when it brings him publicity and rewards him with positions. He dislikes it when he is forced to interact closely with others. For most of these Deputies the enjoyable aspects of politics appeared to overshadow frustrations. One cannot say, however, that these men as a whole are enthusiastic about politics. Although they like politics somewhat more than obligation Deputies, they like it much less than mission and program Deputies.

The dislikes of status Deputies relate solely to intense personal relations with other men. A Centrist and both Socialists complained that people often deceived them or did not keep their word. Two Gaullists told of their distaste for having to meet frequently with their constituents. Two other Gaullists and a Centrist stressed their contempt for the intrigues and deals which they believe dominate Assembly activity. Their suspicion of others coupled with their view of human relations as manipulative leads these men into tense and depressing relations with others.[28]

Status participants do have pleasant moments in politics. *They especially enjoy those experiences which place them at the center of attention without necessitating close interaction with others. The act of public speaking is most likely to give them publicity without entanglements.* Nine of these ten Deputies either stated directly or strongly implied that they loved to speak in public. This action, they clearly believed, brought them glory and made them the center of attention:

> *Deputy, UDR:* I started the campaign alone: then I had five or six helpers, then twenty, then fifty, eighty, one hundred, two hundred militants. There were people around me every night; everywhere I went they came to hear me. In these meetings you become conscious of the influence you can have. It becomes intoxicating. I was terribly excited to find out what I could do.

> *Deputy, UDR:* I find the campaign periods exhilarating. I love these periods. I love the public meetings. My friends in politics think I'm crazy. They say public meetings aren't important any more. You achieve a spectacular success if you draw 500 people, but that's just one per cent of the voters. But *I* think they're important. You get a certain atmosphere created between you and the people. You can feel things building over the course of the campaign like a rolling snowball until the last day when the meeting-hall won't hold all the people. And I find it stimulating to see that when you speak, you have contacts with them through the spoken word and your ideas.

> *Deputy, FGDS (Socialist):* When I was a boy and saw those two men debating, I was struck by the way they dominated the crowd. Since then, I've come to know what a crowd is. I always find an intense satisfaction when I'm before an audience. In the first fifteen minutes you don't know if you're going to be eaten up or if you'll bend them. But after fifteen minutes you feel them relax and give before

you. You hold them in the grip of your hand. You can play with them at will. You've succeeded in mastering them.

This delight in the power of the spoken word was also evident in William Jennings Bryan, a probable status participant. One of his comments sounds very similar to that of the Socialist Deputy above. After coming home from a speaking engagement, Bryan woke his wife and told her: "Mary, I have had a strange experience. Last night I found that I had power over the audience. I could move them as I chose. I have more than usual power as a speaker."[29]

The ability to manipulate others through your public performance, to make them applaud you and follow you, stands out as the single most important enjoyment status Deputies find in politics. They are most happy when stirring others by the power of their voice. Payne has suggested the value to status participants of gaining the public eye through vigorous, even inflammatory speeches.[30] Barber has shown that "Advertisers" spend most of their time in the legislature talking rather than studying and preparing bills.[31] Vocal expression before large groups is clearly a significant element in the syndrome connected with the status incentive.

Conclusion

The status participant seeks to enhance his social prestige by rising in political office. He is identified by his interest in political positions, the techniques necessary for attaining them, and the marks of status connected with them. Correlated with this desire for status is lack of interest in both public policies and ideological doctrines. He is rude and uncooperative during interviews. In seeking to enhance his own status, he is envious of higher leaders, suspicious and distrustful of other politicians, and patronizing of the electorate. The voters, other activists, his own party—these are all instruments which he tries to manipulate for his career advantage. Hence, his relations with others are often tense, unfriendly.

The status participant, then, does not enjoy many aspects of politics. His primary enjoyment comes from public speaking. In performing brilliantly (as he imagines) before masses of people, he gains the publicity and prestige he seeks without having to endure the entanglements of close personal relationships.

As long as he can sway voters and political participants and hence rise in office, the status participant is likely to remain in politics. Few men, however, meet no personal setbacks in politics. The status participant is more likely than other politicians to let political losses upset him, since any loss automatically deprives him of his main goal: status. It appears likely that many status participants will withdraw from politics by middle age as they find their satisfactions in that activity outweighed by their frustrations.

7

Behavioral Differences Among Incentive Types (1): Behavior in the National Assembly

Incentives shape behavior in politics. Different incentive types do not merely think about the political world in different ways (as the previous chapters demonstrate). They also act differently in politics—and in ways consistent with their different needs. This chapter and the next present a variety of evidence on the different behavioral patterns of the four kinds of incentive participant observed in France.

Knowledge of each incentive type's drives and attitudes lead to definite expectations about how these men will behave in the legislature. Program participants are expected to be active in areas of substantive legislative work, while obligation participants are expected to be inactive. The program participant's activism should follow from his enjoyment of political activity and his desire to work on policy-making. The obligation participant's inactivity should follow from his dislike of politics and his wish to avoid intense involvement in what is, to him, a sordid activity.[1]

Status participants are expected to be active in public debates and in struggles for leadership positions, but inactive in areas specifically connected with the mechanics of legislation and policy-making. This behavior should follow from their desire for attention and position, coupled with their lack of interest in influencing policies.[2] Mission participants were expected to be active in most areas of the legislature, driven by their zeal to serve a movement in any way possible.

These expectations represent major hypotheses of incentive analysis. Data on the way French Deputies behave in the National Assembly support these hypotheses (with some minor exceptions to be noted below).

1. Speaking on the Floor of the Assembly

One good indicator of legislative activity is the time each Deputy devotes to participation in floor debate. An effective measure of this activity is, simply, the total amount of space attributed to each Deputy by the *Journal Officiel*'s record of parliamentary debates. The time period chosen for study included the months from July through December, 1968, and October through December, 1969.[3]

Table 7-1 records this evidence on the Deputies' total activity in plenary sessions. Two facts quickly emerge from this table. First, program Deputies are a good deal more active in Assembly debates than other Deputies. Second,

Table 7-1

Differences Among Incentive Types: Speaking on the Floor of the Assembly[a]

	Obligation Deputies	Program Deputies	Mission Deputies	Status Deputies	All Deputies in Sample
Number of Deputies	7	14	19	10	50
Mean Number of Centimeters	267.7	525.6	341.6	397.2	393.9
Median Number of Centimeters	181.5	429.8	323.5	272.8	275.8
Percent from each group *above* median for all Deputies in sample	29%	71%	42%	50%	50%

[a]This table documents the total number of centimeters attributed by the *Journal Officiel* to Deputies in the sample for all acts of participation during plenary sessions of the National Assembly in the period July-December, 1968, and October-December, 1969.

obligation Deputies are a good deal less active than others. The recorded comments of program Deputies average 525.6 centimeters compared to a sample average of 393.9 and an average of 267.7 for obligation Deputies.

Status and mission Deputies occupy an in-between ground. They are clearly active participants on the floor of the Assembly, but fall into a category below that of program Deputies. This evidence does not quite fit my expectations. In the case of mission Deputies I had thought they would be closer to program Deputies in total activity. Later evidence will show that on other dimensions of legislative activity they do participate as much as program Deputies. Only in floor speaking are they less active. This fact may perhaps be explained by the small number of exciting *political* debates in a legislature dominated by one party. In situations of one-party dominance mission types on both sides may see less need for constant struggle to assure their side's success. One group knows it cannot gain victory; the other knows it cannot lose. A comparison with the behavior of mission Deputies in the evenly-balanced 1967 legislature would be instructive.

Status Deputies were expected to be more active in public speaking than they appear in Table 7-1. Later evidence does indicate their high degree of activity in attention-getting areas. Table 7-1 includes all acts of speaking on the floor of the Assembly, including the presentation of *rapports*[4] and discussion on the specific articles of all bills. Evidence presented below shows that status Deputies are inactive in these areas which are directly related to work on policies. On the other hand, they are extremely talkative in general debates. Thus, status Deputies' midway position on Table 7-1 reflects the fact that they are active in speech-making, but inactive in work on the formulation of laws. These facts confirm initial expectations about their behavior.

Table 7-1 compresses a great deal of data. By breaking this data down into component parts, one can gain additional insight into behavioral differences among incentive types. I found it useful to divide Deputies' Assembly comments into three kinds: those which one might properly call prepared public speeches; those comments which are simply interruptions of other speakers; and those intended to bear directly on a law under consideration. Each of these will be discussed in turn.

2. Legislative Speech-making

Deputies have three basic opportunities in which to deliver lengthy remarks before the whole Assembly: after major policy statements by the Government; during the general discussion of a bill (this stage precedes consideration of the bill article by article; during this first stage speeches are formal and prepared); and during the time of oral questions (*questions orales avec et sans débat*). (Unlike procedure in the House of Commons, question time is extremely formal in the Assembly. "Questions" are short speeches; so are the Minister's "answers," and even "replies" to the Minister's answers have been prepared in advance.) These three moments in the life of the Assembly are the only times when Deputies are able to talk at length on broad subjects of political importance. A study of this time period should disclose those Deputies who have a penchant for oratory.

I had expected program Deputies to be somewhat less active in this area than in others, while expecting mission Deputies to be somewhat more active. But my main expectation was to find status Deputies the most active speech-makers. Table 7-2 presents data to sustain these expectations. The case of program Deputies does, it is true, exhibit some ambiguity. They are well ahead of the other types of Deputy in terms of mean centimeters, but well below them all in terms of median centimeters. It appears that a few program Deputies do talk a good deal in the Assembly (thus pulling up the average), but that most of them talk little during these periods of debate. Status Deputies, on the other hand, are obviously the most active speakers, as expected. Mission Deputies, on the whole, seem somewhat more inclined than program Deputies to enter formal debates, if one considers median figures (which are useful for these cases with small numbers). Obligation Deputies were more active than expected, actually exceeding program Deputies in median number of centimeters.

A final set of figures perhaps best illuminates the trend in speech-making: sixty percent of the status Deputies spoke more than the median for the entire sample, compared to forty-seven percent for mission Deputies and forty-three percent for program and obligation Deputies.

Table 7-2

Differences Among Incentive Types: Legislative Speech-making[a]

	Obligation Deputies	Program Deputies	Mission Deputies	Status Deputies	All Deputies in Sample
Number of Deputies	7	14	19	10	50
Mean Number of Centimeters	176.4	291.1	218.4	277.2	244.6
Median Number of Centimeters	179	152.2	199	209.8	199
Percent from each group *above* median for all Deputies in sample	43%	43%	47%	60%	50%

[a]This table documents the total number of centimeters attributed by the *Journal Officiel* to Deputies in the sample during general political debates and general discussions of bills during plenary sessions of the National Assembly in the period July-December, 1968, and October-December, 1969.

3. Expertise and Specialization

All past incentive studies have led to the expectation that program legislators will be far more involved in work on the specific details of bills and policy-making than others. They also lead one to expect the zealous mission participants to be fairly involved in law-making. The status and obligation participants, however, who find little satisfaction in solving problems or manipulating their environment, are not likely to be heavily involved in concrete work on the formulation of laws.

To discover the actual behavior of each type, it was necessary to devise an indicator of legislative expertise and interest in policy-making details. A careful study of Assembly debates suggested such an indicator. A Deputy's behavior in two different capacities should illustrate his interest in affecting legislation. The first involves his work as *rapporteur*.

Each bill reported out of committee is floor-managed by a *rapporteur* appointed by the committee which considered the bill. This man must know more about the bill than any other Deputy. He must explain the bill to the Assembly, elucidate the committee's point of view on every article of the bill, present and argue for committee amendments to the bill,[5] and debate with other Deputies who wish to amend the bill in some way. It seems likely that anyone undertaking this work must have a fair degree of interest in the policy outcomes implied by the legislation.

There is a second area of work for Deputies who wish to influence legislation.

This involves time spent in plenary sessions discussing the meaning of a bill article by article. After the general discussion of a bill, the Assembly examines it in this detailed way. A Deputy concerned about legislative outcomes is likely to take an active part in this phase of Assembly work. On the other hand, Deputies who wish to gain attention by talking will leave this work to others. They are not permitted at this juncture to deliver a "major statement" on the country's problems; nor will they be familiar with the subject matter and significance of an obscure article buried in a bill they found too tiresome to read.

I argue, then, that Deputies concerned about the substance of legislation will seek the job of *rapporteur* and serve actively in this capacity. They will also acquire a degree of expertise in some area of legislation and thus be able to participate effectively when the Assembly discusses the specific articles of bills which interest them. Thus, the amount of time which a Deputy spends as *rapporteur* and discussant of articles should indicate his interest in influencing public policy.

Table 7-3 shows how much time the different types of Deputy spent on these matters. It is clear at a glance that program Deputies are overwhelmingly more active than other Deputies. In fact, by themselves they are more active than mission and status Deputies combined! The fourteen program Deputies totaled 3398 centimeters of print in the *Journal Officiel* for the entire time period; the twenty-nine mission and status Deputies totaled only 3363 centimeters. Obligation Deputies rank well below the others. This table presents striking evidence that program Deputies devote far more time to serious legislative work than other types of legislator in France.

Table 7-3
Differences Among Incentive Types: Expertise and Specialization[a]

	Obligation Deputies	Program Deputies	Mission Deputies	Status Deputies	All Deputies in Sample
Number of Deputies	7	14	19	10	50
Mean Number of Centimeters	91.0	242.7	117.1	113.8	147.9
Median Number of Centimeters	5	162.8	32	11.5	31.8
Percent from each group *above* median for all Deputies in sample	43%	64%	53%	40%	50%

[a]This table is based on the number of centimeters attributed by the *Journal Officiel* to Deputies in the sample during discussion of the articles of bills and the presentation of *rapports* in plenary sessions of the National Assembly in the period July-December, 1968, and October-December, 1969.

Table 7-3 also shows that, as expected, mission Deputies are somewhat more likely than status and obligation Deputies to be active on *rapports* and articles. This fact is somewhat obscured by the startling lead program Deputies have over all other types, but it deserves to be noted.

Table 7-3 conforms so precisely to expectations derived from incentive analysis that it raised my suspicions. To make sure that this data could not be explained by some other variable, I looked for alternate explanations not based on incentive analysis. Only two of these seemed reasonably relevant. When followed up, however, they altered in no way the previous conclusions derived from Table 7-3.

One of these explanations hinged on the position of *rapporteur*. Only members of the existing political majority can attain this position, since others could not present the majority's viewpoint. This led me to suspect that program Deputies are more likely than others to be members of the majority. If this were true, they would naturally be more likely than others to be chosen for the job of *rapporteur*. Their work in this area would thus be explained by their political affiliations and not by their incentives.

This explanation does not take one far. It turns out that program Deputies are, in fact, somewhat more likely than other Deputies to belong to the political majority, but this fact does not begin to explain the huge distance between program Deputies and others. During the time period under consideration one hundred percent of obligation Deputies, seventy-eight percent of program Deputies, sixty-nine percent of status Deputies, and sixty-four percent of mission Deputies belonged to the Assembly majority. Thus, although they had less chance to serve as *rapporteurs* than obligation Deputies, program Deputies did have somewhat more chance than status and mission Deputies to serve in this capacity. This somewhat greater likelihood of being in the majority, however, hardly seems able to account for the huge lead of program Deputies over others, especially when one remembers that work as *rapporteur* makes up only part of the totals shown in Table 7-3. Deputies really concerned with policy-management could easily speak up during discussion of articles; they thus have the opportunity to make up for the fact that they cannot be named *rapporteur*.

It will clearly be instructive to compare the work on articles of Deputies who were unable to present *rapports*. During the entire time period three program Deputies, six mission Deputies, and two status Deputies were never in the political majority. Two of the three program Deputies spoke so much during Assembly discussion of articles alone that they ranked high above the median for all Deputies on articles and *rapports* combined. *None* of the eight mission and status opposition Deputies spoke more than the median. In fact, only two of these eight were attributed more than five centimeters by the *Journal Officiel* during the entire time period. These two were attributed 14.5 and 21.5 centimeters—a status Deputy and a mission Deputy respectively. The two program Deputies mentioned earlier were attributed 135 and 160.5 centimeters!

Thus, opposition program Deputies have the same wide lead over other opposition Deputies that program Deputies as a whole have over all other Deputies. Political affiliation in no way explains why program Deputies are more active than other Deputies in areas requiring legislative expertise.

In searching for another possible explanation of the data in Table 7-3, I studied seniority in the legislature. It may be, I hypothesized, that program Deputies are more experienced legislators than the others. In many legislatures experienced men carry more of the work load than newcomers. Program Deputies may work harder than others simply because they have developed more legislative experience and skills than other, relatively inexperienced, Deputies. This hypothesis is plausible. It is, however, simply false. The data in Table 7-4 show that program Deputies are *less* likely than status and mission Deputies to have experience in the Assembly. Fifty-seven percent of program Deputies, compared to forty-seven percent of mission and forty percent of status Deputies, have served in the Assembly only since 1967. The seniority hypothesis thus has no value in explaining program Deputies' legislative activity.

Neither the seniority hypothesis nor the party affiliation hypothesis can explain why program Deputies appear so much more hard-working than other Deputies. In fact, the simplest explanation of this fact is based on incentive analysis: program participants will work hard on specific pieces of legislation in order to exercise real influence on the policy process.

One final fact deserves noting. Program Deputies not only spend much time on articles and *rapports*; they also spend a large proportion of their time on these matters. Table 7-5 shows the proportion of their talking time in the Assembly that Deputies spent on articles and *rapports*. Status and obligation Deputies spent only 21.7 percent and 22.9 percent of their time, respectively, on these matters, compared to 30.6 percent for mission Deputies and 33.6 percent for program Deputies. Over a third of the work these men do in plenary sessions is spent as *rapporteurs* or discussants of articles.

Table 7-4
Differences Among Incentive Types: Experience in the Legislature

	Obligation Deputies	Program Deputies	Mission Deputies	Status Deputies	All Deputies in Sample
Number of Deputies	7	14	19	10	50
Percent in each group first elected in 1968	43%	36%	32%	10%	30%
Percent in each group first elected in 1967 or 1968	57%	57%	47%	40%	50%

Table 7-5

Differences Among Incentive Types: Proportion of Plenary Session Work Spent on Matters Requiring Legislative Expertise[a]

	Obligation Deputies	Program Deputies	Mission Deputies	Status Deputies	All Deputies in Sample
Number of Deputies	7	14	19	10	50
Average ratio of time on articles and *rapports* to time of all spoken comments in plenary sessions	22.9%	33.6%	30.6%	21.7%	28.6%

[a]The percentage figures listed in this table can be considered indicators of expertise. The higher the percentage, the greater the interest shown in the concrete details of legislation. These figures were obtained for each Deputy by calculating the following ratio:

> Time (measured in centimeters) spent as *rapporteur* or as a discussant of the articles of a bill during plenary sessions

> divided by

> Time (measured in centimeters) spent on all recorded acts of participation in plenary sessions.

Time Period: All plenary sessions of the National Assembly in the period of July-December, 1968, and October-December, 1969.

4. Committee Attendance

Although Assembly committees are not powerful in France, they do meet frequently during regular sessions, examine all bills before they are discussed in plenary sessions, and have some influence on the final form of all legislation. While interviewing Deputies, I found a widespread belief that committees are places where legislative work can get done because the group is small and no one has to worry about publicity. (Committee meetings in France are never open to the public.) There also appears to be a widespread norm that attending committee meetings is an important part of the Deputy's job. One should be able to learn something about the differences among incentive types by discovering who does and who does not attend these committee meetings.

I expected both program and mission Deputies to be assiduous committee-attenders, while expecting status Deputies to avoid these work-centered meetings. Payne, for instance, found very low committee-attendance rates in the Colombian legislature dominated by status participants.[6] I also felt that the more passive obligation Deputies would go to fewer committee meetings than program and mission Deputies.

To check on these expectations, data was gathered from the *Journal Officiel: lois et décrets*. This official Government source appears daily and lists, among many other facts, the names of Deputies and Senators present at all legislative committee meetings. A fairly long time period was selected for study: July-December, 1968, and the month of October, 1969. To learn about the Deputies' overall committee record, I studied not merely their record of attendance at regular standing committees (there are six of these and every Deputy belongs to one only), but also included special internal Assembly committees (such as the committee set up to change Assembly rules of procedure) and joint committees, which are set up for the special purpose of ironing out differences in the final Assembly and Senate versions of a bill. Some Deputies belonged to several special and joint committees, some to none.

To get a true measure of a Deputy's committee performance, I used two indicators. First, I simply counted the number of meetings he attended throughout the entire time period. This indicator shows who are the most active Deputies. A second indicator shows which Deputies are most willing to perform their assigned duties. This indicator was the percentage of all his scheduled committee meetings actually attended by each Deputy. This measure was included because some Deputies were simply unable to attend a large number of meetings, yet faithfully went to almost all they could attend. One Deputy, for instance, went to twenty-four of the twenty-four meetings of the Foreign Affairs Committee in this period. In absolute terms, he appears less active than another Deputy who went to thirty-one of the sixty-two meetings of the Finance Committee. Yet he has a much better committee attendance record. Both the absolute number of meetings attended and the overall attendance record have been included in the data presented below to give a complete view of these Deputies' performances in attending legislative committees.

The data on these two measures of committee attendance are set forth in Tables 7-6 and 7-7. These tables show that the original expectations were correct concerning program, mission, and status Deputies, but incorrect about obligation Deputies. Both tables show exactly the same trend. Program, mission, and obligation Deputies attend about the same number of committee meetings and have about the same record of attendance at those meetings. All three types go to more meetings and have a better record of attendance than status Deputies. The only surprising element in this data is the record of obligation Deputies. On the basis of median number of meetings attended, they even have a slightly better record than mission and program Deputies.

One can only speculate on the reasons for this unexpected fact. Obligation Deputies have a strong sense of duty and believe they should carry out those tasks assigned to them. Since part of the Deputy's job is attending committee meetings, they attend committee meetings. In short, they go through the motions of being a legislator. If their record in committee meetings resembles their record of work in plenary sessions, they are passive, not active, members of those bodies. It appears likely that obligation Deputies shoulder the formal burdens of their job, while making few positive or creative contributions to the work of the legislature.

Table 7-6

Differences Among Incentive Types: Number of Committee Meetings Attended[a]

	Obligation Deputies	Program Deputies	Mission Deputies	Status Deputies	All Deputies in Sample
Number of Deputies	7	14	19	10	50
Mean number of meetings attended	23.6	23.7	24.9	18.8	23.2
Median number of meetings attended	24	21.5	23	11	23
Percent at or over median for all Deputies in sample	71%	50%	53%	40%	50%

[a]This table is based on the total number of committee meetings each Deputy attended in the period July-December, 1968, and October, 1969. Every internal National Assembly committee was included in this count: the six regular standing committees, special assembly committees, and joint committees set up with the Senate for the purpose of resolving Assembly-Senate differences on a particular bill.

Table 7-7

Differences Among Incentive Types: Percent of Committee Meetings Attended[a]

	Obligation Deputies	Program Deputies	Mission Deputies	Status Deputies	All Deputies in Sample
Number of Deputies	7	14	19	10	50
Average attendance record	54.3%	54.6%	53.6%	44.7%	52.3%

[a]This table is based on the percent of all committee meetings which he could actually have attended that each Deputy did, in fact, attend. The time period is: July-December, 1968, and October, 1969. Every National Assembly committee was included in the count: regular standing committees, special committees, and joint committees with the Senate.

5. Questions Submitted to the Government
(*Questions écrites*)

It is now clear that status Deputies are inactive in matters pertaining to legislative work: articles, *rapports*, and committee meetings. They are, however, active speech-makers. It will be instructive to see those areas in which they lead their fellow Deputies. The first category consists of *questions écrites*—written questions which Deputies can submit at any time to particular Cabinet Ministers.

These questions, published frequently in the *Journal Officiel* record of Assembly debates, can touch on any subject and are supposed to be answered by the Minister within thirty days. In practice, many questions are not answered this quickly, but most eventually receive a written reply (also published in the *Journal Officiel*). General agreement exists among observers of the Assembly that these questions are primarily a device whereby Deputies receive free financial and legal aid for their constitutents. They also help to air grievances about administrative mishandling of local problems.[7]

Why would some Deputies ask more questions than others? To answer, one must understand what function these questions serve. There can be little doubt that these questions bring a Deputy local and national publicity, helping him politically. Local papers report on the questions their Deputies ask. Sometimes national newspapers (such as *Le Monde*) give coverage to a Deputy's question when it touches on a national issue.

The Deputy who asks numerous questions thus keeps his name before the public and gives the outward impression of working for his constitutents' interests. Yet these questions can hardly be taken as proof of any programmatic focus. Questions are not hard to write. Indeed, the Deputy may submit a question that came verbatim from a local Mayor or a party worker. Little energy is thus required to submit a question, and once it is submitted, the Deputy need do nothing more about the matter. Questions, then, bring one a certain degree of publicity and may help one politically—particularly with that segment of the public which is most interested in politics and thus aware of the Deputy's activity in this sphere.

Status Deputies are the incentive type most concerned with gaining personal publicity, while mission Deputies are also very much aware of the benefits of publicity for furthering their party's cause. These two types were therefore expected to be more active than program and obligation Deputies in submitting written questions. The incentives of these latter two types would not seem to engender this sporadic and nonpolicy-centered kind of activity.

As Table 7-8 shows, these expectations were confirmed. Status and mission Deputies submit far more written questions to Ministers over time than do program and obligation Deputies. Especially striking is the use status Deputies make of this device. Skillful in keeping themselves before the public eye, these men probably use questions to pose as defenders of the "common man" and local interests against the encroachments of the State and the hated Paris *fonctionnaires*.

6. Disruptive Behavior in the Legislature

In comparison with other Deputies, status Deputies also rank high in disruptive behavior. As is well known, French legislative debates are often characterized by acrimonious bickering, sharp, pungent exchanges across the aisles, and frequent

Table 7-8

Differences Among Incentive Types: Number of Written Questions Submitted to Cabinet Ministers[a]

	Obligation Deputies	Program Deputies	Mission Deputies	Status Deputies	All Deputies in Sample
Number of Deputies	7	14	19	10	50
Mean number of questions submitted	6.1	7.7	11.0	20.8	11.4
Percent of Deputies submitting more questions than the average Deputy	14%	29%	37%	50%	34%
Percent of Deputies in each group who submitted *no* questions during entire period	29%	21%	5%	0%	12%

[a]This table is based on the number of written questions (*questions écrites*) Deputies submitted to Cabinet Ministers during the period July-December, 1968, and October-December, 1969.

interruptions of a speaker by one or many Deputies. These acts hardly contribute to the orderly process of policy-making. Disruptive tactics can only embitter personal relations among Deputies and make working together difficult.

In many legislatures a norm of courtesy moderates the intensity of political conflict between opposing forces. Although Deputies acknowledge this norm in interviews, they often ignore it in practice. Even a cursory reading of Assembly debates uncovers numerous instances of rude and provocative behavior—behavior which lends itself to high drama but not to effective lawmaking. Obviously, some legislators are more likely than others to engage in this disruptive practice. An understanding of the various incentives leads to specific expectations about which types are likely to be rowdy in the legislature.

Program and obligation Deputies are likely to avoid disruptive actions. This activity would neither contribute to effective policy manipulation nor illustrate moral behavior in politics. On the other hand, it seems likely that mission and status Deputies would engage in this type of behavior. A knowledge of their incentives suggests both conscious and unconscious reasons for these actions.

Consciously, the mission Deputy makes the political calculation that he can serve his party by frequently stating its positions and by refuting the central points made by opposing speakers. If he must interrupt others to gain these ends, he will not hesitate to do so. At the unconscious level, mission participants may be unable to control themselves when they hear the spokesman of an opposing philosophy; they must instantly denounce this heresy without concern for the niceties of legislature procedure.

Consciously, the status Deputy tries to gain the attention of others so that he can cut a good figure for himself in public debates and gain the reputation of being *ministrable*. One way to boost himself is to cut others down—by scathing remarks and jibes at appropriate places in opponents' speeches. At the unconscious level, status participants are likely to adopt behavior patterns which assure them the attention of others and prevent people near them from getting this attention. This would lead them to talk a good deal themselves and to have a natural predisposition to break into the conversation of any around them who appear to be gaining the group's admiration.[8]

To test the validity of these expectations, an Index of Disruptiveness was devised. Its construction is explained in Appendix B. The Index was based on three elements: the number of times a Deputy interrupts other speakers in plenary sessions; the amount of time he spends in these interruptions; and the number of interruptions he provokes from others during his own speeches. (This last element was included in the Index because a close reading of legislative debates clearly shows that some Deputies invite interruptions in their speeches by provocative remarks, ad hominem comments, and denigrating slaps at political opponents.)

Each Deputy was given a score on the Index of Disruptiveness ranging from zero (nondisruptive) to twelve (disruptive). Table 7-9 shows the average of these scores for each incentive type. The data in this table lie in the expected direction, although program Deputies rank somewhat higher in disruptiveness than hypothesized. Obtaining average scores of 5.9 and 5.1 respectively, status and mission Deputies rank above the average of 4.6, while obligation Deputies

Table 7-9
Differences Among Incentive Types: Scores on Index of Disruptiveness[a]

	Obligation Deputies	Program Deputies	Mission Deputies	Status Deputies	All Deputies in Sample
Number of Deputies	7	14	19	10	50
Mean Score	2.1	4.2	5.1	5.9	4.6
Median Score	2	4.5	6	5.5	4.5
Percent *above* median for all Deputies in sample	14%	36%	68%	60%	50%

[a]Range is from 0 (nondisruptive) to 12 (disruptive). For explanation of the Index, see Appendix B.

with an average score of 2.1 rank well below average. The scores of program Deputies average 4.2, somewhat below average.

The difference between program Deputies and mission-status Deputies becomes more dramatic when one considers the numbers in each group who scored above the median of 4.5. Sixty-eight percent of mission Deputies and sixty percent of status Deputies scored above the median, compared to only thirty-six percent of program Deputies. Only one obligation Deputy (fourteen percent) scored above the median.

One can only conclude that some program Deputies do not refrain from disruptive behavior when this behavior is a persistent pattern in their legislature. Perhaps the actions of program participants would differ in a legislature with fewer traditions of interruptiveness. In any case, even in the French legislature they are less disruptive than mission and status participants.

7. Leadership in the Legislature

The final indicator of legislative behavior was aimed at discovering the degree of leadership and initiative Deputies exercise in the Assembly. For this purpose an Index of Legislative Leadership and Initiative was developed. It is explained in Appendix C. Essentially, it aims at learning which Deputies are given positions of responsibility by fellow legislators or take on legislative responsibilities by their own action. The scale is constructed from data indicating (1) those Deputies nominated to Assembly leadership positions; (2) those Deputies nominated to special legislative committees; (3) those Deputies nominated as *rapporteurs*; and (4) those Deputies who have introduced private-member bills (*propositions de loi*). The time period chosen for study was July-December, 1968. On this scale each Deputy received a score ranging from zero (low in legislative leadership and initiative) to four (high in legislative leadership and initiative).

Table 7-10 shows the average scores by incentive type. The data in this table shows a clear pattern: status, mission, and program Deputies all score approximately the same on this scale and all score higher than obligation Deputies. The passive obligation Deputy's position is expected, as are the positions of the activist program and mission Deputies.

The high score of the status Deputy is especially interesting. It precisely conforms to the expectations raised by a knowledge of their incentives. These men rank in the same category as program and mission Deputies when it comes to asserting themselves energetically as Assembly leaders and initiators. Yet the previous data has indicated that they do little work in the area of concrete policy-formulation and lawmaking. This data helps to solidify our image of the status Deputy as a man who will work hard to gain positions and prestige without working hard in areas requiring policy expertise.

Table 7-10

Differences Among Incentive Types: Scores on Index of Legislative Leadership and Initiative[a]

	Obligation Deputies	Program Deputies	Mission Deputies	Status Deputies	All Deputies in Sample
Number of Deputies	7	14	19	10	50
Mean score on scale	1.1	1.6	1.7	1.6	1.6
Percent in each group scoring 2-4 (moderate to high in leadership and initiative)	29%	43%	47%	40%	42%

[a]Scores range from zero (low in leadership and initiative) to four (high in leadership and initiative). The index is explained in Appendix C.

8. Conclusion

The basic findings conform closely to initial expectations raised by the study of incentives. Program Deputies are very active in matters requiring concrete knowledge of public policies. Obligation Deputies are less active than any other type, although they are not wholly inactive. They apparently try to fulfill the duties of legislator, but since they have no great enthusiasm for their work, they do not exert themselves strenuously. Status Deputies do little in the way of solid work to shape final legislation, but they do whatever possible to stay in the public eye and to gain leadership positions. The only Deputy who deviates slightly from original expectations is the mission Deputy. This individual was somewhat less active in the legislature than he was originally expected to be. What might account for this fact?

Although one can only conjecture at this early stage in the study of incentives, a plausible explanation comes quickly to mind. Mission Deputies are by far the most party-oriented of the incentive groups. All but four of nineteen have worked for their party for over fifteen years and many have high party positions. Only three of fourteen program Deputies have been party workers for over fifteen years. Mission Deputies are probably party militants first and Deputies second. They spend much time outside the Assembly in party work unrelated to the legislature, and this work cuts into the time they can devote to parliamentary activities.

One example may illustrate this point. One Communist Deputy I interviewed had worked full-time for the party for decades. He now holds one of the party's most important positions. Yet he scored low on several of the indices of legislative activity. Clearly, this mission participant is not an inactive political leader. Rather, he owes more allegiance to his party than to the legislature, and his party duties keep him from playing an active role in the Assembly.

Program Deputies, unlike mission Deputies, accept the job of legislator as their most important one. One might hypothesize that mission Deputies are no less active political leaders than program Deputies; they are simply less active as legislators alone.

Behavioral Differences Among Incentive Types (2): Political Careers of French Deputies

Incentive analysis leads to expectations about the career pattern of each incentive type. Payne listed several hypotheses in *Patterns of Conflict*.[1] Barber deals both explicitly and implicitly with the likely career pattern of his four types.[2] The French interviews provided additional knowledge about the predispositions of each incentive participant, and this knowledge generated new hypotheses about the way incentives might shape political careers.

Happily, data on the careers of French Deputies is readily available.[3] This data can serve as a significant test of the utility of incentive analysis. One wishes to know whether Deputies do, in fact, behave in ways consistent with their incentives. The evidence indicates that they do. It shows that each incentive type in France has a particular career pattern—a pattern one would largely have predicted solely from knowledge of the incentive and its probable consequences.

1. Age at Entering Politics and at Obtaining Public Office

Let us begin with an examination of the ages at which Deputies entered politics and later achieved public office. What pattern would one expect for each type? Payne has already hypothesized that the status incentive will lead to early entry into politics and rapid attempts to gain public positions.[4] Barber's "Advertiser" (a probable status participant) is clearly a young man in a hurry.[5] It seems likely that the status participant—concerned with quickly finding "success" and ascending a ladder of prestigious positions—enters politics early to assure himself the best chance of reaching the top.

The mission participant is also likely to enter politics early—soon after the adolescent period of self-questioning. He solves the young man's concern about what to do with his life by early dedicating himself to a secular cause. Since life for him consists of service to a cause, he will want to begin working toward this noble end as soon as possible.

There seems to be no reason to expect program or obligation participants to enter politics early. Nothing inherent in their incentives provokes a strong, youthful drive for such activity. Both types are likely first to develop separate careers outside politics, then later in life be drawn into politics. The obligation participant specifically considers himself an "amateur" in politics; he is temporarily—but only temporarily—fulfilling his moral duty as citizen. Most obligation

143

participants would not feel the call of this moral commitment until they had established themselves as working adult members of their society. Concerning program participants, Payne explains why one expects them to become interested in politics relatively late in life:

The program satisfaction depends upon an awareness of the outside world. It involves a focus upon, that is, a genuine interest in, substantive matters lying beyond the individual. Consequently this satisfaction is not likely to emerge until the individual lifts his horizon, until he overcomes problems of personal adjustment (characteristic of youth) and achieves the emotional maturity to become interested in matters outside himself.[6]

After entry into politics at different ages, incentive types should also behave differently in seeking office. The status participant has his eyes focused on prestigious positions. Anxious to gain social recognition, he hopes to gain public office quickly and to rise to higher offices as rapidly as possible. He should differ markedly from the mission participant in this regard. The mission participant enters politics early, but with the aim of serving a cause, not gaining a position. His work for a party may eventually bring him into public office, but he does not bend all his efforts in that direction, as does the status participant. Hence, one would expect the mission participant to reach public office, and to rise in office, slowly after his entry into politics.

Program participants should also rise slowly in public office. Intrigued by the possibilities for policy-management at each political level, they should prefer to spend time accomplishing something in one position before trying to rise to a higher one. Obligation Deputies, who do not enjoy politics, should be expected to spend little time in any position. They will probably remain for short periods of time in a given office, leaving it after a term or two with the feeling that they have "done their duty."

The data in Table 8-1 show that these expectations are justified. Status Deputies do enter politics early, advance very quickly to public office, and become Deputies at a very early age. Mission Deputies also enter politics early, but advance very slowly to public office. They average eleven and a half years in politics before gaining a public position and seventeen and a half years in politics before reaching the Assembly. These are significantly greater lengths of time than for the other three types.

Program participants enter politics quite late and advance fairly quickly to a public office. Once they achieve office, they seem content with managing policy at that level. They take, on the average, much longer than the other three types of Deputy to advance from their first public position to the Assembly. Consequently, they first enter the Assembly four years older than obligation Deputies, six years older than mission Deputies, and nearly eleven years older than status Deputies.

Obligation Deputies enter politics late, but advance to the Assembly as

Table 8-1

Differences Among Incentive Types: Ages at Important Career Stages

	Obligation Deputies	Program Deputies	Mission Deputies	Status Deputies	All Deputies in Sample
Number of Deputies	7	14	19	10	50
Average age at entering politics[a]	32.4	32.4	24.2	26.0	28.0
Average age at gaining first public office	39.0	37.8	35.7	29.1	35.4
Average age at entering Assembly	43.6	47.7	41.7	37.0	42.5

[a]The date of entry into politics is based on information supplied by the Deputy during the interview. Total time spent in politics is based on the time between this first political activity and mid-1969. A few Deputies clearly dropped out of politics altogether between their first activities and later ones. This time was not included in the calculations.

rapidly as status Deputies (eleven years after entry). They average less than five years between the time of attaining their first public office and entering the Assembly. This is a significantly shorter period than that taken by other Deputies. It appears that obligation Deputies do not enjoy public office. They will not stay long in one office, although probably in the name of "the public interest" they can be persuaded to go from one office to a higher one—i.e., the National Assembly. (They do not remain long in the Assembly either, as shown by the data in Table 8-2.)

2. Seniority in the Legislature

The study of incentives leads to certain expectations about the length of time different incentive types will stay in the legislature. Since status and obligation participants have some or many negative feelings about politics, compared to the positive attitudes of mission and program participants, one would expect these latter types to have more seniority in the legislature than the former. This expectation follows from the reasoning that men with ambivalent or negative feelings about political activity should expend less effort than others trying to maintain themselves in public office. Eventually, they may simply quit. Mission and program participants, for whom politics is a central and rewarding activity, should do all they can to remain in public office. One hardly expects them to leave of their own accord. These different attitudes toward politics should ultimately be reflected in high legislative seniority for mission and program participants compared to status and obligation participants.

This reasoning is based in part on the findings of Payne and Barber. Barber's "Advertiser" (probable status participant) and "Reluctant" (probable obligation participant) are partially defined by lack of willingness to return to the state legislature for three or more terms.[7] This attitude apparently signifies their lack of enthusiasm for legislative work. Payne explicitly hypothesizes that status participants will remain for less time in legislative office than program participants, and presents data showing enormous legislative turnover in the Colombian Congress dominated by status participants.[8]

The data on seniority in Table 8-2 does not entirely conform to expectations. Status Deputies have as much seniority as program Deputies, and mission Deputies are even more active than anticipated. Obligation Deputies have, as expected, the lowest average seniority.

It is not difficult to explain why mission Deputies have more seniority than program Deputies. The mission incentive appears to stimulate more driving force and lasting dedication than any other incentive. (We shall shortly see that mission Deputies spend more total years in politics than program Deputies.) The more surprising fact in Table 8-2 is the seniority built up by status Deputies. This finding directly contradicts expectations and the evidence of other studies. It clearly calls for some attempt at explanation.

There appear to be two reasons why status participants will remain in the national legislature in a country such as France. First, one is likely to have less status in France as a former Deputy than as a Deputy. Payne shows that this is not the case in Colombia, where "prestige adheres to an ex-representative as well as an incumbent."[9] Thus, in Colombia the status participant has what he wants immediately after his election to national office. If his chances for advancing still higher are slim, he may retire after a term in the legislature and retain the high status of "former Representative" for the rest of his life. It is unlikely that the title of "former Deputy" in France adds much to a man's social status, especially

Table 8-2
Differences Among Incentive Types: Seniority in the Legislature

	Obligation Deputies	Program Deputies	Mission Deputies	Status Deputies	All Deputies in Sample
Number of Deputies	7	14	19	10	50
Average number of years spent in National Assembly[a]	4.0	6.1	8.0	6.0	6.5

[a]Terms not necessarily continuous.

compared to the title of Deputy. French status legislators must remain in office if they wish to retain the social prestige they seek.

French status legislators have an additional reason for remaining in the legislature. Although "former Deputy" may mean little in France, the title of "former Minister" does carry great weight. It is well to recall that status participants see their life as a rapid climb up a steep ladder. In France for most politicians the position of Minister is the highest feasible rung on the ladder. Service in the Assembly has provided the traditional training-ground for French Ministers. It is extremely unlikely that a Deputy who retires or loses an election will be awarded a Ministerial post. To gain this prestigious position in French society, status Deputies must remain in the legislature and must work to stay there.

This variable—seniority in the legislature—produces the one major finding which deviates from previous studies. Although status Deputies spend less time generally in politics than program Deputies (see following section), they do spend an equal amount of time in the National Assembly. It seems likely that the time they spend there is related to their desire to advance to Cabinet positions. In a political system where legislative seniority is required in order to obtain prestigious higher offices, status participants may decide to go ahead and accumulate this seniority, even though they do not enjoy the actual work involved in the position they must hold.

3. Number of Years Devoted to Politics

The same reasoning which led to the expectations on legislative seniority led to similar expectations on over-all time spent in politics. Program and mission Deputies were expected to spend more years in politics—a voluntary activity they like—than status Deputies, who have ambivalent attitudes toward politics, and obligation Deputies, who dislike politics altogether. These particular expectations were wholly supported by the data.

The amount of continuous political activity engaged in by each Deputy was calculated—from the day he entered politics until mid-1969 (time of the interviews). Mission Deputies were by far the most active group. They averaged twenty-five and a half years of political participation. Program Deputies were somewhat less active, averaging over twenty-one years in politics. Status Deputies were still less active, with seventeen years in politics on the average. As expected, obligation Deputies have spent the least time in politics—slightly over fifteen years on the average. It is worth noting that even this low average is inflated by the inclusion of a thirty-year period one obligation Deputy had spent as Mayor of a tiny commune before his election to the Assembly. And this man swore his job as Mayor was "not political." With this man excluded from the calculations, the other six obligation Deputies average only *eleven* years of political activity.

Table 8-3
Differences Among Incentive Types: Time Spent in Politics

	Obligation Deputies	Program Deputies	Mission Deputies	Status Deputies	All Deputies in Sample
Number of Deputies	7	14	19	10	50
Average number of years spent in politics[a]	15.2[b]	21.3	25.5	17.0	21.2

[a]For method of calculating time spent in politics, see footnote a, Table 8-1.

[b]The average time spent in politics for six of these seven obligation Deputies is eleven years.

The data on time in politics is presented in Table 8-3. This data shows clearly that status and obligation participants spend less time in politics than program and mission participants and that mission participants spend more time in politics than the others.

4. Party-oriented Career Activity

A crucial variable in a man's political career is the degree to which his actions are party-oriented. Some men are dedicated party workers; others have minimal or no ties to a party. The variation is particularly strong in France where many different types of party have coexisted and where it is still possible to be a national politician with no party ties at all. If different incentive types have differing tendencies for party activity, it should be especially easy to see these different tendencies among French participants.

It appeared certain that mission Deputies would be party activists; they would feel best able to serve a cause by joining a political organization. Obligation Deputies were expected to shun parties, which, especially in France, have the reputation of being divisive elements serving narrow interests. Wishing to serve "the public good," these men should avoid party involvement.

It was less clear what to expect with program and status Deputies. Their work in a party would depend on whether this work served their respective ends of policy-management and self-promotion. In a country with weak parties, such as France, party backing may not be essential. Program participants may be able to gain policy-oriented positions (such as Mayor) and status participants may be able to gain high public office without proving themselves first to be dedicated party workers. Thus, it seemed likely that these men would show less devotion to a French political party than mission participants.

Data on party activity indicates that these expectations were generally correct. I first examined the beginning of these men's careers. Entry into politics through a party is one sign of a man's party orientation. Some men, of course, may join a party simply to boost their chances for election in the near future. In order to separate these types from others, I isolated all Deputies who had begun their political career by joining a party and working in that party's organization for two or more years before gaining any public office. This distinction should pinpoint men for whom party was a significant initial reference-point and not simply an immediate means to office.

Twenty-eight of the fifty Deputies met this requirement of early party work. As expected, mission Deputies are strong party men. Fifteen of the nineteen mission Deputies (seventy-nine percent) began their career in this way. On the other hand, only two of the seven obligation Deputies (twenty-nine percent) followed this path. Status and program Deputies occupy a middle position. Forty percent of status Deputies and fifty percent of program Deputies entered politics in this way.

This trend is solidified when one considers lifetime party activity. Table 8-4 shows for each incentive group the number of years Deputies have engaged in sustained political activity for a party. Mission Deputies clearly have the best record for long-time party activity, while obligation Deputies clearly have no penchant for party work. Seventy-nine percent of mission Deputies, compared to fourteen percent of obligation Deputies, have worked in a party for over fifteen years. The figures for status and program Deputies are forty percent and thirty-six percent, respectively.

On the other hand, seventy-one percent of obligation Deputies but only eleven percent of mission Deputies have worked for less than five years in a party. The figures for status and program Deputies are forty percent and forty-three percent, respectively.

Table 8-4
Differences Among Incentive Types: Party Activity

	Obligation Deputies	Program Deputies	Mission Deputies	Status Deputies	All Deputies in Sample
Active in Party or Movement:					
Less than 5 years	5(71%)	6(43%)	2(11%)	4(40%)	17(34%)
5-10 years	1(14%)	1(7%)	1(5%)	0(00%)	3(6%)
10-15 years	0(00%)	2(14%)	1(5%)	2(20%)	5(10%)
More than 15 years	1(14%)	5(36%)	15(79%)	4(40%)	25(50%)
Totals	7(99%)[a]	14(100%)	19(100%)	10(100%)	50(100%)

[a]Figures do not add to 100% because of rounding.

5. Entry at the Top

Another piece of information on Deputies' careers is illuminating. It appears that status Deputies are much more likely than others to enter politics from positions close to the top of the political ladder. This fact was discovered by accident. I had been attempting to learn whether particular political positions—such as Mayor—attracted some incentive types and not others. No correlations at all appeared for most public offices. A striking fact did appear, however, when I focused on Ministerial *cabinets* (staffs). *Most status Deputies began their political careers on the staff of a Cabinet Minister, while no other incentive type showed this pattern.*

A Minister's *cabinet* is his official, personal staff. It is usually composed of two or three of his long-time associates and several others—often bright, young men with some business or administrative experience. A *cabinet* position is a perfect opportunity for an ambitious man to break into politics. He enters near the top, works for a Minister, has dealings with other Ministers and high civil servants, and can make many political contacts. Enjoying a high social rating, he can easily become a "man about town" in Paris. This position would surely appeal to individuals with a status incentive. The facts lend strong support to this hypothesis.

Seven out of the fifty Deputies in the sample *entered politics* by joining a Minister's staff. This was their first political act. Ten Deputies (including these seven) gained their *first public position* by serving on a Minister's staff. (Three of these Deputies, in other words, had had some political experience but no public office before gaining the staff position.) In these two groups of seven and ten Deputies, status Deputies are vastly overrepresented. *Six of the seven* (eighty-six percent) who entered politics through a Minister's staff are status Deputies. *Seven of the ten* (seventy percent) for whom a staff position was their first public office are status Deputies.

These facts indicate that six of ten interviewed status Deputies (sixty percent) entered politics through a Minister's staff; and for seven of these ten status Deputies (seventy percent) the staff position was their first public office. This evidence strikingly illustrates how status Deputies in France began their political careers: as near the top as possible.

6. Type of Legislative District

I held no specific expectations about the type of district different incentive participants might represent. Research in this area was prompted by a trend I noted in reading over the interviews. It appeared that, while many Deputies represented districts with dozens or hundreds of communes (and hence Mayors), mission Deputies tended to have few communes in their districts. They therefore had few Mayors to deal with as part of their job. Since for practical purposes the more communes in a district, the more rural it is, it appeared that mission Deputies were more likely than others to represent urban areas.

I decided to check on this possibility. Facts had been gathered during each interview on the number of communes in the Deputy's legislative district. Table 8-5 makes use of this variable as an indicator of urbanism. Districts with fewer than twenty communes are defined as "urban districts"; districts with twenty or more communes are defined as "nonurban districts."

Data in this table show that urban districts are likely to be represented by mission Deputies. Nonurban districts are likely to be represented by other incentive types, but not by mission participants. The relationship is strong and statistically significant. Fourteen of the nineteen mission Deputies come from urban areas; fourteen of the twenty-two Deputies who come from urban areas are mission Deputies.

Clearly, urbanism does not cause men to hold a mission incentive. It seems likely, however, that an urban environment makes it easier for a movement dominated by mission participants to take root and grow. This type of movement thrives on strong organization, secrecy, and frequent interaction of its members. The urban setting—in France, at least—may be more congenial than sparsely populated rural areas, where distance alone prevents rapid communication among party members.

In any case the data in Table 8-5 suggest how an urban setting can help to *sustain* a mission incentive in experienced political leaders. It has already been shown that mission Deputies, more than others, make hostile and intransigent statements about politicians outside their own party. They are intolerant toward outside political leaders. This intolerance may well be related to communication patterns in mission participants' districts.

Table 8-5
Relation Between Mission Incentive and Urbanism[a]

	Deputies Who Come From:		
	Urban Legislative Districts	Nonurban Legislative Districts	Total
Deputies holding a mission incentive	14	5	19
Deputies holding other incentives	8	23	31
Total	22	28	50

Chi-square = 8.5. Significant at .01 level.
Goodman and Kruskal's Tau = 0.701 (70.1% error reduction knowing incentive).

[a]Urbanism is here determined by the number of communes in a Deputy's district. "Urban legislative districts" are those which contain fewer than twenty communes. "Nonurban legislative districts" are those which contain more than twenty communes.

In these urban districts mission Deputies work in well-developed party machines and spend much of their time with adherents to their cause. They see few politicians outside their movement on a regular basis. Often the few communes within their district are dominated by their own party. Hence, these men do not face the same experience as other Deputies: meeting dozens of political leaders (Mayors) every month who are wholly outside their own party and who come seeking political favors.

This insulation from daily interaction with politicians outside their party must, at the least, help mission Deputies maintain their intransigence toward the outside world. It does not cause this intransigence. Yet it keeps these men from being constantly and intimately exposed to men with differing points of view, a situation which can ultimately lead to erosion of one's ideological beliefs.

Mission participants enter politics early and remain active for years. If their beliefs were not constantly reinforced, their initial dedication might waver. The strong, urban party organization seems an excellent tool for welding men together and sheltering them from opposing ideas. This situation is symbolized by the few contacts mission Deputies have with Mayors—men who often have different party affiliations from their Deputy. This insulation of mission Deputies may well help them to maintain the *pur et dur* orientation of the ideal party militant.

7. Conclusion

Each type of Deputy exhibits a different career pattern and one which is largely predicted on the basis of incentives:

a. *Mission Deputies* are long-time activists: they enter politics early, spend more time in politics and in the legislature than others, and devote more of their time than others to political party work.

b. *Obligation Deputies* enter politics late, spend little time in politics, spend little time in any particular political position, and have little to do with political parties.

c. *Status Deputies* enter politics early, usually near the top via a Minister's staff, advance quickly to other public offices and to the Assembly; they have moderate ties with a party and do remain fairly long in the Assembly, presumably in hopes of gaining Ministerial position.

d. *Program Deputies* enter politics late, advance slowly to the Assembly, remain there for a fairly long period of time, and have only moderate ties with political parties, presumably because they do not see parties in France as policy-oriented.

The extensive evidence in this and the preceding chapter shows that each incentive type engages in a particular pattern of action in politics. This behavioral pattern, summarized in Table 1-3, appears to follow from the basic need which led each type into politics. Incentives, in short, help predict how men will act in the political arena.

Toward an Incentive Analysis of French Politics (1): Incentives and the French National Assembly

Incentives can help one understand institutional, as well as individual, behavior. They would appear especially useful in explaining the capacity of legislatures to reduce internal conflict so as to facilitate involvement in policy formulation. Incentives clearly affect the way political leaders view each other and act in the legislature. Hence, they may go a long way toward explaining why different norms, roles, and customs evolve in different legislatures. And these norms, roles, and customs appear directly related to the ability of a legislature to reduce internal disputes and focus on the management of public policy.

I have earlier[1] discussed Payne's thesis on the relation between incentives and legislative behavior. He concluded that status participants sustain conflict-provoking behavior which diminishes a legislature's capacity for participating in policy-formulation; while program participants sustain conflict-reducing norms which assist a legislature to play a role in solving public problems.[2] As real-world examples, Payne contrasted patterns in the Colombian Congress (status participants dominant) with those in the U.S. Congress (program participants dominant).

Payne's reasoning shows the possibilities inherent in incentive analysis. Using his knowledge of incentives, he offered a broad, persuasive explanation for differences in the political patterns of two national legislatures. There are, however, shortcomings in this first formulation of incentive analysis. Perhaps the weakest element in the Colombia study was the restricted view of the number of possible incentives. Payne reduced them to two: program and status. Subsequent study has identified seven incentives among political leaders in five different countries.[3] These later findings complicate the task of the political analyst.

Payne's incentive typology contained a second weakness. He assumed that most political groups will be composed almost entirely of one or another incentive type. This assumption does not now appear realistic. All other studies done of incentives and all the studies which appear closely related to incentive analysis have found two or more motivational types coexisting within the same setting or institution.[4] It now seems reasonable to conclude that most political groups of any size will be composed of at least two and perhaps several incentive types. Attempts to theorize about incentives and group behavior must take this fact into consideration.

Several incentive types, then, coexist in most legislatures. Knowing this fact, the scholar must seek to learn the mix of incentive types in a given legislature and the effect of this mix on the norms of that body. A legislature dominated by program and obligation types, for instance, would probably differ considerably from one dominated by status and mission types.

The term "dominated by" offers a clue toward explaining the behavior of groups composed of multiple incentive types. In making generalizations based on the mix of incentives in a political group, one must concentrate on the major components of this mix. The minor groups of incentives may be ignored for analytical purposes.

Take a legislature composed of the following incentive types: thirty-seven percent program, thirty percent status, twenty-six percent mission, five percent obligation, and two percent game. In generalizing about this legislature's behavior, one would almost certainly ignore the obligation and game incentives and state that the legislature was dominated by program, status, and mission types. By this statement one would mean that these types influence group behavior, while the obligation and game types would have no important effect on the group. "Domination," then, merely refers to relative size.[5]

If five percent of a group has little impact in shaping its characteristics but twenty-six percent of the group does have a major impact, then there would seem to be a critical point at which an incentive ceases to be unimportant and begins to affect group norms. If two percent, say, of a given legislature in 1920 were program participants but ninety-eight percent of that same legislature were program participants by 1960, one would expect to find drastic internal changes in that body—such as greatly increased committee workloads and growth of the norm of expertise.[6] The central problem is identification of the threshold at which incentive types start to influence group norms.

Given the present state of the social sciences, one would be naively optimistic to believe it possible to pinpoint exactly when part of a group starts to influence the group as a whole. One might, however, postulate a *critical range*, below which an incentive type will have little effect on the legislature and above which it will have a major impact. In principle, it seems reasonable to assume the existence of such a range. Although only additional studies can locate it accurately, I would at present speculate that this critical range would be approximately twenty to thirty percent. When an incentive type composes less than one-fifth of a legislature (group), it probably has little overall effect on it; when it approaches one-third of the legislature (group), it undoubtedly will have some impact. The threshold at which an incentive type passes from unimportant to influential probably lies somewhere in this twenty to thirty percent range.[7]

It is, of course, possible that this critical range would differ among incentive types. Perhaps program participants will begin to influence a group's behavior when they compose only eighteen percent of it, while obligation participants might not affect a group until they composed thirty-two percent of it. Again, this question can be resolved only by future study. At this point in time it is simply the principle of a critical range that should be established. Until future research shows otherwise, the range will be assumed the same for each incentive type.

The need to establish the principle of a critical range stems from a desire for elegance and simplicity—elements essential for satisfactory theory-building. The threshold, or critical range, idea produces the following simplifying propositions: each incentive type either is or is not a "dominating" incentive type in a given legislature; and it becomes a dominating type only when its numbers reach at least one-fifth of the members of the legislature. These assumptions drastically reduce the potential number of incentive mixes within a legislature.

Added to these assumptions, another simplifying principle—reasonably derived from the evidence presented above—helps lead to a suggestive typology of legislatures. This principle states that, for analyzing the effect of incentives on legislative norms, one may concentrate on two categories of incentive types. The first category is simply the program type. The reasons for this type's importance in understanding legislative norms should by now be clear. This type is highly active, deeply involved in legislative work, and strongly supportive of conflict-reducing legislative norms. When the number of program-motivated legislators passes the critical threshold, these men will almost certainly have a strong influence on legislative behavior, and this influence will be directed toward conflict-reducing norms and legislative output. The existence or nonexistence of such a group of legislators is a vital fact which must be established before one can effectively analyze a given legislature.

The second category necessary for understanding a legislative system are those incentive types whose presence insures strong internal conflicts and decreased effectiveness for policy-management. Those which fall into this category are the status, mission, and adulation types.[8] One might label these the "conflict-producing incentives." If at least one of these types were dominant in a legislature, it would have a negative effect on that body's stability and capacity for problem-solving.

The contrast between these two categories is striking: the program type with his practical emphasis on solid legislative work; the status, mission, and adulation types with their taste for loud, flashy rhetoric and their lack of interest in the substance of most bills. No characteristic of the other incentive types seem as relevant as these for influencing a legislature's effectiveness.

Other incentives, then, can be ignored. Given the characteristics of other incentive types, it is probable that they will be inactive and thus have little impact on the legislature (obligation and conviviality participants), or they will adapt quickly to whatever norms are imposed by others (game participants). To understand a legislature's norms and capabilities for policy management, the important thing is to concentrate on the conflict-reducing (program) and conflict-provoking (status, mission, adulation) incentives.

Our limiting assumptions now lead to an economical typology of legislatures. This typology is outlined in Table 9-1. It is based on the two dichotomous variables already discussed: conflict-reducing and conflict-provoking incentive types; dominance and nondominance of these types in a legislature. This typology allows for the comparison of different legislatures and places the French National Assembly into comparative perspective.

Table 9-1

Typology of Legislatures Based on Numbers of Conflict-Reducing and Conflict-Provoking Incentive Types

		Conflict-Provoking Types (Mission, Status, Adulation)	
		Dominant	Not Dominant
Conflict-Reducing Types (Program)	Dominant	I. Mixed-elements legislature. (Elements of both orderly and disorderly behavior.) Example: French National Assembly	II. Stable and orderly legislature. Example: U.S. Congress
	Not Dominant	III. Unstable and ineffective legislature. Example: Colombian Congress	IV. Uncertain: probably orderly but weak and ineffective legislature (probably rare). Example: Canadian Senate? English House of Lords?

Definition of Terms:

1. Dominant—the numbers of the particular incentive type in a given legislature fall within or above the hypothesized critical range (twenty to thirty percent) necessary to affect legislative behavior.

2. Not dominant—numbers of incentive type fall below critical range.

3. Conflict-reducing types—refers to legislators who hold the program incentive.

4. Conflict-provoking types—refers to legislators who hold the status, mission, or adulation incentives.

The typology suggests that on the dimension of internal norms, one may usefully conceive of four basic types of legislature. A legislature dominated only by conflict-reducing participants (Type II) will evolve norms emphasizing hard work, specialization, reciprocity, courtesy, and depersonalization of conflict which facilitate its involvement in the making of policy. The U.S. Congress would be an example of a Type II Legislature.[9]

A legislature dominated by conflict-provoking participants (Type III) will develop few stable internal norms. Most of its activities will center on acrimonious floor debates where members strive for publicity to enhance themselves, strengthen their movement, or attract adoring followers. The Colombian Congress would illustrate a Type III Legislature.[10]

One can only speculate about the characteristics of a Type IV Legislature. No study relating to incentives has uncovered a political group with less than twenty percent of each of the four crucial incentive types. (A Type IV Legislature would theoretically contain fewer than twenty percent of each of these four types: program, mission, status, and adulation.) Since each of these types is highly active and has been found in several settings, it is difficult to imagine an important political group which did not contain at least twenty percent of one of these four types. Some nonpowerful groups, however, might contain few of these types. It may be that the weak, essentially symbolic, Canadian Senate is dominated by men such as Barber's "Spectators"—men who hold, say, a conviviality incentive.[11] The English House of Lords may be a similar example. Men in these bodies may wish to sit together in a convivial, prestigious group after a political life spent watching others act and supporting party leaders whenever called upon. Some city councils or school boards may be composed largely of obligation participants, recruited to "serve the community." Based on this reasoning and knowledge of these incentive types, one can conjecture that a Type IV Legislature would be a nondynamic, noninnovative, weak political unit. Its members would do little more than carry out their formal duties.

The task now centers on explaining the Type I Legislature, dominated by both conflict-reducing and conflict-provoking participants. The French National Assembly can apparently be placed in this category. Mission, program, and status participants all appear to be dominant forces there.[12] What, then, are the characteristics of this Type I Legislature and how does its incentive mix help to explain these characteristics?

The purpose of the following discussion is not simply to list the well-known characteristics of the National Assembly[13] but to suggest how these characteristics may be traced to the incentive mix in that body. Emphasis will be placed on those internal norms and structures of the Assembly which affect its capacity for involvement in the policy-making process.

Both conflict-reducing and conflict-provoking types coexist in the National Assembly. This fact may explain what I call the contradictory nature of that body. It suggests that French politics is more complex than politics in the U.S. or Colombia. Major forces within the Assembly are pulling in contradictory directions. On the one hand, program legislators are trying to set up structures and procedures which will involve them in the work of formulating laws on subjects which interest them. On the other hand, mission and status legislators are actively seeking to use the legislature for the promotion of a secular cause or advancement to higher office. The orientations of mission and status legislators cause them to act differently from program legislators and often at odds with them.

Since the program-motivated legislator wants to work on legislation, he will take time to develop legislative procedures which facilitate this task. These will include specialized legislative units (committees, study groups) devoted to particular subject areas, and norms such as hard work, specialization, reciprocity, and courtesy. Because these structures and norms form an integral part of the policy-making process, they will come to have independent importance for the program type and he will devote many of his resources to creating or preserving them.

Status and mission types will behave quite differently. Since neither type gives high priority to facilitating the legislative process, neither will place high value on procedures designed toward that end. They will see structures and rules in tactical and opportunistic terms. Those which benefit them or their movement at a given moment will be accepted. Those which disadvantage them will be fought viciously. Since the operating procedures of any legislature will at any given time work to the detriment of some political group, and since most groups in France will probably contain some status or mission types, it follows that there will always be a significant number of conflict-provoking legislators working to destroy the legislation-facilitating procedures introduced by the program legislators.

These two legislative types work at cross-purposes in another important way. The program legislator has a positive attitude toward productive interaction. Because he enjoys working with others and seeing the fruits of collective labor, he wants to make the legislature an efficient place for transacting public business. Status and mission types see the world differently. For them politics is a ceaseless struggle for scarce rewards: office, prestige, power, political control of the nation. Constantly competing with others for these rewards, these men are unlikely to foster cooperative action in the legislature. Furthermore, they will view with suspicion the motives of those who do undertake to bring men together to shape public policy.

Finally, program legislators will attempt to mitigate social conflicts, channeling them into the public sphere and there pressing for governmental actions to deal with the problems which gave rise to the conflicts. Status and mission legislators will exacerbate social divisions by trying to make themselves the loud spokesmen for those groups which are most discontent and potentially powerful.

Thus, in terms of their goals, the legislative procedures they support, and their attitudes toward social demands, these two types of legislator will usually work toward directly opposite ends with directly contradictory strategies.

What are the institutional results of these divergent activities? All studies of the program participant have stressed his drive and devotion to hard work.[14] Given the wide-ranging activity of these men, it seems certain that soon after their numbers in any legislature reach the critical range, they will succeed in formally setting up the procedures they consider necessary to influence legislation. In a Type I Legislature, however, they will never wholly be able to overcome what they will consider to be obstructionist activities by conflict-provoking legislators. These men will hinder the work of program participants. They will bend legislative structures to their own ends (e.g., status participants will use committees to enhance their chances of gaining higher office, not to fashion laws). They will ignore legislative norms or pay lip service to them while acting in contrary ways.

The institutional result of this *mélange* of activities will be: the formal existence of internal mechanisms often associated with effective legislatures; actions on the part of some legislators to use these mechanisms to make public policy; and actions on the part of other legislators which undermine these legislation-facilitating mechanisms. As a result the legislature will only sporadically and inefficiently do what program legislators want it to do: work on laws dealing with social problems and oversee their implementation. Frequently, legislative work will break down in violent floor debates between bitter and recriminating opponents. And just as often, it will come to a complete halt as legislators vote out a government while disagreeing on a successor, or refuse to pass a budget.

This overview of the mixed-incentives legislature generally describes the National Assembly since 1946. I speculate that there has been no change in the Assembly's incentive mix since at least that date. The drastic change in Assembly powers and operations since 1958 can be understood entirely in terms of political and institutional changes. That is, since 1958 the Assembly has behaved the way a mixed-incentives legislature would behave when its powers have been radically cut. Before 1958 it behaved in the manner of a mixed-incentives legislature with strong powers.

This speculation about the continuity of the incentive mix is based on several regularities in Assembly behavior since 1946—regularities (discussed below) directly related to the incentive mix observed in my sample of Deputies. The differences which do exist between the Fourth and Fifth Republic Assemblies can be traced to factors unrelated to incentives. The basic difference lies in the weakness of the present Assembly. Three major factors account for this weakness: (1) constitutional restraints on the power of the Assembly (such as the constitutionally-required limit on the number of committees to six); (2) new institutions (such as the direct election of the President) which center national power in the executive branch and independent of the legislature; and (3) political developments in the nation as a whole (notably the growth of a large, fairly regular vote for one conservative party, the UDR).

All of these factors weaken the Assembly's powers, yet none relate to its incentive mix. One can explain the Assembly's loss of power after 1958 by factors outside the realm of incentive analysis. The Assembly's power was weakened by these developments, but there is no reason to assume that they also worked to change its incentive mix.

In fact, it appears likely that the incentives prevalent in a national institution reflect deep cultural and political trends in that nation and are not subject to rapid change. The incentive mix at the highest levels of a polity probably changes quickly only during major social upheavals. The political change in 1958 cannot be described in those terms. The 334 newly-elected Deputies of that year were not political novices. As Dogan has shown, all but thirty-three of these men had held important political positions or been actively involved in politics before

1958.[15] They were an integral part of the reservoir of French activists from which Deputies are traditionally recruited. Since there took place in 1958 no evident transformation of the type of men who form the French legislative elite, and since legislative patterns both before and after 1958 appear typical of a mixed-incentive pattern (under different institutional arrangements), I have drawn the tentative conclusion that no change in the incentive mix of the National Assembly took place in that year.

Although this conclusion can only be speculative, a certain amount of evidence appears to support it. It would appear that along five major dimensions directly affected by the incentive mix, the Fourth and Fifth Republic Assemblies show similar patterns of behavior, even though they operated under vastly different institutional systems.

1. Floor Debates

Action on the Assembly floor during both the Fourth and Fifth Republics follows two major patterns. Rowdy, boisterous shouting matches during major political debates alternate with long periods of calm (to the point of dullness) during which handfuls of Deputies discuss and pass bills of a "minor, technical" nature. Most observers associate the frenzied debates with the Fourth Republic, colorless monologues with the Fifth. Yet this is a misleading view. The observer who studies numerous Fifth Republic debates—such as those on the Algerian War, the *force de frappe*, the Government's request for emergency powers after the 1967 elections, the May Events, and the Government's monetary policy in the fall of 1968—will find the same intense emotional atmosphere of charge and counter-charge, name-calling, and lack of courtesy as that which characterized the "great" debates of the Fourth Republic.

On the other hand, one can exaggerate the importance of this type of debate in the Fourth Republic. Chronic absenteeism was a well-known fact among Fourth Republic Deputies.[16] The lack of a crowd has a singularly inhibiting effect upon would-be orators. Presumably, the consistent absence of many Deputies prevented the too-frequent occurrence of fiery debates before a packed Assembly. In fact, as in the Fifth Republic, a very large number of bills were passed by the Fourth Republic Assembly with no debate and no political obstruction:

Minor and uncontentious measures could be dealt with by an unopposed bills procedure, *vote sans débats*, by which after the committee report the Assembly passed each clause and then the whole bill without any discussion. It was used extensively: *in 1947 two-fifths of the bills passed, and in 1956 over half, went through in this way.*[17] (Emphasis added.)

This pattern reminds one of the present Assembly, where much of the time only a handful of Deputies are present on the floor to shepherd through that body the "minor" bills which interest them.[18]

The alternation of styles on the floor of the Assembly probably owes much to its mixed-incentive structure. The behavior of both status and mission types will create the spectacular debates. This atmosphere is congenial to status types, who can gain publicity within and outside the Assembly by scoring points off opponents before a packed house, and to mission types, who feel that in merciless combat with their enemies they are best serving their cause. Yet, unlike the Colombian legislature, work does get done in France, bills are passed, order and parliamentary rules are restored. This aspect of the Assembly probably owes much to the program types, who want to create a stable legislative process. Unable to restrain the status and mission types during major debates on national issues, program legislators probably do what they can to keep the debate in hand, then assert themselves after the issues have been talked out, the tired orators leave for a night's rest, and the press turns its attention to the latest ghastly murder. Thus, the wild debates interrupt but do not prevent the continuous, orderly work of the legislature.

The major difference between the Fourth and Fifth Republic debates is simply that there are fewer periods of clashing rhetoric and more periods of calm in the latter. This fact derives entirely from the institutional changes since 1958. The weakness of the Assembly, the Government's control of agenda and procedures, the inability of Deputies to make any *political* changes through Assembly debate—these changes have calmed the oratorical zeal of status and mission legislators. Yet this zeal can spring up again at the first sign of Government weakness. The legislative sharks smell blood from the slightest Government wound. The basic pattern of debate continues; it is simply under more rigid institutional restriction for the moment.

2. Committees

Committees are the working units of any legislature. Here differences of opinion are first aired, information gathered, the details of legislation thrashed out, and bills actually written. These structures are central to program legislators, who will devote much time to them. Yet for status and mission legislators committees have meaning only to the extent that they can be used to promote one's position or hamper one's enemies. What actions they take in committee are unlikely to contribute to the orderly process of lawmaking. On the whole, however, one would not expect them to devote consistent attention to committee activities, since many of these activities would have no political significance for them.

These differing attitudes toward committees are reflected in committee operations of both the Fourth and Fifth Republics. Committee attendance has been low since 1946. Yet each committee has retained a solid core of hard-working legislators who attend most of its meetings and do most of its work. In two different studies of these two Republics Williams makes the same point:

On most committees [during the Fourth Republic] a nucleus of a dozen or fifteen members [out of 44] attended regularly, drafted most reports, and spoke often in the house on the committee's subject.[19]

[In the Fifth Republic, Assembly committees] are much larger—and therefore much less cohesive—than they used to be. . . . At first some of them overcame this drawback . . . by setting up sub-committees under another name. . . . But as parliamentary absenteeism spread, an older practice revived: increasingly committee meetings were attended only by members interested in the bill to be discussed.[20]

I believe it likely that program legislators comprise most of this minority of regular, working members.

Several pieces of evidence reinforce this expectation. My study of a seven-month period in 1968 and 1969 shows that, on the average, forty-one percent of the members of each committee attend each committee meeting. Obviously, the percent of each committee which attends meetings consistently is somewhat below this figure. This finding ties in with what I was told by one of the highest-ranking civil servants attached to the Assembly, a man who had worked in both Republics with many of the Assembly committees:

> *Civil servant:* Only one-fifth of the Deputies are genuinely concerned with technical problems of the laws they vote on. . . . All the Deputies work hard on constituency problems because they want to be re-elected. But for more general matters, of those who really work and study the laws their committee deals with, only one-fifth of the Deputies fall into this category. The rest go along with the waves; they follow the trends. They are just there to vote the way the majority or their party leaders decide. At committee meetings the number of Deputies who come is generally between one-third and two-thirds, depending on the controversy of the topic. But the one-fifth are there all the time.

Williams' estimate of committee workers in the Fourth Republic differs little from this opinion. He suggests that twenty-seven to thirty-four percent of committee members did most of the committee work.[21] Finally, it should be recalled that program legislators made up twenty-eight percent of my sample. Since there is widespread agreement that only twenty to forty percent of the legislators apply themselves to committee work, and since one expects that most of the program Deputies will be committee workhorses, one would expect them to form a large percentage of these members.

Thus, to the extent that French committees play a role in legislating, they probably do so through the efforts of program Deputies. In both the Fourth and Fifth Republics political and institutional factors unrelated to incentives kept committees from gaining the powerful position they hold in the U.S. Congress.

They have been especially weak under the Fifth Republic for institutional reasons. But the incentives of French Deputies have probably also had a hand in weakening committees. The existence of many status and mission Deputies who probably work little in committees, ignore committee recommendations on the floor of the Assembly, or use committees for partisan and personal advantage, surely must weaken the prestige and effectiveness of those bodies.

Perhaps the most obvious weakening of the committees would come from the attempts of status Deputies to use them to bolster their national reputation. Many Deputies see committee leadership positions as useful steps on the ladder up to a Government post. In the Fourth Republic,

chairmen of important committees were always men of standing in the house and party. Those who were not already ex-ministers became *ministrables* by virtue of their election. . . .[22]

The finance committee was . . . a rival centre of leadership to the cabinet. . . . It harassed and hampered most governments, and some of its early querulousness was due to rising young politicians using it as a springboard for promotion.[23]

If newspaper articles and Parisian political conversations signify anything, they suggest that this tendency of status-motivated Deputies to use committee positions to gain or retain political prominence has not diminished. (I interviewed two status Deputies who were chairman and vice-chairman of the same committee. One was a former Minister, the other very anxious to become one. Both were dissatisfied with their legislative positions and looked longingly at those inside the charmed circle of the Government. It was clear that they hoped to use their committee position to gain, or regain, Ministerial office, not to influence legislation.)

To the extent that men such as these gain control of committees, it becomes more difficult for program legislators to use them for their ends. Nevertheless, some solid work does emanate from committees. All bills are discussed and many revised there. Even the weak committees of the Fifth Republic meet on the average fifty-eight times a year, which does not compare badly with the average 117 meetings a year for each American committee.[24] Despite institutional factors and the presence of many conflict-provoking incentive types, French committees do engage in important legislative work and participate, at times effectively, in the making of laws. The presence of a critical number of program Deputies insures that committees have at least some significance in the French legislative process.

3. Staffing and Research Facilities

American Congressmen would find Deputies scandalously unequipped for legislative work. For instance, they have no allocation for personal assistants.

Many Deputies spend a good deal of their precious time laboriously opening every piece of mail and replying to each letter by hand. Each political group in the Assembly has a small sum of money for hiring a skeleton crew of secretaries. Nevertheless, the Deputies' situation has been slowly improving since 1946. Once, a Deputy was not even given an office. In 1968-69 most Deputies shared an office in the Assembly building with one to three other colleagues. The aim of a recent administrative reform is to give each Deputy his own office in the near future. Thus, slow improvements are taking place in the Deputy's working conditions.

Deputies who are *sérieux* are not entirely without resources. The Assembly library, a small, somber set of rooms off the main corridor of the Assembly building, can hardly compare to the Library of Congress. Still, it does contain many official documents and seems to be used with some frequency. A large staff of civil servants is attached to the Assembly, and through them Deputies can gain information, publications, and technical assistance. In short, Deputies can receive some, though relatively little, material aid for their work.

One would expect that those resources they do have have been gained through the efforts of program legislators. Other incentive types have little interest in enhancing their chances to influence the bulk of legislation through gaining solid technical knowledge of the subject matter and the existing laws and regulations relating to it. Thus, program Deputies must struggle against the indifference of all other legislators and the positive animosity of all Governments, who can only see in backbenchers' attempts to gain independent sources of information and staff assistance a serious threat to governmental powers. (The Gaullist Government, for instance, has remained hostile to all attempts to reform the Assembly in this direction. In 1969 a suggestion by conservative Gaullist Deputies to increase slightly the number of Assembly committees was quickly quashed by their own Government. An increase in Assembly committees, of course, would probably increase the Deputies' power.)

I suspect that program Deputies have been largely responsible for those small gains in staffing and research facilities that have been made since 1946. It also appears likely that additional small gains in this area will continue over the years as the consistent efforts of program Deputies pay off in minor reforms wrenched from an unwilling Government.

4. Overseeing the Bureaucracy

Program legislators like to learn how laws they have passed are carried out. This desire, carried to its logical conclusion, implies strong powers to investigate administrative behavior. It would take a large group of consistently determined legislators to set up effective machinery for this task in a nation with a centuries-old tradition of centralized, rational, "nonpolitical" administration. No such machinery has existed in either the Fourth or Fifth Republics. In fact, most authors stress the fact that Assemblies in both Republics delegated their powers wholesale to the executive branch.[25]

Given the institutional setting it is understandable that program Deputies in the Assembly have been unable to assert any authority over the French bureaucracy. Yet the sweeping delegation of powers to administrators with no consistent efforts to check their actions does not fit with the program legislator's behavior patterns. These actions would, rather, follow from status and mission incentives. The status Deputy has no desire to spend time on the "petty" details of policy-making and willingly delegates complicated matters to administrators; mission Deputies will delegate powers to their leaders in the Government, when asked to do so. These are the men who may have been most responsible for the Assembly's present weak position *vis-à-vis* the administration. (Some weight is lent to this speculation by the fact that sixty percent of Gaullist Deputies in the sample are either status or mission legislators, and Gaullist Deputies have done more than any others to weaken the Assembly and strengthen the Executive.)

One would expect program Deputies to be less eager than others to relinquish the Assembly's powers. Congruent with this expectation is the fact that the only attempts during the Fourth and Fifth Republics to control the executive branch have come from legislative committees, which are probably dominated by program types. Of the Fourth Republic, Williams states: "... for influencing (governments') day-to-day activities ... (t)he committees were the most effective instrument of scrutiny."[26] Given the high rate of absenteeism in committee meetings and the subordinate position of committees in the Assembly, it is unlikely that committees were, in fact, really effective in this role. Controlled by program Deputies, they apparently did what they could to act as a watchdog on the bureaucracy but made little headway against the indifference of other Deputies, the French tradition of administrative power, and the trend toward the expansion of executive power in all modern nations.

In the Fifth Republic both the legislature as a whole and its committees in particular have been reduced in power. Committees are now a very weak structure from which to oversee administrators. Nevertheless, Ministers still appear regularly before committees, and outside experts are often brought in to testify before these bodies. Despite all the roadblocks, program Deputies in these committees are apparently still making determined efforts to maintain a modicum of legislative control over the Government.

5. Legislative Norms

There has been no systematic study of Assembly norms in the manner of the classic studies of Matthews, Fenno, and Wahlke et al.[27] The one attempt—by Leites[28]—to enumerate the "rules of the game" in the Assembly has been described by many French scholars as exaggerated and misleading.[29] It is difficult to generalize about norms in the National Assembly—perhaps because, as the evidence suggests, there simply are no widely accepted rules for personal behavior in that body.

As previous chapters show, each incentive type has a different view of his role and the way he should relate to other Deputies. Program Deputies emphasized such norms as hard work, specialization, and courtesy. Mission Deputies stressed the need to support their party and its leaders. Status Deputies were reluctant to discuss informal rules of behavior at all; when they did so, they discussed them in terms of personal strategy, emphasizing the intricacy of the rules and the importance of knowing them if one were to succeed as a legislator. Some status Deputies had apparently never thought systematically about the subject. Others seemed to feel it was too delicate a matter to discuss with a stranger.

What strikes one who sets out to learn about the agreed-upon rules for legislative behavior is that a set of rules does not exist. The National Assembly has evolved no well-articulated norms for personal conduct. Different types of Deputy enunciate different informal customs or do not even perceive such customs. This lack of a well-defined set of norms and roles is characteristic of a poorly-integrated group, one unable to solve problems effectively without internal conflict. As social psychologists have shown, the more cohesive the group, the more likely it will be to solve problems and attain group goals. And according to Newcomb, Turner, and Converse, two of the most important characteristics of a "highly cohesive group" are:

. . . .
2. shared attitudes, including *shared acceptance of rules* (normativeness), concerning group-relevant matters;
3. well-developed structural integration; members' *role relationships*, including those of leadership, *are understood*, accepted, and smoothly coordinated.[30] (Emphasis added.)

My findings show little "shared acceptance of rules" or "understood and accepted role relationships" in the National Assembly. This lack of a stable set of roles and norms derives from the program-mission-status incentive mix and leads directly to the Assembly's inability to organize for effective involvement in the policy process.

Conclusion

This explanation of Assembly behavior may help to place in perspective the varied analyses that have been offered of French national politics. Many well-known views of French politics seem based on the assumption that only one of the three dominant types in the Assembly controls politics there. Other studies show clearly that the three types exist but fail to make this point analytically.

Nathan Leites has been intrigued with the behavior of the status-motivated politician.[31] He is fascinated by the complexity of their political maneuverings, but he ignores all other types of politician in France and simply assumes that status types are the only major actors. My data show that status Deputies do indeed exist but that one would be making a serious error to interpret all of French politics as a struggle for position among status politicians.

One would also be making a serious error to assume that French politics is primarily ideological. This is the traditional view of French analysts.[32] Yet only a minority of Deputies in the sample could be classed as "ideologues"—that is, as men with a mission incentive. For most, the political faith of their party was not the governing force behind their political actions. It would be misleading to interpret in terms of an ideological commitment the behavior of these numerous Deputies who do not hold the mission incentive.

It would also seem misleading to interpret French politics as if most Deputies were moved by programmatic concerns. In fact, views of French politicians as solely status-hungry, or ideological, or programmatic, are all correct in a way, but all miss the broader point. There are *three* major types of Deputy in France. It is only in the interaction of all three that French political patterns can be understood.

The best works on France illustrate this point clearly. Duverger, for instance, makes it clear that three different kinds of people staff his three kinds of party.[33] Cadre party leaders seem primarily interested in gaining office; mass party leaders seek to implement progressive social programs; and devotee party leaders struggle for the political victory of their ideology. I would label Duverger's cadre party leaders as status participants, his mass party leaders as program participants, and his devotee party leaders as mission participants.

The foreigner who best understands the National Assembly is Philip Williams.[34] Throughout his works on this subject one constantly senses the variety of political leaders inhabiting the Palais Bourbon. Sometimes they are seen as ambitious; at other times they are hard-working; at still other times they are demagogic ideologues. Williams does not make explicit the diverse motivations of the politicians he analyzes. But many of his descriptions of the way these men interact support my contention that the modern National Assembly has been a mixed-incentive legislature—shaped by the behavior peculiar to status, program, and mission participants.

10 Toward an Incentive Analysis of French Politics (2): Incentives and French Political Parties

If the incentives dominant in a legislature affect the workings of that body, there is every reason to assume that the incentives in any political group will have major consequences for that group's behavior. One might, for instance, use incentives to study political parties. Parties were not the focus for this research, but in the course of studying motives and behavior in the National Assembly a good deal of information was incidentally gathered on French party politics. Statements about French parties based on this data must remain in the realm of speculation. Nevertheless, the patterns discovered among French Deputies suggest some interesting explanations for French party behavior.

Table 10-1
Incentive Distribution by Party

Party[a]	Number of Deputies	Number of Deputies as % of Sample	Incentive Distribution Within Party
Non-Ins.	1	2%	1 Mission
RI app	1	2%	1 Obligation
RI	9	18%	6 Program 2 Mission 1 Obligation
UDR app	3	6%	1 Program 1 Status 1 Obligation
UDR	22	44%	9 Mission 5 Status 4 Program 4 Obligation
PDM	3	6%	2 Status 1 Mission
FGDS	5	10%	3 Program 2 Status
PC	6	12%	6 Mission
TOTAL	50	100%	19 Mission 14 Program 10 Status 7 Obligation

[a]For explanation of abbreviations, see List of Abbreviations.

1. The Mission Incentive and French Parties

My evidence suggests that the French Communist Party contains many mission participants. All six of the six interviewed PCF Deputies held this incentive. This fact, plus an understanding of the mission incentive, can help to explain several well-known patterns in the PCF: its strict adherence to an outdated ideology, the blind obedience of members to the party, its emphasis on close comradeship of party members, its stress on constant struggle against dedicated enemies. These characteristics would appear to follow from the presence of numerous mission participants within the PCF. Other incentive types find no need for an all-encompassing ideology, for accepting complete subordination to their party as an organization, for accepting the view that politics is a comradeship-in-arms against opponents who must be destroyed.

The significance for French politics of the mission-dominated Communist Party becomes clear when one examines the political loyalties of other mission participants. Mission participants in France gravitate toward the two major parties of the Fifth Republic: the PCF and the UDR. All mission Deputies on the Left are Communists. Seventy-five percent of mission Deputies on the Right (nine of twelve) are members of the UDR. Three of the remaining four mission Deputies are Gaullist supporters. Only one of nineteen mission Deputies is in neither the Gaullist nor Communist camp. This clear pattern may foreshadow ominous political developments.

Mission participants thrive on healthy opponents. Lack of political enemies reduces the stimuli which impel them to action; it may discourage many potential mission participants from entering politics at all. The existence of many mission types in two irreconcilably opposed parties produces the opposite effect. This pattern may set off a chain reaction which is difficult to stop. Mission opponents perceive an enemy (a threat to their movement); they are thus stimulated to take action against this enemy; their actions stimulate the enemy to defend himself and counterattack; the enemy's actions in turn stimulate the first group to further action; and this continuing set of activities draws into politics on both sides additional mission-motivated individuals. If this cycle is not stopped, the eventual result is likely to be civil war among bitterly-opposing forces or the repression of one force by the other.

I believe it no exaggeration to say that France has since World War II more than once entered such cycles and stood on the verge of civil war. In each case almost accidental factors prevented this final result. The presence of a determined Jules Moch at the Ministry of the Interior did much to prevent the spread of Communist violence in 1948-49. The hesitation and indecision of PCF leaders in May, 1968, kept the major anti-Gaullist forces from attempting a political coup which would surely have resulted in widespread violence. It is far from certain, however, that chance circumstances will always prevent open political warfare in the future. If the two major parties in the country are in fact staffed by large numbers of mission participants, and if electoral trends continue to favor these two parties at the expense of others, political stability in France may again soon be put to a severe test.

2. The Program Incentive and French Parties

Political loyalties of program Deputies show nearly the opposite pattern from that of mission Deputies. They tend to shun the PCF and the UDR, apparently feeling little desire to mingle closely with mission participants.

Program participants in the sample belonged to the following parliamentary groups:

Table 10-2
Party Distribution of Program Deputies

RI	UDR app	UDR	FGDS	Total
6	1	4	3 (2 Socialists, 1 Radical)	14

One must not conclude from this finding that program participants gravitate to the Right. Program Deputies appear more likely to come from the Right simply because more Right Deputies as a whole were interviewed. As Table 10-3 shows, the percentage of program Deputies from both Right and Left parties is nearly the same. Of eleven Left Deputies interviewed, three were program participants. Of thirty-six Right Deputies, eleven held this incentive. Thus, 27.3 percent of Left Deputies and 30.6 percent of Right Deputies in the sample were program-motivated. This small difference is hardly enough to justify any conclusion about the side of the political spectrum to which program Deputies will commit themselves.

What *is* striking is the apparent low appeal to program Deputies of the two major parties in France: the UDR and the PCF. Not one program Deputy belongs to the PCF, although six of the eleven interviewed Left Deputies do. Program Deputies of the Right clearly prefer to avoid the main organizational structure of Gaullism, the UDR. Seven of these eleven Deputies have made definite choices to remain outside of (or minimally attached to) this party.[1] The tendency of Right program Deputies to avoid the UDR is seen dramatically in Table 10-4. Six of nine RI Deputies, compared to only four of twenty-two UDR Deputies, are program-motivated. Thus, 66.7 percent of RI Deputies and only 18.2 percent of UDR Deputies are program participants. (When one includes *apparenté* Deputies, these figures become sixty percent and twenty percent.)

Table 10-3
Distribution of Program Deputies: Right, Left, Center

Area on the French Political Spectrum	Number of Deputies Interviewed	Number of Program Deputies Interviewed	Percent of Deputies with Program Incentive
Left	11	3	27.3%
Center	3	0	00.0%
Right	36	11	30.6%

Table 10-4
Distribution of Program Deputies: Right

Legislative Party Group	Number of Deputies Interviewed	Number of Program Deputies Interviewed	Percent of Deputies with Program Incentive
UDR			
UDR and UDR *apparenté*	22	4	18.2%
	25	5	20.0%
RI	9	6	66.7%
RI and RI *apparenté*	10	6	60.0%

The relationship is clear. Among Right Deputies, those with a program incentive prefer the loosely-organized party of Independent Republicans to the structured and disciplined UDR.

Why are program Deputies attracted in significantly small proportions to the UDR and the PCF? Program Deputies probably see these parties as dominated by mission participants. When they refer to the UDR or the PCF, they mention the "sectarian spirit" and the "intransigence" of their leaders. They see UDR or PCF leaders as men zealously dedicated to their own cause and uncompromising toward those outside it. These are terms a program participant might use to designate mission politicians. Repelled by the attitudes of these men, program Deputies dislike the rigid control they exercise when they gain power in an organization. Program participants fear that this control will hinder their own ability to work for policy goals, as well as prevent the kind of independent, open relations they like to have with other men. They are thus likely to avoid organizations dominated by mission leaders.

It seems probable, then, that those program Deputies who are conservative will be attracted to the RI rather than to the UDR—seeing the RI organization as a conservative alliance of independent, cooperating individuals not dominated by a strong rigid leader. By the same token, program Deputies who situate themselves to the Left of the political spectrum will avoid the Communist Party—seeing that structure as rigid, authoritarian, and nonprogram-oriented.

These speculations suggest an answer to a question that has intrigued observers of French politics for years: why are French politicians never able to construct a truly "united Left?" The answer may lie in the incompatibility of Left non-Communist program participants and mission Communists. These two types may simply be unable to construct a stable, unitary political structure. Their goals and methods are probably too incompatible to allow them to develop voluntarily an organization which satisfies their different needs.

3. The Status Incentive and French Parties

Status participants seem more likely than any others to exert a disruptive influence on their political party. This results from their highly personal orientation toward politics. They clearly use parties for their own aim of self-advancement. Thus, they are likely to join those parties which provide them the best chances of rising to the top of the political ladder, but they will have little intrinsic loyalty to those parties. They may well leave their parties or create factions within them if these actions serve their own perceived interests.

The calculating, career-conscious orientation of status Deputies toward their parties can hardly be doubted. Six of the ten status Deputies (sixty percent) are members of the UDR, yet none joined the Gaullist movement before its ascendancy in 1958. (In contrast, seven of the nine mission Deputies in the

UDR, and nine of the twelve mission Deputies who can be called Gaullists, were working in the movement before that year.) The two Socialists with a status incentive entered politics at times when the SFIO either formed part of the Government or was the major political force in their region. The two status Centrists entered politics by joining the strongest party in their regions; both played active roles in bringing French Centrists into the governing majority after Pompidou's Presidential election (thus increasing their chances for gaining Ministerial posts). All but one of the status Deputies (the oldest Socialist) have gained a good deal of press coverage since 1968 concerning their political activities—activities calculated to gain them reputations as party leaders. These reputations will insure that they are not forgotten when party or Government rewards are distributed. It is noteworthy that no status Deputy was found in the PCF. This party, which has little chance of gaining political power in France, would hold little appeal for a status participant.

The presence of a sizable number of status participants in France may help explain a number of phenomena which have been associated with French politics. The most obvious of these would be the instability of Governments under the Third and Fourth Republics. Constantly maneuvering for Cabinet offices, status participants in those years undoubtedly aggravated the political instability fostered by French institutions, social conflicts, and weak parties. Cabinet instability was extremely useful for status participants. The frequently-changing positions at the highest level of the polity enhanced their own chances for advancing to those positions.

The presence of status participants in France may help to explain another French phenomenon: the "flash party." The sudden rise and fall of various French parties owes much, of course, to the lack of stable party identification.[2] It also owes something to the existence of political leaders who are willing to leap on the bandwagon of a rapidly-rising party. If a flash party is to exist, it must attract party leaders and active followers. It seems likely that these men will be heavily recruited from the ranks of those who wish to rise quickly and do not wish to spend years working their way up in well-structured party organizations: i.e., status participants. They will also be recruited from status participants already in other parties but willing to accept a good thing when they see it. Status participants, in short, are likely to join a rapidly rising party, even if they must leave their own party in order to do so.

The quick disappearance of the flash party can also be explained, in part, by the behavior of status participants. When these parties fail to attain the dominant position they need to provide Government posts for their backers, status participants within them may fade away—rejoining their former party or joining whatever political grouping next appears to offer them the best chance for rapid promotion. Desertion of the status participants weakens the flash party still further. By the time of the next election the party has few active leaders to promote its fortunes before the fickle French voter.

The overwhelming Gaullist victory in 1958 prevented the UNR (now UDR) from going the way of other flash parties in France, because it actually gained control of the government and thus was able to distribute rewards to its followers and hold out the hope of rewards to others. Once inside a successful and governing party, status participants would normally have little interest in deserting it.

Another likely effect of status participants on French politics follows from what has already been said. The traditionally weak French political parties probably owe this weakness in part to the continued presence in French politics of a large number of status participants. Men who maneuver for office within their party and change political affiliations to suit their own ambitions are unlikely to help build strong party organizations. Men who are scornful or envious of other political participants are unlikely to foster close organizational contacts based on mutual cooperation. Status politicians are likely to aggravate the tensions and differences which exist within any political organization, encourage internal rivalries, and engender party splits. In short, their actions make it difficult for a party to build a solid, coherent base. It is interesting again to note that no status Deputies belonged to the party with the strongest organization in France—the PCF. The absence of status participants in that party surely contributes to its ability to maintain internal cohesion.

4. The Obligation Incentive and French Parties

All seven obligation participants were Gaullists. They were either members of the UDR or closely aligned with it. This fact should hardly be surprising. Of all party doctrines in France today, Gaullist ideology should be most attractive to obligation participants. Stressing devotion to "the national interest" and abjuring "divisive party politics," Gaullists have a unique appeal in French politics to men who feel the need to serve their country or their community. Of all the parties, only the UDR stresses the appeal to civic duty and "nonpolitical public service" which attracts obligation participants.

It does not seem reasonable to conclude, however, that obligation participants will never be found on the Left side of the spectrum in France. The seven obligation Gaullists are men of relatively conservative outlooks. It appears likely that there are French citizens with less conservative orientations who might enter politics because of an obligation incentive and who would want to join a Center or Left political grouping. There are several reasons which might explain why these men were not noted in the sample.

First, the sample can tell little about behavior patterns on the Center of the spectrum or within the non-Communist Left. Among these groups only three (disparate) Centrists, one Radical, and four Socialists were interviewed. One can make no generalizations about intraparty trends on the basis of this information.

It is possible that obligation participants do belong to these various groupings but simply did not appear among the small number of their members in the sample.

Second, if obligation participants ever join the Communist Party, it is probably very rare that they rise to the Assembly in the PCF. French Communists are promoted only after years of faithful party service. Since obligation participants do not stay long in politics, it is likely that those who do join the PCF would drop out of politics long before attaining the post of Deputy. One would therefore not expect to find obligation participants as PCF Deputies. (Obligation participants in the PCF could simply not follow the pattern of three of the obligation Gaullist Deputies who found themselves in the National Assembly one or two years after their first political act.)

Third, the behavior of the obligation participant tends to be unstable and erratic. He enters politics when he perceives a vital moral issue to be at stake, when he perceives grave national danger, or when he perceives a "man of principle" desperately needing his support. Under just what conditions large numbers of obligation participants will come to hold these perceptions is uncertain. It is also uncertain when these perceptions will no longer be held, leading to the exit of obligation participants from politics.

Although it is difficult to pinpoint, it does appear that few conditions have existed in recent years which would bring obligation participants into French politics on the Left side of the spectrum. No "man of principle" above politics has emerged there to call forth their dutiful activity. (One of Mitterand's problems in uniting the Left is the aura he projects of the "compleat politician." His well-earned reputation as a skilled political maneuverer hinders his attempts to project a statesmanlike image to the mass of potential Left voters.) No party on the Left has been able to capitalize on any of the crises of recent years to present itself as a "party of national unity" around which good French citizens should rally. In fact, Gaullists have succeeded in stigmatizing the parties of the Left as responsible for all the ills of the Fourth Republic; potential obligation participants are not likely to think they could fulfill a civic duty within parties dominated by "petty politicians."

Few stimuli exist, then, to trigger the entry into French politics today of Left-leaning obligation participants. One can, however, imagine such stimuli in the past. It seems likely that the popular enthusiasm raised in the early days of the Popular Front or at the beginning of the Fourth Republic, when men dreamt of building a glorious new France, must have stimulated the entry of Left obligation participants into politics. The rapid decline of these movements would also be congruent with the exit from politics of those same obligation participants, disenchanted with the daily compromises and piecemeal solutions of the political world.

Left obligation participants may not have been entirely missing from the political scene in the 1960s. The interesting "club" phenomenon of that era suggests their presence.[3] The political clubs which sprang up after 1958 were clearly staffed by "amateurs" who wished to avoid established political parties and hoped to "inject new life" into French politics by "reforming" the old political institutions. One can speculate that many Left obligation participants became members of these bodies. Some may even have worked their way up to the position of Deputy within the *Convention des institutions républicaines,* a political alliance of some of these new clubs with some older French politicians. Had Deputies in the 1967 Assembly been interviewed, some Left obligation Deputies might have been found among the twenty or so CIR Deputies elected that year. One nonsample interview with a former CIR Deputy in fact indicated that he was a probable obligation participant.

Political trends since 1967 have scarcely been encouraging to obligation participants on the French Left. The chances for the reforms they sought appear dimmer than ever. The established Left parties are no closer to unity, having spent the ensuing years in personal and political squabbles. These conditions have undoubtedly discouraged many Left obligation participants. The decline of the clubs probably indicates their departure from the present political scene.

5. The Political Future of the Gaullists

One would very much like to know the incentive mix within each French political party. This information helped generate a number of hypotheses about the National Assembly. If one could know the incentive mix within the subgroups of the French political system (e.g., political parties), one could suggest explanations for numerous other aspects of French politics. Unfortunately, the sample of fifty Deputies was too small to allow valid generalizations about subsets of that sample, although they have led to some interesting speculations. Of all the party members interviewed, the number of Gaullists was large enough to allow for some attempt at explanation and prediction.

Of the twenty-five members of the UDR Assembly group interviewed (including three *apparentés*), nine (thirty-six percent) held the mission incentive, six (twenty-four percent) held the status incentive, and five each (twenty percent) held the program and obligation incentives. These figures may portend ominous developments for future party unity.

It would appear that mission Gaullists have dominated policy-making and organizational positions in the UDR to this date. This tentative conclusion follows from the likelihood that de Gaulle surrounded himself with faithful mission-motivated Gaullists and insured the political leadership of these men. (Probable mission participants like the unpopular Michel Debré, for instance, could never have achieved their power without de Gaulle's backing.) Furthermore, it is likely that mission Gaullists held the party together in the lean years before 1958 and were thus ready to man the top party positions once it achieved power. Status Gaullists, working their way up as political figures since 1958, were undoubtedly held partly in check by de Gaulle himself. Despite de Gaulle's departure from politics, the divisive elements within the UDR have managed to hold themselves together, but one wonders for how long UDR cohesion can last.

One major possibility for cleavage within the UDR centers on mission Gaullists. It has been pointed out that an agreed-upon, unified ideology is crucial for mission participants and that disagreements over the ideology can lead to schisms and organizational disruptions for these men. Yet Gaullists do not agree on all the tenets of their belief system. Doctrinal quarrels could thus lead to future internal division. The split over the "correct solution" to the Algerian problem led to numerous resignations and expulsions from the party.[4] For years, however, the party could usually hold together because de Gaulle—the founder of the faith—was there to act as final arbiter and enunciator of what the doctrine "really" was. With his retirement and death doctrinal disputes have begun to flare up. *"L'affaire Vallon"* provided the first post-de Gaulle example of Gaullist internal conflict based on ideological differences. Louis Vallon, a leading "Left Gaullist," published a book soon after Pompidou's Presidential victory. Entitled *L'Anti-de Gaulle*, this work accused Pompidou of "betraying" the real meaning of Gaullism. For his brashness Vallon was expelled from the UDR group in the Assembly.

One could cite several other indicators of internal unrest in the UDR due to doctrinal differences. Up to the present, however, no major splits have taken place. There are probably three major reasons for this fact. First, the party has discovered a new strong leader and interpreter of the ideology in President Pompidou. Second, since the party is in power, strong pressure can be applied to possible dissenters by reminding them that their actions could cause the downfall of the movement to which they have dedicated their lives.[5] Finally, the party has not had to confront any major new social dilemma or political problem since de Gaulle's resignation. Thus, party leaders have been spared the necessity of using their doctrine to explain a major historical development. Any dramatic interpretation of the ideology at a tense political moment could alienate large numbers of mission Gaullists who might interpret that doctrine differently. If in the future one or more of these three conditions were to change, serious ideological struggles might well take place within the UDR.

These statements by no means imply the imminent demise of the UDR. The three conditions which promote present unity could endure for some time. If the party remains in power with a strong leader for a long, stable period, party ideology may come to take a definite, clearly-agreed-upon form. It could then no longer serve as a potential weapon in internal power disputes. Furthermore, not all Gaullists are mission participants. Nonmission Gaullists are unlikely to leave the party over a simple ideological debate. Future ideological conflicts could occasionally lead (as they have in the past) to the loss of a few mission participants, but these developments will not necessarily weaken the party irreparably.

The most serious situation the Gaullists could face would be *a doctrinal dispute combined with a future loss of power*. One quarter of the interviewed Gaullist Deputies held the status incentive, and this figure may be less than the true proportion, since of all types status participants are least willing to grant interviews. In any case a sizable proportion of Gaullists appear to be status participants. The interviews show that these men were not attracted to Gaullism for ideological reasons, did not work for the movement before it came to power, and remain with it only as long as it helps enhance their chances for gaining Cabinet posts. Were Gaullist numbers in the Assembly to decline—especially to the point where they could no longer form the Government—it seems very likely that status Gaullists would start asking themselves what they had to gain by continuing to support the UDR. They might look for ways in which they could ease themselves into the new majority, even at the expense of leaving the party.

If this development occurred at the same time as an intense ideological dispute within the party, the results could be a disastrous party split. Many mission Gaullists might resign to start a new party, while status Gaullists would desert a sinking ship. At the same time, obligation Gaullists within the party would find themselves confronted with a highly uncomfortable (for them) "political" situation—factional infighting, personal recriminations, and the apparent neglect of the party's once high ideals. In such a situation few of them are likely to remain active within the UDR.

The departure of status and obligation participants and a number of mission participants from the UDR in such a situation would leave only the ideologically victorious mission Gaullists and the normally party-loyal program Gaullists in command of a greatly weakened UDR. The party's fortunes would then depend on the ability of those remnants to cooperate in holding the organization together and preventing irreparable damage to the party's large block of supporters in the French electorate. It is possible that those remaining in the party after a major split could remain together and be able to stabilize the party's share of the vote at some level (say, twenty percent) which would insure its continuation as a power in French politics. Clearly, the UDR would then have a diminished role in the French system. It might, however, be able to remain for years as the major party of the Right, as the Communists have been the major party of the Left, although it would be unable to dominate Governmental majorities as it has in the past.

6. Conclusion

It appears that different incentive types are attracted to different parties. Mission participants seek to serve parties which act as secular religions or proclaim with dogmatic certainty all-encompassing ideologies. Program participants are unlikely to be attracted to ideological parties, gravitating toward more pragmatic and flexible ones. Status participants will join successful parties in order to boost their chances for rising in politics; they are also likely to create party factions or switch parties when these actions facilitate their own self-advancement. Obligation participants are the most unstable of these political actors, entering and leaving parties and politics in line with their perceived moral duties. In general, they will be attracted to parties which proclaim service to "the national interest" and which style themselves "nonpolitical."

These last two chapters together must be seen as tentative, early attempts to develop incentive-based explanations of French politics. Much additional work is necessary on both incentives and France. I have attempted to show in this book that information about the incentives present in a political system leads to a host of speculations and hypotheses about political behavior in that system. These in turn may generate new insights into the politics of that nation.

Incentives appear useful for understanding several aspects of politics in France. Indeed, incentives probably constitute a key variable for understanding politics in any setting. For that reason it is hoped that this study of French Deputies will encourage others to investigate the potential of incentives for improving political analysis.

Appendixes

Appendix A: Summary Description of the Four Incentive Types in France

1. The Mission Participant

This participant is concerned with the purpose of life. By serving a transcendental cause, he seeks to give meaning to his own life and actions. He is identified by his strong desire to express commitment to a movement and explain the movement's ideology. Correlated with this commitment is his glorification of movement leaders, who embody the ideas of the movement and lead it in battle against its enemies. This participant sees politics as a bitter struggle between those who have the truth and those who oppose it. Politicians outside the movement are bitter enemies who must be defeated. Fellow party members are brothers in combat. Combat, expressed in political conflict, is sought as proof of one's dedication; enemies prove the need for the saving doctrine of one's party. Mission participants of opposing parties thrive on each other, since they provide each other with the hated enemy necessary to sustain and justify their political involvement.

2. The Program Participant

This participant enjoys learning about his environment and solving problems in it. He is identified by his strong interest in constructing public policies and overseeing their application. Correlated to this interest is his respect for leaders who "can get things done," although he is not psychologically dependent on those above him. He cooperates with other politicians in order to achieve his policy ends. He supports his political party, since it can help him influence policies. If he criticizes others, he does so because they are hindering his attempts to manage policy. Usually able to find outlets for his programmatic interests, the program participant enjoys his political activity.

3. The Obligation Participant

This participant seeks to live up to his beliefs about how men should act. His interest in politics springs from his belief that the good citizen *ought* to participate. This concern for moral consistency and normatively correct behavior identifies the obligation participant. He is concerned about the way things are done in politics, the *style* of decision-making. Correlated with his moral concern is his lack of interest in the ends of policy making: public programs. He usually sees other politicians as immoral and opportunistic. Politics is an evil world to the obligation participant. His dislike for this activity leads him to withdraw from it quickly, feeling either that he has fulfilled his obligation or that his efforts at reform simply cannot succeed and he must keep his own hands pure.

4. The Status Participant

This participant seeks to enhance his social prestige by rising in political office. He is identified by his interest in political positions, the techniques necessary for attaining them, and the marks of status connected with them. Correlated with this desire for status is a complete lack of interest in the details of public policies. He is rude and uncooperative during interviews, suspicious of other politicians, and envious of those in higher positions. These attitudes reflect his constant desire to appear of higher status than those around him. He has little loyalty to his party, seeing it only as an instrument to advance his own career. He does not really enjoy politics, which he sees as a war of all against all, but he will remain active as long as he finds opportunities to rise to higher positions.

Appendix B: Construction of the Index of Disruptiveness

For French Deputies one can obtain three convenient indicators of legislative disruptiveness. Since Assembly debates are faithfully recorded, one can learn from the *Journal Officiel* (1) who disrupts these debates, (2) for how long they disrupt them, and (3) how often a Deputy's speeches incite others to disruptive behavior. Three separate scales were built from these indicators. On each scale each Deputy was rated from zero (nondisruptive) to four (disruptive). (These scales are explained below.) Each Deputy's final score on the entire index could thus range from zero to twelve. The median score was 5.5. Deputies with higher scores were considered disruptive. Those with lower scores were judged nondisruptive.

An explanation follows of each of the three scales used to construct this index.

Scale 1: This scale is based on the number of times each Deputy interrupted speakers without their permission during all plenary sessions in the period July-December, 1968, and October-December, 1969.

Number of Interruptions	Score	Number of Deputies in Range
0	0	21
1	1	5
2-3	2	8
4-9	3	9
10 or above	4	7

Scale 2: This scale is based on the amount of time a Deputy spent interrupting speakers without their permission. The measure is the number of centimeters attributed to each Deputy by the *Journal Officiel* for all his interruptive comments in plenary sessions of the National Assembly during the time period July-December, 1968, and October-December, 1969.

Number of Centimeters	Score	Number of Deputies in Range
0	0	21
0.5-1	1	10
1.5-3	2	8
3.5-6	3	7
above 6	4	4

Scale 3: This scale is based on the number of interruptions each Deputy provokes during his own speeches. Deputies who specialize in provocative statements, badgering the opposition, demagoguery, and publicity-seeking invite interruptions from other Deputies during debates. This measure is designed to show who provokes such interruptions. It shows the number of times other Deputies interrupt each Deputy in the sample without his permission. Interruptions are counted whenever the Deputy had the legitimate right to speak (i.e., recognition by the Assembly President) and was interrupted by another Deputy or by a Minister without granting his permission. The time period is: all plenary sessions of the National Assembly during the period July-December, 1968, and October-December, 1969.

Number of Interruptions	Score	Number of Deputies in Range
0	0	14
1	1	8
2-4	2	11
5-10	3	8
above 10	4	9

Appendix C: Construction of the Index of Legislative Leadership and Initiative

This index represents an attempt to judge a Deputy's leadership qualities. Four types of legislative actions were chosen as indicative of a Deputy's drive and initiative. Deputies were given a score of one for each of these which they accomplished. Scores thus ranged from zero (low in leadership and initiative) to four (high in leadership and initiative). Thirty Deputies had scores of zero or one and were judged generally low on this scale; twenty had scores of two to four and were judged moderate to high on the scale. Only four Deputies obtained scores of four. The time period chosen for study was July-December, 1968. Data was gathered from the *Table du Journal Officiel de la République Française, Assemblée Nationale, 4e Législature—Sessions de 1968, Table Nominative.*

Each Deputy's score depended on the number of the following four criteria he met:

1. Deputy holds at least one Assembly leadership position—such as committee chairman (includes fourteen Deputies in sample).
2. Deputy has been appointed by Assembly to at least one of the many special committees of the Assembly—including extra-parliamentary committees and joint committees with the Senate (includes twenty-six Deputies in sample).
3. Deputy has been appointed to write at least one *rapport* or *avis* for his standing committee (includes twenty-one Deputies).
4. Deputy has introduced into the Assembly at least one private-member bill (*proposition de loi*) (includes fifteen Deputies).[1]

Each Deputy was scored as follows:

Number of Criteria Met	Score	Number of Deputies in Range
Met none of above criteria	0	11
Met 1 of above criteria	1	19
Met 2 of above criteria	2	7
Met 3 of above criteria	3	9
Met 4 of above criteria	4	4

[1] The introduction of private-member bills, which played an important part in the Fourth Republic, has declined drastically in Fifth Republic France. During the three-year period 1962-64, for example, only 470 private-member bills were introduced in the National Assembly and a mere twenty-one adopted. Compare this with the period 1950-52, when 3,124 bills were introduced by individual members of the Assembly and 240 adopted! (These figures are calculated from data in the study by Paul Cahoua, "Le Droit d'initiative en France," which can be found in Jean-Luc Parodi, "Les Fonctions du parlement dans les démocraties occidentales contemporaines: esquisse de bilan de deux années de recherche" (mimeographed: Paris: Institut d'Études Politiques, 1967), pp. 127-38.)

Appendix D: Interview Schedule and Procedure

The incentive interview should be run on an open, flexible basis. The aim is to probe role satisfactions, motivations, interests, and attitudes of each respondent. Since respondents differ radically in these orientations, one must be able to improvise questions to fit the situation and to probe in the respondent's obvious area of interest. One should also, of course, cover a number of similar points with each respondent to allow for meaningful comparisons.

Questions were designed with these aims in mind. The interview schedule reproduced here served as a rough guide to the interview. It was neither possible nor necessary to formally ask each of these questions of each Deputy. I used as many of these questions as necessary to encourage the Deputy to open up and talk about those areas of politics he found especially satisfying and those he found repugnant. The number used in any interview would vary—depending on the loquaciousness of the Deputy and the time he allowed for the conversation.

The questions which follow do provide an idea of the kind of topics one wishes to learn about in incentive interviews and the way of approaching those topics. Some of these questions were, of course, more useful than others and were asked in every interview. One must always, for instance, in trying to learn about incentives, ask how and why a man entered politics, what aspects of his present position most interest him, and what things he finds enjoyable and unenjoyable about politics.

Despite abundant evidence to the contrary a persistent myth exists in academic circles that French politicians will not grant interviews. My own experience leaves me greatly encouraged about the possibility of gaining useful information from interviews in France. With persistent effort and a good knowledge of spoken French I found it possible to obtain very satisfactory and often excellent interviews with dozens of French politicians.

The interviews themselves varied considerably, in time and in tone. Thirty-nine of the fifty lasted over an hour, and the average interview took nearly an hour and a half. Half of the Deputies were interviewed in their provincial constituency, half in Paris (usually at the Assembly). A full set of notes was taken during each interview, and the entire interview was written up in detail immediately afterward—usually in the nearest café. All quotations in this study were taken from these write-ups. All interviews were conducted in French. The translations are my own. Throughout this book I have made every effort to disguise the identity of respondents, even going so far as to alter slightly any facts which might conceivably be used to identify these individuals.

189

Interview Questions

1. First Political Position. Before asking you about your legislative work, I would like to talk with you about your political career. I am already familiar with the principal stages of your career, and in this interview I am particularly interested in your personal feelings and views as a politician. First, let's talk about your entry into political life. Your first political position was, I think, _____ . Could you tell me what led you to (enter the political arena at that time) (run for this office)? Why did you want to be _____ ?

2. First Interest in Politics. We've talked about your first political position. I would like to go back even farther into the past. When did you first get interested in politics? At that time, what was there about politics that especially attracted you? What is your first memory relating to politics? At what age did you first become aware of the legislature? What did the legislature mean to you at that time?

3. Political Party Membership(s). Let's go back to your political career. I know you are (were) a member of the _____ Party. What attracted you to that party? What led you to join? When did you become a member of the _____ Party? In your estimation, what are some of the major accomplishments of your party? What are the party's present goals? Are you planning to continue working within the party? If you wanted to vote a certain way in the Assembly, but your local party organization wished you to vote otherwise, what would you decide? (Why have you never been a member of any party? Why did you quit the _____ Party?)

4. Decision to Run for Deputy. Concerning your decision to enter the National Assembly, for what reason did you run for the legislature the first time? What did you take into consideration when you decided to become a candidate? What were the pros and cons? When you began speaking with political leaders about your candidacy, what were their reactions? Did they encourage you? How did you become your party's candidate? (For those elected under Fourth Republic: what was your position on the party list? Why did you receive that position?)

5. Political Situation in District. At the time of your first campaign, what was the political situation in your district? What was the relative importance of the parties? Was the election hotly contested? How do you explain your (victory) (defeat)? Outside the party, do you have friends and sympathizers who support you on the local level?

6. His Feelings About Campaigns. What do you think of electoral campaigns? Do you like them? Why? During the last campaign, what was your party's strategy (or: your strategy) in your district? (Would you say that the national tactics of the party helped or hindered you?) In general, during campaigns, do parties have much contact with the voters?

7. His Relation to Constituents. Are your constituents well-informed on political issues? What is your relationship with the voters? For what reasons do you see them? Are they familiar with your legislative work? If you wanted to vote one way in the Assembly and you thought that your constituents wanted you to vote the other way, what would you do? What is your relationship with local political leaders? When do you see them?

8. Legislative Activities. I'd like to go on to your activities in the National Assembly. What aspect of your work interests you most? What have been your main activities in the Assembly up to now? Have you introduced any bills? Do you speak often during floor debates? Do you like to speak on the floor? In your opinion, what is the function of legislative debates?

9. Committees. Let's talk a little about committees. What is the importance of committees in the context of legislative work? Could you tell me about a specific question that your committee has examined recently? Do you enjoy your work on the committee?

10. Contacts with Administrators. For its background work, does your committee need to have frequent contacts with administrators? For what reasons? Do the administrators give Deputies all the information they desire on technical questions? In your estimation, do conflicts often arise between administrative and legislative interests? Do you feel the Deputies exercise a real check on administrators? What other contacts do you have with administrators?

11. Deputy's Role and Satisfactions. All things considered, what is the Deputy's role? What satisfactions have you found in your legislative experience?

12. Personal Relations in the Assembly. In all countries, there are people who adapt better than others to legislative action. In your view, what must a Deputy do to be able to work with others in the Assembly? What is the legislative future of those who cannot work with others? Do most of the Deputies get along well? And do you yourself get on well with the other Deputies? Including members of other parties? Have you made a lot of friends through your political activities? Do you have any enemies in politics?

13. Rules of the Game. Every legislature, it is said, has its "rules of the game," its particular customs. Could you cite some of the unwritten rules of the National Assembly? What do you think is the function of these rules?

14. Qualities of a Good Deputy. All in all, what are the characteristics of a good Deputy? How do you rate yourself in relation to an ideal Deputy? It has been noted that there are several kinds of Deputies, including those who want to further their personal career and those who are only interested in their legislative work. Do you know Deputies who correspond to these two types? Are there fundamental differences between them?

15. Issues. Up to now, we have been speaking in rather general terms. Now, I'd like to go on to more specific questions. What particular political issues have concerned you recently? What have you done about these problems, at the Assembly or elsewhere? Do you often talk about these problems with other politicians? Are there many Deputies who specialize in a given area? If a Deputy wanted to work to get a bill passed—let's say, for a new national highway—what would he do? How would he go about getting a new school in his town?

16. Interest Groups. Social and economic interest groups are always concerned with political issues. Do Deputies have much contact with representatives of these groups? Do you? Do you think the action of these groups is a help or a hindrance to the Assembly?

17. Ideology. In speaking of politics, people often use the terms "right," "center," and "left." Do you feel that these terms are still useful for an understanding of present-day French politics? Is there a public interest which outweighs the influence of diverse political forces? How could the social conflicts that exist in France today be reduced?

18. Work in Parliamentary Group. You are a member of the _____ Party in the Legislature. Have you participated actively in party meetings? Have you supported your leaders? How do the leaders help the party members? Do they help to reduce group conflicts? What is their main role? Do you find the group leadership to be effective? What is your colleagues' opinion? What is the influence of the national party on the legislative party? In legislative balloting, why do the party members almost always vote together? If you wanted to vote one way, but your party caucus decided to vote otherwise, what would you do?

19. Attitude Toward Becoming a Leader. Would you like to hold a leadership position in your party group or at the Assembly? What would you do in that position? Are there other public offices you would like to hold? Which ones? Why? Why would anyone want to be a Deputy and a Mayor at the same time?

20. View of Leaders. We've talked about political leaders. In your opinion, what are the qualities of an ideal leader? What is it necessary to do to succeed in politics in France? Among the great figures of French history, what man do you admire the most? (Not a living leader.) Why?

21. Attitude Toward Existing Political Procedures. Let's go on to broader issues. What do you think of the present relations between the National Assembly and the Government? Would you propose far-reaching reforms for the Assembly? What changes would you like to see made in the present political system?

22. His Conception of French Politics. All in all, what is the main characteristic of political life in France? Why would anyone want to enter political life in France? What does politics mean to you?

23. Most Enjoyable Experience. I've asked you a lot of questions about your political activities. Finally, I'd like to ask you to consider the whole of your political experience up to now. Which of your experiences was the most agreeable? Which of your political experiences was the most disagreeable? All things considered, do you like politics? What do you like about it? What do you dislike?

Are there important aspects of your legislative work or your political career I've neglected in this interview?

Notes

Notes

Chapter 1
Incentive Analysis and French Politics

1. For the best expressions of this point of view, see: Roy C. Macridis, "France," in Roy C. Macridis and Robert E. Ward, eds., *Modern Political Systems: Europe* (Englewood Cliffs, New Jersey: Prentice-Hall, Inc., 1963), pp. 135-365; Stanley Hoffmann, et al., *In Search of France* (New York: Harper & Row, 1965), pp. 1-117; Charles Morazé, *The French and the Republic* (Ithaca, New York: Cornell University Press, 1958); Jacques Fauvet, *The Cockpit of France*, trans. by Nancy Pearson (London: Harvill, 1960); Maurice Duverger, *The French Political System* (Chicago: University of Chicago Press, 1958); and René Rémond, *The Right Wing in France: From 1815 to DeGaulle* (Philadelphia: University of Pennsylvania Press, 1966). For further discussion of the role of ideology in French politics, see: Philip E. Converse and Georges Dupeux, "Politicization of the Electorate in France and the United States," *Public Opinion Quarterly* 26 (1962): 1-23; Emeric Deutsch, Denis Lindon, and Pierre Weill, *Les Familles politiques aujourd'hui en France* (Paris: Les Editions de Minuit, 1966); Harvey Waterman, *Political Change in Contemporary France: The Politics of an Industrial Democracy* (Columbus, Ohio: Charles E. Merrill Publishing Company, 1969); and William H. Hunt, "Legislative Roles and Ideological Orientations of French Deputies" (paper presented at the Sixty-Fifth Annual Meeting of The American Political Science Association, New York City, September 2-6, 1969).

2. See in particular: Nathan Leites, *On the Game of Politics in France* (Palo Alto, California: Stanford University Press, 1959); and Constantin Melnik and Nathan Leites, *The House without Windows: France Selects a President* (Evanston, Illinois: Row Peterson, 1958).

3. James L. Payne, *Patterns of Conflict in Colombia* (New Haven: Yale University Press, 1968).

4. This research includes: a study by Payne of political leaders in the Dominican Republic; another study by Payne of Virginia city councilmen; a study by Michael McCullough of Brazilian Deputies; my own study of Connecticut state legislators, as well as my work on French Deputies. The written material which has emerged from this research on incentives includes: Payne, *Patterns of Conflict*; Woshinsky, "Incentives to Political Action: Connecticut Legislators" (unpublished, 1968); Payne, "Toward the Valid and Reliable Determination of the Incentives of Political Participants" (unpublished, 1968); Michael P. McCullough, "The Brazilian Congress" (unpublished, 1969); Payne, *Incentive Theory and Political Process: Motivation and Leadership in the Dominican Republic* (Lexington, Mass.: D.C. Heath and Company, Lexington

Books, 1972); Woshinsky, "The Political Incentives of French Deputies" (Ph.D. dissertation, Yale University, 1971); and Payne, "Determining the Incentives of Political Participants: A Reliability Study" (mimeographed, Washington, D.C.: School of Advanced International Studies, 1972). Two other studies contributed directly to the present formulation of incentive analysis, although neither study specifically used the incentive approach. These are: James D. Barber, *The Lawmakers: Recruitment and Adaptation to Legislative Life* (New Haven and London: Yale University Press, 1965); and Aaron Wildavsky, "The Goldwater Phenomenon: Purists, Politicians, and the Two-Party System," *The Review of Politics* 27 (1965): 386-413. For other works closely related to the study of incentives, see the citations in footnotes 9 and 12, this chapter.

5. James L. Payne and Oliver H. Woshinsky, "Incentives for Political Participation," *World Politics* 24 (1972): 518-46.

6. The term "political leader" in incentive analysis simply refers to anyone who holds, or actively aspires to hold, one of his nation's higher political positions. See the discussion in Payne, *Patterns of Conflict*, pp. 25-28.

7. Payne and Woshinsky, "Incentives," p. 519.

8. Ibid., pp. 519-20.

9. See, for example: Peter Clark and James Q. Wilson, "Incentive Systems: A Theory of Organizations," *Administrative Science Quarterly* 6 (1961): 129-66; John H. Fenton, *People and Parties in Politics* (Glenview, Ill.: Scott Foresman & Co., 1966); Robert R. Alford and Harry M. Scoble, "Sources of Local Political Involvement," *American Political Science Review* 62 (1968): 1192-1206; Frank J. Sorauf, *Political Parties in the American System* (Boston and Toronto: Little, Brown, 1964), pp. 81-97; Samuel J. Eldersveld, *Political Parties: A Behavioral Analysis* (Chicago: Rand McNally, 1964), pp. 222ff.; and James David Barber, *The Presidential Character: Predicting Performance in the White House* (Englewood Cliffs, N.J.: Prentice-Hall, Inc., 1972). For other recent studies which focus on motivation for explaining political behavior, see the works cited in Table 1-2 and in footnote 12 of this chapter. On the relation between incentive analysis and motivational psychology, see Woshinsky, "French Deputies," pp. 34-41. Harold Lasswell was, of course, one of the first to suggest the need for systematic study of politicians' motives. See in particular *Psychopathology and Politics* (Chicago: University of Chicago Press, 1930). For an excellent introduction to the general field of personality and politics, see Fred I. Greenstein, *Personality and Politics* (Chicago: Markham Press, 1969).

10. Payne and Woshinsky, "Incentives," p. 519.

11. See Barber's description of the "Spectator" in *The Lawmakers*, pp. 23-66. Barber's "Spectator" appears to hold the conviviality incentive.

12. It is interesting that a number of scholars have proposed classifications of politicians which correspond closely or partially with the incentive typology. In addition to the material cited in footnote 9 of this chapter and in Table 1-2, see: M. Margaret Conway and Frank B. Feigert, "Motivation, Incentive Systems, and

the Political Party Organization," *American Political Science Review* 62 (1968): 1159-73; Lewis Bowman, Dennis Ippolito, and William Donaldson, "Incentives for the Maintenance of Grassroots Political Action," *Midwest Journal of Political Science* 13 (1969): 126-39; Oliver Garceau and Corinne Silverman, "A Pressure Group and the Pressured," *American Political Science Review* 48 (1954): 672-91; Allan Kornberg, "Caucus and Cohesion in Canadian Parliamentary Parties," *American Political Science Review* 60 (1966): 83-92; Kenneth Prewitt and William Nowlin, "Political Ambitions and the Behavior of Incumbent Politicians," *Western Political Quarterly* 22 (1969): 298-308; Robert H. Salisbury, "The Urban Party Organization Member," *Public Opinion Quarterly* 29 (1965-66): 350-64; Leo M. Snowiss, "Congressional Recruitment and Representation," *American Political Science Review* 60 (1966): 627-39; and Samuel C. Patterson and G.R. Boynton, "Legislative Recruitment in a Civic Culture," *Social Science Quarterly* 50 (1969): 243-63.

13. This conclusion is drawn in part from study of the following works: Raymond A. Bauer, Ithiel de Sola Pool, and Lewis Anthony Dexter, *American Business and Public Policy: The Politics of Foreign Trade* (New York: Atherton Press, 1964), pp. 401-58; Donald R. Matthews, *U.S. Senators and Their World* (New York: Vintage Books, 1960); Robert L. Peabody and Nelson W. Polsby, eds., *New Perspectives on the House of Representatives* (Chicago: Rand McNally, 1963); Richard F. Fenno, Jr., *The Power of the Purse* (Boston: Little Brown, 1964); John F. Manley, "The House Committee on Ways and Means: Conflict Management in a Congressional Committee," *American Political Science Review* 59 (1965): 927-39; Charles L. Clapp, *The Congressman: His Work as He Sees It* (Washington, D.C.: The Brookings Institution, 1963); Aaron Wildavsky, *The Politics of the Budgetary Process* (Boston: Little Brown, 1964); and Donald G. Tacheron and Morris K. Udall, *The Job of the Congressman*, 2d ed. (Indianapolis: The Bobbs-Merrill Company, Inc., 1970). See also John C. Wahlke, Heinz Eulau, William Buchanan, and LeRoy C. Ferguson, *The Legislative System* (New York: John Wiley & Sons, 1962).

14. See Payne, *Patterns of Conflict*, pp. 19-20, 238-67.

15. Ibid., p. 266.

16. Barber, *The Lawmakers*.

17. Ibid., p. 209.

18. Ibid., pp. 113-14.

19. Ibid., p. 159.

20. Ibid., p. 66.

21. Ibid.

22. Both Payne and I have been conducting reliability experiments with our students. For some of the first results of the attempt to achieve reliability in classifying political leaders, see Payne, "A Reliability Study."

23. See Payne, *Patterns of Conflict*, pp. 19-20, 238-67.

24. The literature on this subject is vast. For an excellent introduction to

role analysis, see Theodore M. Newcomb, Ralph H. Turner, and Philip E. Converse, *Social Psychology: The Study of Human Interaction* (New York: Holt, Rinehart and Winston, Inc., 1965), pp. 322-56 and 393-427. For a good example of the way role analysis can be used to understand politics, see Andrew S. McFarland, "Role and Role Conflict," in Aaron Wildavsky, ed., *The Presidency* (Boston: Little, Brown and Company, 1969), pp. 3-17. The most thorough attempt to apply role analysis to the study of legislatures is Wahlke, et al., *The Legislative System.* See also the sources cited in these three works.

25. They may, however, be very active for short periods of time. Their sporadic outbursts of great activity are likely to come during moments of unusual political tension or excitement: revolutionary events or crucial elections. Obligation participants in the U.S. have probably been heavily involved in politics during recent Presidential elections and at the national conventions.

26. The relationship between incentives and career patterns is a central theme in Payne, *Patterns of Conflict*. See in particular pp. 17-20, 25-50, and 103-107.

27. Ibid., pp. 17-20 and 103-107.

28. Altogether, the Assembly had 487 members. These included the 470 members from metropolitan France and 17 members from the Overseas Departments and Territories. Three additional seats from metropolitan France have been added since my interviews.

29. For further discussion of the interview procedure and the interview schedule, see Appendix D.

Chapter 3
The Mission Participant

1. It is not possible to cite the vast literature on these topics. For some of the better works which suggest the characteristics and consequences of mission participants in politics, see: Bertram D. Wolfe, *Three Who Made A Revolution* (Boston: Beacon Press, 1948); Avrahm Yarmolinsky, *Road to Revolution: A Century of Russian Radicalism* (New York: Collier Books, 1962); Gabriel A. Almond, *The Appeals of Communism* (Princeton: Princeton University Press, 1954); Eric Hoffer, *The True Believer* (New York and Evanston: Harper, 1951); and Robert C. Tucker, "The Dictator and Totalitarianism," *World Politics* 17 (1965): 555-83.

Five autobiographies which appear to illustrate the mission incentive are: Whittaker Chambers, *Witness* (New York: Random House, 1952); Arthur Koestler, *Arrow in the Blue: An Autobiography* (New York: The Macmillan Company, 1952); Jules Humbert-Droz, *Mon évolution du tolstoïsme au communisme* (Paris: La Baconnière, 1970); Virgile Barel, *Cinquante années de lutte* (Paris: Editions Sociales, 1967); and Malcolm X, with the assistance of Alex Haley, *The Autobiography of Malcolm X* (New York: Grove Press, 1966).

2. Payne and Woshinsky, "Incentives," p. 533. For an excellent illustration of the way religious needs can lead a man into political activity, see Whittaker Chambers's explanation of why he became a Communist: *Witness*, p. 196.

3. This account bears a striking resemblance to Tucker's description of those "attributes of the radical mind" which lead to involvement in Marxist movements. See Robert C. Tucker, "The Deradicalization of Marxist Movements," *American Political Science Review* 61 (1967): 343-58.

4. Bertrand Russell, *Bolshevism: Practice and Theory* (New York: Harcourt, Brace & Howe), quoted in Milovan Djilas, *The New Class* (New York: Frederick A. Praeger, Publishers, 1959, p. 127). See also the illuminating statement of a former American Communist in Frank S. Meyer, *The Moulding of Communists: The Training of the Communist Cadre* (New York: Harcourt, Brace & World, 1961), p. 53. Almond produces impressive evidence on the importance of ideology to people who were probably mission participants; see *The Appeals of Communism*, table on p. 243.

5. Tucker has suggested that continued, even intensified, verbal commitment to the old ideology goes hand in hand with the "deradicalization of Marxist movements." See Tucker, "Deradicalization."

6. Payne and Woshinsky, "Incentives," p. 534.

7. The denial that they have personally benefitted, or even intended to benefit, from their political involvement is a common theme in autobiographies of probable mission participants. See, for example, Malcolm X, *Autobiography*, pp. 290-94, and Chambers, *Witness*, pp. 694-95 and 714-15.

8. Compare these statements about de Gaulle with similar statements of Malcolm X about Elijah Muhammed in Malcolm X, *Autobiography*, p. 365.

9. See Marie-Pierre Herzog, "L'Appel," in *Le Monde* 16 July 1968, reprinted in Jacques de Montalais, *Qu'est-ce que le gaullisme?* (Paris: Maison Mame, 1969), pp. 209-13.

10. Maurice Duverger, *Les Partis politiques* (6th ed.; Paris: Librairie Armand Colin, 1967), p. 147 [my translation].

11. Russell, quoted in Djilas, *The New Class*, p. 127.

12. See, for instance, Hoffer, *The True Believer*, p. 122; Almond, *The Appeals of Communism*, pp. 28-32; Meyer, *The Moulding of Communists*, p. 17; and de Montalais, *Qu'est-ce que le gaullisme?*, pp. 19ff. and 101ff.

13. On the nondemocratic nature of the PCF, see Annie Kriegel, *Les communistes français* (Paris: Editions du Seuill, 1968), pp. 158-77. On the nondemocratic nature of the UDR, see Jean Charlot, *L'Union pour la nouvelle république: étude du pouvoir au sein d'un parti politique* (Paris: Librairie-Armand Colin, 1967), pp. 242-54. Concerning discipline, there is some evidence that Gaullists and Communists, along with the Socialists, have been the most disciplined groups on roll-call votes in the Assembly since 1956. See David M. Wood, "Majority vs. Opposition in the French National Assembly, 1956-65: A Guttman Scale Analysis," *American Political Science Review* 62 (1968): 88-109.

14. The interpretation of Fourth Republic history in this and the following

paragraph draws heavily on Georgette Elgey, *Histoire de la IVe République: la république des illusions, 1945-1951* (Paris: Fayard, 1965), pp. 393-412.

Chapter 4
The Program Participant

1. Smith, Bruner, and White, *Opinions and Personality*, p. 41 and passim.

2. Fenton, *People and Parties in Politics*, pp. 50-65.

3. Sorauf, *Political Parties in the American System*, p. 85.

4. Browning, "The Interaction of Personality and Political System," pp. 97-104.

5. Wahlke, et al., *The Legislative System*, p. 255; for a complete description of the "inventor," see pp. 254-56.

6. Undoubtedly the best of these is Benjamin Franklin, *The Autobiography of Benjamin Franklin*, edited by Leonard W. Labaree, Ralph L. Ketcham, Helen C. Boatfield, and Helene H. Fineman (New Haven and London: Yale University Press, 1964). Other probable program participants are revealed in the following autobiographies: Sol Bloom, *The Autobiography of Sol Bloom* (New York: G.P. Putnam's Sons, 1948); Raymond E. Baldwin, *Let's Go Into Politics* (New York: The Macmillan Company, 1952); and Frank E. Smith, *Congressman from Mississippi* (New York: Random House, 1964).

7. Barber, *The Lawmakers*, pp. 163-211.

8. Ibid., p. 181.

9. Payne, *Patterns of Conflict*, pp. 3-24 and 96-107.

10. See Chapter 1 in this book and Table 1-1 in particular.

11. For elaboration of this theme, see Payne, *Patterns of Conflict*, passim., and Chapter 9 in this book.

12. For a strikingly similar interview which Payne conducted with a program participant in Antioquia, Colombia, see *Patterns of Conflict*, pp. 98-99.

13. Numerous passages in Benjamin Franklin's *Autobiography* illustrate the program participant's attention to policy details and his eagerness to work on these matters. See in particular a delightful passage in which Franklin describes how he helped get a street paved: pp. 202-03.

14. Barber, *The Lawmakers*, p. 183.

15. Ibid., p. 182.

16. Both Barber and I recorded comments exactly similar to this one among program participants in Connecticut. See Barber, *The Lawmakers*, pp. 164-65, and Woshinsky, "Incentives to Political Action," p. 7.

17. In any case this view that legislators in Fifth Republic France "have no power" is exaggerated. For a balanced account of the role of the modern French legislature, see Philip M. Williams, *The French Parliament, 1958-1967* (London: George Allen and Unwin Ltd., 1968). Williams argues that French legislators

have had more impact on policy-making than is generally believed. See in particular pp. 84-97.

18. The two best sources on French parties are: Duverger, *Les Partis politiques*; and Philip M. Williams, *Crisis and Compromise: Politics in the Fourth Republic* (Garden City, N.Y.: Doubleday & Company, Inc., Anchor Books, 1966). On the negative view of voters toward political parties, see Converse and Dupeux, "The Politicization of the Electorate in France and the United States"; and Sidney Tarrow, "The Urban-Rural Cleavage in Political Involvement: The Case of France," *American Political Science Review* 65 (1971): 341-57.

19. *Votes bloqués* [block votes] are votes in which the Government can declare that an entire bill, or an entire set of amendments, must be voted on as a whole. Through this device the Government can force Deputies to accept unpopular features of a bill which, on the whole, the Deputies wish to see passed. The unpopular parts are grouped with the entire bill and cannot be voted on individually.

20. Barber, *The Lawmakers*, p. 211.

Chapter 5
The Obligation Participant

1. The first full-length study of this type was: James Q. Wilson, *The Amateur Democrat* (Chicago: University of Chicago Press, 1962). Since Wilson's initial statement, several other studies have focused on the "amateur" in American politics. See, for example: John W. Soule and James W. Clarke, "Amateurs and Professionals: A Study of Delegates to the 1968 Democratic National Convention," *American Political Science Review* 64 (1970): 888-98; Jeff Fishel, "Ambition and the Political Vocation," *Journal of Politics* 33 (1971): 25-56; Richard C. Hofstetter, "The Amateur Politician," *Midwest Journal of Politics* 15 (1971): 31-56.

2. The "purist" term derives from a study of delegates at the 1964 Republican National Convention; see Wildavsky, "The Goldwater Phenomenon." Wildavsky also observed this "purist" orientation among McCarthy supporters at the 1968 Democratic National Convention; see Aaron Wildavsky, "The Meaning of 'Youth' in the Struggle for Control of the Democratic Party," in Wildavsky, *The Revolt Against the Masses and Other Essays on Politics and Public Policy* (New York: Basic Books, 1971), pp. 270-87. The term "Reluctant" is taken from Barber's study of Connecticut freshman state legislators; see Barber, *The Lawmakers*, pp. 116-62. "Moralizer" is the term Riesman gives to his "inner-directed man" when that type enters politics; see David Riesman, Nathan Glazer, and Reuel Denney, *The Lonely Crowd: A Study of the Changing American Character* (Garden City, New York: Doubleday & Company, Inc., Doubleday Anchor Books, 1953).

3. Several studies suggest the existence of an obligation type in politics. Browning describes a type with "policy-concerned behavior" who has some of the characteristics of the obligation participant; see Rufus P. Browning, "The Interaction of Personality and Political System in Decisions to Run for Office: Some Data and a Simulation Technique," *Journal of Social Issues* 24 (1968): 93-110. Some of Keniston's "young radicals" at times sound like obligation participants; see Kenneth Keniston, *Young Radicals: Notes on Committed Youth* (New York: Harcourt, Brace and World, Inc., 1968), in particular quotations on pp. 114-15, 123, 158-59, 210-11, and 216. Some of the role orientations described by Wahlke, et al., would probably be adopted by obligation participants: e.g., "ritualist," "resister" to pressure groups; see *The Legislative System*, pp. 249-52 and 323-28. For autobiographical works which give evidence of the obligation participant's focus on morally consistent behavior, see: William F. Buckley, Jr., *The Unmaking of a Mayor* (New York: Bantam Books, 1967); M.K. Gandhi, *Gandhi's Autobiography: The Story of My Experiments with Truth*, translated by Mahadev Desai (Washington, D.C.: Public Affairs Press, 1948); and Stephen Spender, in *The God That Failed*, edited by Richard Crossman (New York: Bantam Books, 1950), pp. 208-48.

4. Compare this specific explanation of why *French* obligation Deputies get into politics with an earlier (and more general) statement by Payne: "The obligation incentive can be stimulated in at least three ways: 1) an issue arises (Vietnam) on which one feels it is his duty to participate; 2) a candidate emerges who clearly possesses high principles, morals and civic virtues whom it is one's duty to support (Barry Goldwater); 3) one is pressed into service by the apparent absence of anyone else to do a job (Barber's Reluctants?)." Payne, "Determination of the Incentives of Political Participants," p. 20.

5. A Dominican obligation participant explained his entry into politics in almost exactly the same way; see the quotation in Payne and Woshinsky, "Incentives," p. 539.

6. For other statements by political activists motivated by the need to behave in a manner consistent with their principles, see Barber, *The Lawmakers*, p. 141, and Keniston, *Young Radicals*, p. 122.

7. For quotations from other studies which indicate the obligation participant's emphasis on personal integrity and correct behavior, see: Wildavsky, "The Goldwater Phenomenon," p. 394; Barber, *The Lawmakers*, p. 141; Keniston, *Young Radicals*, p. 115; and Payne, "Determination of the Incentives of Political Participants," p. 22.

8. This attitude appeared widespread among obligation-motivated supporters of Goldwater in 1964 and McCarthy in 1968. For suggestive quotations, see: pro-Goldwater Washington Delegate cited in Payne and Woshinsky, "Incentives," p. 538; and Wildavsky, "Struggle for Control of the Democratic Party," pp. 282-3.

9. Barber, *The Lawmakers*, p. 142.

10. For Wylie's description of attitudes toward politics in the French village of "Peyrane," see Laurence Wylie, *Village in the Vaucluse* (Cambridge: Harvard University Press, 1957), pp. 206-39.

11. *Conseil Général*: the very weak legislative body in each of France's ninety-five *départements*.

12. Obligation participants in other settings make the same negative comments about politics. See the Dominican politician cited in Payne and Woshinsky, "Incentives," p. 540, and the Connecticut politician quoted in Barber, *The Lawmakers*, p. 143.

Chapter 6
The Status Participant

1. Payne, *Patterns of Conflict*, pp. 11-12.

2. This fact has been demonstrated in survey after survey. See, for instance, the data cited in Robert W. Hodge, Paul M. Siegel, and Peter H. Rossi, "Occupational Prestige in the United States, 1925-63," *American Journal of Sociology* 70 (1964): 286-302, especially Table 1, p. 290. (Note that a "U.S. Supreme Court justice" ranks higher than a "physician," but this concerns an office, not an occupation.)

3. On the prestige of high political offices in several nations, see the data and sources cited in Payne, *Patterns of Conflict*, pp. 33-36. See also Alex Inkeles and Peter H. Rossi, "National Comparisons of Occupational Prestige," *American Journal of Sociology* 61 (1956): 329-39; and Hodge, Siegel, and Rossi, "Occupational Prestige in the United States."

4. Payne, *Patterns of Conflict*, p. 12. For an excellent example of this emphasis on external appearance, see the status participant quoted by Payne in *Patterns*, p. 25.

5. Ibid.

6. Barber, *The Lawmakers*, p. 69; see pp. 67-115 for a complete description of the "Advertiser."

7. See Table 1-1 in this book; and Payne and Woshinsky, "Incentives," pp. 543-46.

8. Since this participant resembles the popular stereotype of the politician, one frequently finds superficial references (especially among journalists) to this type. One also finds hints of this incentive in many serious works. The type of Senator which Matthews calls the "Agitator," for instance, would appear to be a status participant; see Matthews, *U.S. Senators*, pp. 64-66. Browning describes a political type with "status-oriented behavior," characterized by "vigorous activity when *position* is at stake, otherwise little interest in influencing or in policy;" his "principal gratification" comes from having "deference, recognition, position;" see Browning, "Interaction of Personality and Political System," p. 103 (emphasis added).

Additional insights into the status participant's outlook can be gleaned from the personal disclosures of William Jennings Bryan and Benjamin Disraeli; see *Memoirs of William Jennings Bryan* (Philadelphia: John C. Winston, 1925), and Disraeli's introspective first novel, *Vivian Grey*.

9. Payne has suggested some of the conditions which cause status participants to enter politics; see *Patterns of Conflict*, pp. 25-50. See also my discussion in Chapter 8 of this book.

10. This argument was advanced in Payne, *Patterns of Conflict*, pp. 17-18 and 103-07.

11. Barber, *The Lawmakers*, p. 83.

12. Ibid., p. 69.

13. Status participants in other settings also betray this desire to obtain higher office for its own sake and nothing else. Payne reports: "In one interview with a Colombian politician the discussion repeatedly came back to this conclusion: 'I want to be mayor of Bogotá' (and this was a respondent whose chances of getting anywhere near the position in the immediate future were nil)." See Payne, "Determination of the Incentives of Political Participants," p. 9. See also Barber's description of the long-range ambitions of one of his "Advertisers" in *The Lawmakers*, p. 84; and the Connecticut State Representative cited in Payne and Woshinsky, "Incentives," p. 525.

14. Barber, *The Lawmakers*, p. 84.

15. Barber noted this same lack of interest in the details of legislation among his "Advertisers;" see in particular the dialogue quoted in ibid., p. 99.

16. Ibid., p. 114.

17. *Memoirs of William Jennings Bryan*.

18. Ibid., p. 85. The entire chapter is found on pp. 85-96.

19. Ibid., p. 86.

20. Barber, *The Lawmakers*, p. 86.

21. Both Payne and Barber noted this rude, uncooperative interview behavior among status participants. See Barber's description of an interview with an "Advertiser" in *The Lawmakers*, pp. 77-78. See Payne's contrast between the interview behavior of status and program participants in Colombia, *Patterns of Conflict*, p. 97.

22. Payne, *Patterns of Conflict*, p. 12.

23. See Barber's comments on attitudes toward leaders among "Advertisers": *The Lawmakers*, pp. 94-95.

24. See ibid., pp. 91-92.

25. See the similar attitude expressed by a Connecticut State Representative quoted in Payne and Woshinsky, "Incentives," p. 528.

26. Leites' thesis was discussed in Chapter 1 of this book. See Leites, *On the Game of Politics in France*, and Melnik and Leites, *The House Without Windows*. The latter work contains an illuminating "Guide to the 'Rules of the Game,'" (pp. 339-50) which codifies the way Deputies behave in the Assembly (according to Leites).

27. For a description of the game participant, see Payne and Woshinsky, "Incentives," pp. 540-43, and Woshinsky, "Incentives to Political Action," pp. 29-41. For another illustration of a probable game participant, see John F. Manley, "Wilbur D. Mills: A Study in Congressional Influence," *American Political Science Review* 63 (1969): 442-64.

28. A Dominican status participant claimed that politics breaks up friendships and even families. Payne and Woshinsky, "Incentives," p. 528.

29. *Memoirs of William Jennings Bryan*, pp. 248-49.

30. Payne, *Patterns of Conflict*, pp. 246-48.

31. Barber, *The Lawmakers*, pp. 111-15.

Chapter 7
Behavioral Differences Among Incentive Types
(1): Behavior in the National Assembly

1. Barber found that his "Lawmakers" (probable program participants) were active in the legislature, while his "Reluctants" (probable obligation participants) were inactive; see *The Lawmakers*, pp. 18-20 and passim. Payne suggests that program participants will be very active in the legislature on substantive policy matters; see *Patterns of Conflict*, pp. 276-78 and passim.

2. This is a major theme in Payne, *Patterns of Conflict*, pp. 238-67. A fair reading of Barber's chapter on the "Advertiser" (probable status participant) suggests that most of this type's activity in the legislature centers on attention- and position-getting behavior, rather than substantive legislative work; see *The Lawmakers*, pp. 67-115.

3. In conducting this phase of the research, I measured the length (in centimeters) of each remark by each Deputy in my sample for the entire time period indicated. Luckily, the *Journal Officiel, débats parlemetaries* provides a good record of what actually happens in the French legislature, since Deputies are not allowed to edit remarks they make on the floor. The period of time chosen for study included two regular fall sessions of the Assembly (its busiest time), a two-week special session in July, 1968, and a one-week special session in September, 1968.

4. *Rapports* are presentations before the full Assembly by Deputies chosen by their committees to floor-manage bills. A *rapport* sums up the main arguments for or against a given bill.

5. Most bills discussed before the Assembly are the Government's (*projets de loi*), except for a few private-member bills (*propositions de loi*). Committees cannot amend Government bills. They must be discussed on the floor of the Assembly exactly as the Government has written them. If a committee wishes to change a Government bill, it must present amendments on the floor of the Assembly and persuade a majority of the Assembly to adopt them.

6. Payne, *Patterns of Conflict*, pp. 245-6.

7. See the discussion of *questions écrites* in two standard sources: François Goguel, *Les Institutions politiques françaises* (Paris: Institut d'Etudes Politiques, Les Cours de Droit, 1968), pp. 642-43; and Jean Gicquel, *Essai sur la pratique de la Ve République: bilan d'un septennat* (Paris: Pichon et Durand-Auzias, 1968), pp. 338-40.

8. These expectations follow from an understanding of each type's psychological structure. Both Barber and Payne reach similar conclusions about the way some of these types should behave in the legislature. See Payne, *Patterns of Conflict*, pp. 246-48; and Barber, *The Lawmakers*, pp. 111-15, 159-62, 205-11.

Chapter 8
Behavioral Differences Among Incentive Types
(2): Political Careers of French Deputies

1. Those relevant to this study are discussed in the course of this chapter. For a complete list of Payne's incentive-relevant hypotheses, see *Patterns of Conflict*, pp. 330-33.

2. For explicit career profiles of Barber's four types, see *The Lawmakers*, pp. 25-27, 69-71, 119-21, and 166-68. Throughout his four chapters on these types, Barber also makes numerous comments on their likely career patterns.

3. The best source is a set of career sketches on each Deputy published by the Sociétés Générale de Presse, 9-11-13 Avenue de l'Opéra, Paris 1, France, under the title *Assemblée Nationale*. Additional information was gleaned from *Who's Who in France*, from the interviews themselves, and from a close reading of the Paris press—in particular, *Le Monde*.

4. Payne, *Patterns of Conflict*, pp. 17-18 and 103-07.

5. Barber, *The Lawmakers*, pp. 67-72.

6. Payne, *Incentive Theory*, p. 130. For an earlier formulation of this same idea, see Payne, *Patterns of Conflict*, pp. 17-18 and 104.

7. Barber, *The Lawmakers*, pp. 17-20.

8. Payne, *Patterns of Conflict*, pp. 238-43.

9. Ibid., p. 241.

Chapter 9
Toward an Incentive Analysis of French Politics
(1): Incentives and the French National Assembly

1. See Chapter 1.

2. Payne, *Patterns of Conflict*, pp. 238-67.

3. See Chapter 1 and especially Table 1-1.

4. See the studies cited in both Table 1-1 and 1-2.

5. In emphasizing relative size of an incentive group, I am purposely ignoring the institutional position of that group. Clearly, a group with only five percent of legislators but one hundred percent of committee chairmanships would have an impact on the legislature. This possibility appears relatively unlikely, however, and has been omitted from the discussion for analytical clarity.

6. This kind of development probably occurred in the U.S. Congress, over a longer period of time. Nelson Polsby has shown the slow change over time of major behavior patterns in that body. He documents the slow growth of Congressional institutions which facilitate hard work on legislation and which minimize internal political conflict. One would speculate that over time a slow increase in the number of program participants preceded and helped create this new pattern—which Polsby calls "institutionalization." See Nelson W. Polsby, "The Institutionalization of the U.S. House of Representatives," *American Political Science Review* 62 (1968): 144-68.

7. This speculation is not entirely idle. It is based on examination of the motivational studies listed in Table 1-2. A close reading of these works leads to the tentative twenty-percent hypothesis. In Barber's *The Lawmakers*, for example, the two groups which compose over thirty percent of his Connecticut freshman legislators seemed to have an effect on the legislative system. "Lawmakers" helped sustain the orderly consideration of proposed legislation, and "Spectators" helped reduce internal conflict. The two groups which composed less than twenty percent of the sample ("Advertisers" and "Reluctants") appeared to have little impact on the legislature.

8. The adulation participant has been observed in the Dominican Republic by Payne and in Brazil by McCullough. See Table 1-1 for citations. See Payne and Woshinsky, "Incentives," pp. 521-24, for a short description.

9. For works from which this conclusion has been drawn, see footnote 13 to Chapter 1 of this book.

10. This conclusion is drawn from Payne, *Patterns of Conflict*, pp. 238-78.

11. On "Spectators," see Barber, *The Lawmakers*, pp. 23-66. On the Canadian Senate, see F.A. Kunz, *The Modern Senate of Canada* (Toronto: The University of Toronto Press, 1965).

12. Mission participants composed thirty-eight percent, program participants twenty-eight percent, and status participants twenty percent, of the sample of fifty Deputies. Although the number of status participants is at the lowest limit of the hypothesized critical range, they are included in that range because they are probably underrepresented in the sample. I suspect that many Deputies who made it impossible for me to interview them were in fact status participants. This likelihood follows from the status Deputy's uncooperative interview behavior (see Chapter 6).

13. For some of the best works on this subject, see: Williams, *Crisis and Compromise* and *The French Parliament, 1958-1967*; Gicquel, *Essai sur la*

pratique de la Ve République; Goguel, *Les Institutions politiques françaises;* Leites, *On the Game of Politics in France;* Pierre Avril, *Le Régime politique de la Ve République* Paris: R. Pichon et R. Durand-Auzias, 1967); Jean-Luc Parodi, *Les Rapports entre de législatif et l'exécutif sous la Ve République* (Paris: Fondation Nationale des Sciences Politiques, 1962); Nicholas Wahl, "The French Constitution of 1958, II: The Initial Draft and Its Origins," *American Political Science Review* 53 (1959): 358-82, and "The French Parliament: From Last Word to Afterthought," in *Lawmakers in a Changing World*, edited by Elke Frank (Englewood Cliffs, New Jersey: Prentice-Hall, 1966); and Eliane Guichard, Charles Roig, and Jean Grangé, *Etudes sur le parlement de la Ve République* (Paris: Presses Universitaires de France, 1965).

14. See, for instance, Barber, *The Lawmakers*, pp. 205-11.

15. This information is drawn from Mattei Dogan, "Changement de régime et changement de personnel," in *Le Référendum de septembre et les élections de novembre 1958*, edited by Association Française de Science Politique (Paris: Librairie Armand Colin, 1960), pp. 241-79.

16. This point can be found frequently in the numerous writings of Philip Williams on French politics; see, for example, his comments in *Crisis and Compromise*, p. 257.

17. Ibid., p. 273.

18. Low attendance rates constitute a well-known fact about the present Assembly. See, for example, François Goguel, "Nothing but Opposition," in *Patterns of Opposition in Western Democracies*, edited by Robert Dahl (New Haven: Yale University Press, 1966). I can personally testify to this pattern, having witnessed a number of undistinguished sessions of the National Assembly—sessions in which five to ten Deputies were on the floor at any given time.

19. Williams, *Crisis and Compromise*, p. 257.

20. Williams, *The French Parliament, 1958-1967*, p. 63.

21. Estimated from information on p. 257, Williams, *Crisis and Compromise*.

22. Ibid., p. 257.

23. Ibid., p. 266.

24. I compiled the data on French committees from information in the *Journal Officiel, lois et décrets*. The yearly average was estimated from the monthly average of committee meetings in the period from July through December, 1968. Data on committee meetings of the U.S. House of Representatives comes from Appendix A, Joint Committee on the Organization of Congress, *Final Report* (Washington, D.C.: Government Printing Office, 1966), pp. 59-74, cited in Tacheron and Udall, *The Job of the Congressman*, p. 183.

25. This argument is found throughout the literature on French politics. One of the best statements of it can be found in Andrew Shonfield, *Modern Capitalism: The Changing Balance of Public and Private Power* (New York and London: Oxford University Press, 1965), p. 130: "Here was a parliament which voluntarily handed over to the permanent administration the authority to get on with certain things, and denied itself the right to interfere with them."

26. Williams, *Crisis and Compromise*, p. 234.

27. Matthews, *U.S. Senators*; Fenno, *The Power of the Purse*; and Wahlke, et al., *The Legislative System*.

28. Leites, *On the Game of Politics in France*.

29. In a typical comment on this work Williams dismisses it as "a subtle analysis of dubious evidence," showing "only the seamy side" of French politics; *Crisis and Compromise*, p. 505.

30. Newcomb, Turner, and Converse, *Social Psychology*, p. 486; see also pp. 380-86 and 486ff.

31. See Leites, *On the Game of Politics in France*, and Melnik and Leites, *The House Without Windows*.

32. See the sources cited in footnote 1, Chapter 1, of this book.

33. See Maurice Duverger, *Political Parties*, translated by Barbara and Robert North (New York: John Wiley and Sons, 1954), passim.

34. See in particular his *Crisis and Compromise* and *The French Parliament, 1958-1967*.

Chapter 10
Toward an Incentive Analysis of French Politics
(2): Incentives and French Political Parties

1. Six of these seven belong to the RI party; the seventh is connected with the UDR parliamentary group but *apparenté* (attached) only. This seventh Deputy has many ties with the Independents (including their leader, Giscard d'Estaing) and emphasized those ties in the interview.

2. See Converse and Dupeux, "Politicization of the Electorate in France and the United States."

3. A good description of the French political clubs can be found in Frank L. Wilson, "The Club Phenomenon in France," *Comparative Politics* 3 (1971): 517-28.

4. See Charlot, *L'U. N. R.*, pp. 29-84.

5. Stalin used this psychological technique very effectively to curb dissent on the part of long-time members of the Russian Communist Party. By making them believe that rebellion against him would negate their life's work in the Communist movement, he obtained obedience and, when necessary, public admission of error. This theme is dramatically illustrated in Arthur Koestler's novel, *Darkness at Noon*.

Selected Bibliography

Selected Bibliography

Almond, Gabriel A. *The Appeals of Communism.* Princeton: Princeton University Press, 1954.

Ardagh, John. *The New French Revolution.* New York: Harper and Row, 1969.

Aron, Raymond. *France, Steadfast and Changing: The Fourth to the Fifth Republic.* Cambridge: Harvard University Press, 1960.

Avril, Pierre. *Le Régime politique de la Ve République.* Paris: R. Pichon et R. Durand-Auzias, 1967.

Baldwin, Raymond E. *Let's Go Into Politics.* New York: The Macmillan Company, 1952.

Barber, James D. *The Lawmakers: Recruitment and Adaptation to Legislative Life.* New Haven and London: Yale University Press, 1965.

_____. "Classifying and Predicting Presidential Styles: Two Weak Presidents." *Journal of Social Issues* 24 (1968): 51-80.

_____. "The President and His Friends." Paper delivered at the 65th annual meeting of The American Political Science Association, New York City, September, 1969.

_____. *The Presidential Character: Predicting Performance in the White House.* Englewood Cliffs, N.J.: Prentice-Hall, 1972.

Barel, Virgile. *Cinquante années de lutte.* Paris: Editions Sociales, 1967.

Bauer, Raymond A.; Pool, Ithiel de Sola; and Dexter, Lewis Anthony. *American Business and Public Policy: The Politics of Foreign Trade.* New York: Atherton Press, 1963.

Berelson, Bernard, and Steiner, Gary A. *Human Behavior: An Inventory of Scientific Findings.* New York: Harcourt, Brace & World, 1964.

Berger, Suzanne; Gourevitch, Peter; Higonnet, Patrice; and Kaiser, Karl. "The Problem of Reform in France: The Political Ideas of Local Elites." *Political Science Quarterly* 84 (1969): 436-60.

Birch, David, and Veroff, Joseph. *Motivation: A Study of Action.* Belmont, California: Brooks/Cole, 1966.

Boyd, James. "Harry Dent, the President's Political Coordinator." *The New York Times Magazine*, 1 February 1970, p. 12.

Brown, Bernard E. "Elite Attitudes and Political Legitimacy in France." *Journal of Politics* 31 (1969): 420-42.

Browning, Rufus P. "Businessmen in Politics: Motivation and Circumstances in the Rise to Power." Ph.D. dissertation, Yale University, 1960.

_____. "The Interaction of Personality and Political System in Decisions to Run for Office: Some Data and a Simulation Technique." *Journal of Social Issues* 24 (1968): 93-110.

_____, and Jacob, Herbert. "Power Motivation and the Political Personality." *Public Opinion Quarterly* 28 (1964): 75-90.

Bryan, William Jennings. *The Memoirs of William Jennings Bryan*. Philadelphia: John C. Winston, 1925.

Buckley, William F., Jr. *The Unmaking of a Mayor*. New York: Bantam Books, 1967.

Buron, Robert. *Le Plus beau des métiers*. Paris: Plon, 1963.

Chambers, Whittaker. *Witness*. New York: Random House, 1952.

Chandernagor, André. *Un Parlement, pour quoi faire?* Paris: Gallimard, 1967.

Charlot, Jean. *L'Union pour la Nouvelle République: etude du pouvoir au sein d'un parti politique*. Paris: Librairie Armand Colin, 1967.

_____. *Le Phénomène gaulliste*. Paris: Fayard, 1970.

Clapp, Charles L. *The Congressman: His Work as He Sees It*. Washington, D.C.: The Brookings Institution, 1963.

Clark, Peter, and Wilson, James Q. "Incentive Systems: A Theory of Organizations." *Administrative Science Quarterly* 6 (1961): 129-66.

Converse, Philip E., and Dupeux, Georges. "Politicization of the Electorate in France and the United States." *Public Opinion Quarterly* 26 (1962): 1-23.

_____. "Eisenhower et de Gaulle: les généraux devant l'opinion." *Revue française de science politique* 12 (1962): 54-92.

Converse, Philip E., and Pierce, Roy. "Basic Cleavages in French Politics and the Disorders of May and June, 1968." Paper presented at the Seventh World Congress of Sociology, Varna, Bulgaria, September, 1970.

Crossman, Richard, ed. *The God That Failed*. New York: Bantam Books, 1949.

Crozier, Michel. *The Bureaucratic Phenomenon*. Chicago: The University of Chicago Press, Phoenix Books, 1969.

Deutsch, Emeric; Lindon, Denis; and Weill, Pierre. *Les Familles politiques aujourd'hui en France*. Paris: Editions de Minuit, 1966.

DiRenzo, Gordon J. *Personality, Power, and Politics: A Social Psychological Analysis of the Italian Deputy and His Parliamentary System*. Notre Dame, London: University of Notre Dame Press, 1967.

Dogan, Mattei. "Les Candidats et les élus." In *Les Elections du 2 janvier 1956*, edited by Maurice Duverger, François Goguel, and Jean Touchard. Paris: Librairie Armand Colin, 1957.

_____. "Changement de régime et changement de personnel." In *Le Référendum de septembre et les élections de novembre 1958*, edited by Association Français de Science Politique. Paris: Librairie Armand Colin, 1960.

_____. "Political Ascent in a Class Society: French Deputies, 1870-1958." In *Political Decision-Makers*, edited by Dwaine Marvick. Glencoe, Ill.: The Free Press, 1961.

_____. "Note sur le nouveau personnel parlementaire." In *Le Référendum d'octobre et les élections de novembre 1962*, edited by François Goguel. Paris: Librairie Armand Colin, 1965.

_____. "Le Personnel politique et la personnalité charismatique." *Revue française de sociologie* 6 (1965): 305-24.

_____. "Les Filières de la carrière politique en France." *Revue française de sociologie* 8 (1967): 468-92.

Duverger, Maurice. *The French Political System.* Translated by Barbara and Robert North. Chicago: University of Chicago Press, 1958.

_____. *Les Partis politiques.* 6th ed. Paris: Librairie Armand Colin, 1967.

Earle, Edward Mead, ed. *Modern France, Problems of the Third and Fourth Republics.* Princeton: Princeton University Press, 1951.

Ehrmann, Henry W. *Politics in France.* Boston: Little, Brown, 1968.

Elgey, Georgette. *Histoire de la IVᵉ République: la république des illusions, 1945-1951.* Paris: Fayard, 1968.

_____. *Histoire de la IVᵉ République: la république des contradictions, 1951-1954.* Paris: Fayard, 1968.

Farley, James A. *Behind the Ballots.* New York: Harcourt, Brace and Co., 1938.

Fauvet, Jacques. *The Cockpit of France.* Translated by Nancy Pearson. London: Harvill, 1960.

Fenno, Richard F., Jr. "The House Appropriations Committee as a Political System: The Problem of Integration." *American Political Science Review* 56 (1962): 310-24.

_____. *The Power of the Purse.* Boston: Little, Brown, 1966.

Fenton, John H. *People and Parties in Politics.* Glenview, Ill.: Scott, Foresman, 1966.

Fichelet, Monique; Fichelet, Raymond; Michelat, Guy; and Simon, Michel. *Premiers résultats d'un programme de recherche en psychosociologie politique: les français, la politique et le parti communiste.* Pamphlet. Paris: V. Michaut, n.d. (Contains material from two articles printed in the December, 1967, and the January, 1968, issues of *Cahiers du communisme.*)

Franklin, Benjamin. *The Autobiography of Benjamin Franklin.* Edited by Leonard W. Labaree, Ralph L. Ketcham, Helen C. Boatfield, and Helene H. Fineman. New Haven and London: Yale University Press, 1964.

Gandhi, M.K. *Gandhi's Autobiography: The Story of My Experiments with Truth.* Translated by Mahadev Desai. Washington, D.C.: Public Affairs Press, 1948.

Gicquel, Jean. *Essai sur la pratique de la Vᵉ République: bilan d'un septennat.* Paris: Pichon et Durand-Auzias, 1968.

Goguel, François. *France under the Fourth Republic.* Translated by Roy Pierce. Ithaca, New York: Cornell University Press, 1952.

_____. *Les Institutions politiques françaises.* Paris: Institut d'Etudes Politiques (Les Cours de Droit), 1968.

Greene, Thomas H. "The Communist Parties of Italy and France: A Study in Comparative Communism." *World Politics* 21 (1968): 1-38.

Greenstein, Fred I., ed. "Personality and Politics: Theoretical and Methodological Issues." *The Journal of Social Issues* 24 (July, 1968).

_____. *Personality and Politics.* Chicago: Markham Publishing Company, 1969.

Greenstein, Fred I., and Tarrow, Sidney G. "The Study of French Political Socialization: Toward the Revocation of Paradox." *World Politics* 22 (1969), 95-137.

_____ , and Lerner, Michael, eds. *A Source Book for the Study of Personality and Politics.* Chicago: Markham Publishing Company, 1971.

Grosser, Alfred. "France: Nothing But Opposition." In *Political Oppositions in Western Democracies*, edited by Robert A. Dahl. New Haven: Yale University Press, 1966.

Guichard, Eliane; Roig, Charles; and Grangé, Jean. *Etudes sur le parlement de la Ve République.* Paris: Presses Universitaires de France, 1965.

Hoffer, Eric. *The True Believer.* New York and Evanston: Harper & Row, 1951.

Hoffmann, Stanley, et al., *In Search of France.* New York: Harper & Row, Harper Torchbooks, 1963.

Humbert-Droz, Jules. *Mon évolution du tolstoïsme au communisme.* Paris: La Baconnière, 1970.

Hunt, William H. "Legislative Roles and Ideological Orientations of French Deputies." Paper presented at the 65th annual meeting of The American Political Science Association, New York City, September 2-6, 1969.

Jouvenal, Robert de. *La République des camarades.* Paris: Bernard Grasset, 1914.

Kanter, Arnold. "The European Defense Community in the French National Assembly: A Roll Call Analysis." *Comparative Politics* 2 (1970): 203-28.

Keniston, Kenneth. *Young Radicals.* New York: Harcourt, Brace and World, 1968.

Kesselman, Mark. *The Ambiguous Consensus: A Study of Local Government in France.* New York: Knopf, 1967.

_____ . "The Recruitment of Rival Party Activists in France." Paper presented at the Eighth World Congress of the International Political Science Association, Munich, Germany, August 31-September 5, 1970.

Koestler, Arthur. *Arrow in the Blue: An Autobiography.* The Macmillan Company, 1952.

Kriegel, Annie. *Les Communistes français.* Paris: Editions du Seuil, 1968.

Lasswell, Harold D. *Psychopathology and Politics.* Chicago: University of Chicago Press, 1930.

_____ . *Politics: Who Gets What, When, How.* New York: P. Smith, 1950.

Leites, Nathan. *On the Game of Politics in France.* Palo Alto, California: Stanford University Press, 1959.

_____ . *The Rules of the Game in Paris.* Translated by Derek Coltman. Chicago and London: The University of Chicago Press, 1966.

Lieberman, Joseph I. *The Power Broker.* Boston: Houghton Mifflin, 1966.

Luethy, Herbert. *France Against Herself.* Translated by Eric Mosbacher. New York: Frederick A. Praeger, Inc., 1955.

McClelland, David C. "Some Social Consequences of Achievement Motivation."

In *Nebraska Symposium on Motivation*, edited by M.R. Jones. Lincoln, Neb.: University of Nebraska Press, 1955.

————. *The Achieving Society*. Princeton: D. Van Nostrand, 1961.

McConaughy, John B. "Certain Personality Factors of State Legislators in South Carolina." *American Political Science Review* 44 (1950): 897-903.

MacRae, Duncan, Jr. *Parliament, Parties, and Society in France, 1946-1958*. New York: St. Martin's Press, 1967.

McCullough, Michael P. "The Brazilian Congress." Unpublished, 1969.

Macridis, Roy C. "France." In *Modern Political Systems: Europe*, edited by Roy C. Macridis and Robert E. Ward. Englewood Cliffs, New Jersey: Prentice-Hall, 1963.

Manley, John F. "The House Committee on Ways and Means: Conflict Management in a Congressional Committee." *American Political Science Review* 59 (1965): 927-39.

————. "Wilbur D. Mills: A Study in Congressional Influence." *American Political Science Review* 63 (1969): 442-64.

Marvick, Dwaine, ed. *Political Decision-Makers: Recruitment and Performance*. Glencoe, Ill.: The Free Press, 1961.

Maslow, Abraham H. *Motivation and Personality*. New York: Harper, 1954.

Matthews, Donald R. *The Social Background of Political Decision-Makers*. Garden City, New York: Doubleday, 1954.

————. *U.S. Senators and Their World*. New York: Random House, Vintage Books, 1960.

Melnik, Constantin, and Leites, Nathan. *The House Without Windows: France Selects a President*. Evanston, Illinois: Row Peterson, 1958.

Merton, Robert K.; Fiske, Marjorie; and Kendall, Patricia L. *The Focused Interview*. Glencoe, Ill.: The Free Press, 1956.

Michels, Robert. *Political Parties*. Translated by Eden and Cedar Paul. New York: The Free Press, 1962.

Morazé, Charles. *The French and the Republic*. Translated by Jean-Jacques Demorest. Ithaca, New York: Cornell University Press, 1958.

Murray, Henry A. *Explorations in Personality*. New York: Oxford University Press, 1938.

Parodi, Jean-Luc. "Les Fonctions du parlement dans les démocraties occidentales contemporaines: esquisse de bilan de deux années de recherche." Mimeographed. Paris: Institut d'Etudes Politiques, 1967.

Payne, James L. *Patterns of Conflict in Colombia*. New Haven: Yale University Press, 1968.

————. "Toward the Valid and Reliable Determination of the Incentives of Political Participants." Unpublished, 1968.

————. *Incentive Theory and Political Process: Motivation and Leadership in the Dominican Republic*. Lexington, Mass.: D.C. Heath and Company, Lexington Books, 1972.

220

Payne, James L. "Determining the Incentives of Political Participants: A Reliability Study." Mimeographed. Washington, D.C.: School of Advanced International Studies, 1972.

_____, and Woshinsky, Oliver H. "Incentives for Political Participation." *World Politics* 24 (1972): 518-46.

Peabody, Robert L., and Polsby, Nelson W., eds. *New Perspectives on the House of Representatives*. Chicago: Rand McNally, 1963.

Pineau, Christian. *Mon cher député*. Paris: René Julliard, 1959.

Polsby, Nelson W. "The Institutionalization of the U.S. House of Representatives." *American Political Science Review* 62 (1968): 144-68.

Prewitt, Kenneth. "Political Socialization and Leadership Selection." *The Annals of the American Academy of Political and Social Science* 361 (1965): 96-111.

Putnam, Robert David. "Politicians and Politics: Themes in British and Italian Elite Political Culture." Ph.D. dissertation, Yale University, 1970.

Riesman, David; Glazer, Nathan; and Denney, Reuel. *The Lonely Crowd: A Study of the Changing American Character*. Garden City, New York: Doubleday & Company, Inc., Doubleday Anchor Books, 1953.

Ripley, Randall B. *Power in the Senate*. New York: St. Martin's Press, 1969.

Rustow, Dankwart. "The Study of Elites: Who's Who, When and How." *World Politics* 18 (1966): 690-717.

Seligman, Lester. "Political Recruitment and Party Structure." *American Political Science Review* 55 (1961): 77-86.

Siegfried, André. *France: A Study in Nationality*. New Haven: Yale University Press, 1930.

Smith, Frank E. *Congressman From Mississippi*. New York: Random House, 1964.

Smith, M. Brewster. "A Map for the Analysis of Personality and Politics." *Journal of Social Issues* 24 (1968): 15-28.

_____; Bruner, Jerome; and White, Robert. *Opinions and Personality*. New York: John Wiley & Sons, Inc., 1956.

Sorauf, Frank J. *Political Parties in the American System*. Boston and Toronto: Little, Brown, 1964.

Tacheron, Donald G., and Udall, Morris K. *The Job of the Congressman*. 2nd ed. Indianapolis: Bobbs-Merrill, 1970.

Thibaudet, Albert. *Les Idées politiques de la France*. Paris: Stock, 1932.

Thompson, David. *Democracy in France since 1870*. 5th ed. London: Oxford University Press, 1969.

Tocqueville, Alexis de. *The Old Régime and the French Revolution*. Translated by Stuart Gilbert. Garden City, New York: Doubleday and Company, Doubleday Anchor Books, 1955.

Tucker, Robert C. "The Dictator and Totalitarianism." *World Politics* 17 (1965): 555-83.

_____. "The Deradicalization of Marxist Movements." *American Political Science Review* 61 (1967): 343-58.

Viansson-Ponté, Pierre. *Les Gaullistes: rituel et annuaire.* Paris: Editions du Seuil, 1963.

Wahl, Nicholas. "The French Parliament: From Last Word to Afterthought." In *Lawmakers in a Changing World*, edited by Elke Frank. Englewood Cliffs, New Jersey: Prentice-Hall, 1966.

Wahlke, John C.; Eulau, Heinz; Buchanan, William; and Ferguson, LeRoy C. *The Legislative System.* New York: John Wiley & Sons, 1962.

Waterman, Harvey. *Political Change in Contemporary France: The Politics of an Industrial Democracy.* Columbus, Ohio: Charles E. Merrill, 1969.

Wildavsky, Aaron. *The Politics of the Budgetary Process.* Boston: Little, Brown, 1964.

_____. "The Goldwater Phenomenon: Purists, Politicians, and the Two-Party System." *Review of Politics* 27 (1965): 386-413.

_____. "The Meaning of 'Youth' in the Struggle for Control of the Democratic Party." In *The Revolt Against the Masses, and Other Essays on Politics and Public Policy.* New York and London: Basic Books, Inc., Publishers, 1971.

Williams, Philip M. *Crisis and Compromise: Politics in the Fourth Republic.* Garden City, New York: Doubleday & Company, Inc., Anchor Books, 1966.

_____. *The French Parliament, 1958-1967.* London: George Allen and Unwin, 1968.

Wood, David M. "Majority vs. Opposition in the French National Assembly, 1956-65: A Guttman Scale Analysis." *American Political Science Review* 62 (1968): 88-109.

Woshinsky, Oliver H. "Incentives to Political Action: Connecticut Legislators." Unpublished, 1968.

_____. "The Political Incentives of French Deputies." Ph.D. dissertation, Yale University, 1971.

Wylie, Laurence. *Village in the Vaucluse.* Cambridge: Harvard University Press, 1957.

X, Malcolm, with the assistance of Alex Haley. *The Autobiography of Malcolm X.* New York: Grove Press, 1966.

Index

Index

Absenteeism: in Colombian Congress, 11; in National Assembly, 160, 162, 165, 210n

Activists, other political, 17, 20; attitude of mission Deputies toward, 72-75; attitude of obligation Deputies toward, 104-05; attitude of program Deputies toward, 89-90; attitude of status Deputies toward, 120

Administrative oversight, 164-65, 210n

Adulation incentive, 3, 5, 7, 155-57

"Advertiser", 4, 7, 11-12, 111-12, 118, 126, 143, 146, 206n, 207n, 209n

Age: at entering politics, 143-45; at obtaining public office, 143-45. *See also* Career, political

"Agitator", 8, 205n

Alford, Robert R., 198n

Almond, Gabriel A., 200n, 201n

Alternate (*suppléant*), 24n

Amateur (in politics), 8, 97, 101-02, 143, 177, 203n. *See also* Obligation incentive

"Amateur Democrat", 7, 203n

L'Année politique, 24n

Antioquia (Colombia), 4, 202n

L'Appel du 18 juin 1940, 70

Assembly, National, 22-25, 156, 187n; attitude of mission Deputies toward role within, 76; attitude of obligation Deputies toward role within, 105-06; attitude of program Deputies toward role within, 91-93; attitude of status Deputies toward role within, 122-24; behavior in, by the four incentive types, 127-42; distribution of incentives within, 26-27; explanation of behavior in, 153-67; number of members in, 200n. *See also* Deputies, French

Association Française de Science Politique, 24n

Attitudes, political. *See* Correlates, attitudinal (of incentives)

Avril, Pierre, 210n

Baldwin, Raymond E., 202n

Barber, James D., 4, 5, 7, 9, 11-12, 81, 87, 96, 105, 111-12, 118, 126, 143, 146, 157, 198n, 199n, 202n, 203n, 205n, 206n, 207n, 208n, 209n, 210n

Barel, Virgile, 200n

Bauer, Raymond A., 199n

Behavior, conflict-provoking, 11-12, 153-67

Behavior, conflict-reducing, 10, 12, 93, 138, 153-67, 209n

Behavior, legislative, 15, 127-42, 153-67

Behavior, political: associated with different incentives, 15, 18-19, 127-52; explained by incentives (motives), 1, 3, 6-12, 22, 198n

Bernstein, Eduard, 63

Bills, private-member: handling of, in National Assembly, 160-61, 187n

Bloom, Sol, 202n

Bolshevism, 63, 71

Bowman, Lewis, 199n

Boynton, G.R., 199n

Brazil, 5, 81, 197n, 209n

"Broker," 8

Browning, Rufus P., 7, 9, 81, 202n, 204n, 205n

Bruner, Jerome, 9, 202n

Bryan, William Jennings, 118, 126, 206n, 207n

Buchanan, William, 199n

Buckley, William F., Jr., 204n

Cabinet (staff), Ministerial, 150

Cadre party, 8, 167

Cahova, Paul, 187n

Canadian Senate, 156-57

Career, political, 19, 22, 143-52

Center (in French politics), 73, 172, 175-76. *See also* PDM

Centrists. *See* PDM

Chambers, Whittaker, 200n, 201n

Charlot, Jean, 8, 9, 201n, 211n

Christian Socialism, 61

Clapp, Charles L., 199n

Clark, Peter, 198n
Clarke, James W., 203n
Clubs (political), in France, 176-77
Colombia, 2, 4, 10-11, 81, 111, 134, 146, 153, 156, 161, 206n
Committees (National Assembly), 187, 210n; attendance at, 134-36; number of, 164; operation of, 161-63, 165. *See also* Finance Committee; Foreign Affairs Committee
Communism: criticized by Duverger, Russell, 71. *See also* Communists; PCF
Communists (French): comradeship within party, 72-73; need for strong opponents, 79-80; relations with Socialists, 35, 63; worship of leaders, 71-72. *See also* Mission incentive; PCF
Communist Party, France. *See* PCF
Compromise: norm of, 10
Conflict-provoking behavior, 11-12, 153-67
Conflict-reduction (in legislature), 10, 12, 93, 138, 153-67, 209n
Congress, Colombian, 10-11, 146, 153, 156, 161
Congress, U.S., 10-12, 153, 156, 162, 163, 209n, 210n
Connecticut, 4, 5, 81, 112, 197n, 202n, 203n, 206n, 209n
Conseil Général, 56, 108, 205n
Convention des institutions républicaines, 177
Converse, Philip E., 166, 197n, 200n, 203n, 211n
Conviviality incentive, 3, 5, 7, 12, 155, 198n
Conway, M. Margaret, 198n
Correlates, attitudinal (of incentives), 15-18, 20-22; of mission incentive, 67-80; of obligation incentive, 102-09; of program incentive, 85-96; of status incentive, 115-26
Correlates, behavioral (of incentives), 15, 18-19, 127-52
Courtesy: norm of, 10, 92, 138, 156, 157, 166
Crossman, Richard, 204n
"Cult of personality", 71
Customs, legislative. *See* Norms, legislative

Dahl, Robert, 210n
Debate, legislative, 12, 15, 18, 127-30, 137-40, 160-61
Debré, Michel, 41, 177
Defferre, Gaston, 51
de Gaulle, General Charles, 24, 54, 55, 56, 58, 64, 65, 68, 73, 86, 88, 97-98, 100-01, 104, 119, 177, 178, 201n; Schweitzer's attitude toward, 39, 41-42; hero-worship of, by Gaullists, 69-72
de Montalais, Jacques, 201n
Denney, Reuel, 203n
Départements: number in France, 24
Depersonalization of conflict: norm of, 10, 93, 156
Deputies, French: as mission participants, 61-80; as obligation participants, 97-109; as program participants, 81-96; as status participants, 111-26; careers of, 143-52; distribution of incentives among, 26-27; four incentive types found among, 3; identification and classification of, 13-15; interviews with four, 29-59; legislative activity of, 127-42; party distribution of, by incentive type, 169-180; political types in other studies similar to those among, 6-9; turnover rate among, 23-24; two interpretations of motives of, 1. *See also* Types of political leader
Deutsch, Emeric, 197n
Devotee party, 8, 72-73, 167
Dexter, Lewis Anthony, 199n
Disraeli, Benjamin, 206n
Disruptiveness, 18, 137-40, 173-75, 185-86. *See also* Conflict-provoking behavior
District, legislative: type of, 19, 150-52
Djilas, Milovan, 201n
Dogan, Mattei, 24n, 159, 210n
Dominican Republic, 4, 5, 81, 112, 197n, 209n
Donaldson, William, 199n
Dupeux, Georges, 197n, 203n, 211n
Dupont, Michel (pseudonym for French mission-motivated Deputy): interview with, 29-35
Duverger, Maurice, 8, 9, 24n, 167, 197n, 201n, 203n, 211n

Eldersveld, Samuel J., 198n
Elections (France), 22-24, 78, 88
Elgey, Georgette, 202n
Engels, Friedrich, 71
Enjoyment of politics, 17, 21-22. *See also* Orientation toward politics
Eulau, Heinz, 199n
Expertise, legislative, 15, 18, 92, 130-34, 154. *See also* Specialization
Externalization, 9

"Facilitator", 8
Fascism, 65, 71
Fauvet, Jacques, 197n
Fédération. See FGDS
Feigert, Frank B., 198n
Fenno, Richard F., Jr., 165, 199n
Fenton, John H., 7, 9, 81, 198n, 202n
Ferguson, LeRoy C., 199n
FGDS (coalition of non-Communist Left), 25, 27, 62, 73, 82, 98, 112, 169, 171; Deputies in, quoted, 84, 86, 89, 92, 93, 114, 120, 121, 125
Fifth Republic: elections in, 22-24; comparison of National Assembly in Fourth Republic and in, 159-67. *See also* Assembly, National; Politics (France)
Finance Committee (National Assembly), 135, 163
Fishel, Jeff, 203n
"Flash party", 174-75
Foreign Affairs Committee, 58, 135
Fourth Republic, 79-80, 176, 187n; comparison of National Assembly in Fifth Republic and in, 159-67
France, 4, 5, 81, 112; elections in, 22-24; legislative behavior in, by the four incentive types, 127-52; legislative committees in, 134-36; legislative debates in, 137-40; party politics in, 169-80; possibility of civil war in, 170-71. *See also* Assembly, National; Politics (France)
Frank, Elke, 210n
Franklin, Benjamin, 202n
Game incentive, 3, 5, 7, 123, 155
Gandhi, M.K., 204n
Garceau, Oliver, 199n
Gaullism, 61, 65, 68, 70, 85-86; attitude of status Gaullists toward,

115-16; ideology of, 66-67, 106, 116-17; lack of ideological unity within, 178-79; political future of, 177-79. *See also* Gaullists; UDR
Gaullists, 36, 44, 79-80; discipline of, 201n; glorify leader, 69-72; ideology of, 106; ideology of, congenial to obligation participants in France, 175-76; leaders of, hostile to Assembly reforms, 164; political future of, 177-79; thrive on anti-Communism, 79-80. *See also* Gaullism; UDR
"Gaullistes de foi", 8
"Gaullistes doctrinaires", 8
"Gaullistes empiristes", 8
Gicquel, Jean, 208n, 209n
Giscard d'Estaing, Valéry, 41, 88, 211n
Glazer, Nathan, 203n
Goguel, François, 24n, 208n, 210n
Goldwater, Barry, 204n
Grangé, Jean, 210n
Greenstein, Fred I., 198n
Guesde, Jules, 63
Guichard, Eliane, 210n

Haley, Alex, 200n
Herriot, Edouard, 88
Herzog, Marie-Pierre, 201n
Hodge, Robert W., 205n
Hoffer, Eric, 8, 9, 200n, 201n
Hoffmann, Stanley, 197n
Hofstetter, Richard C., 203n
House of Commons, 129
House of Lords, 156-57
Humbert-Droz, Jules, 200n
Hunt, William H., 197n

Ideology: emphasis on, as main identifying characteristic of mission participant, 61-67, 201n; importance of, in French politics, 1, 197n; of Gaullists, 116-117; of Gaullists, attractive to obligation participants in France, 175-76; quarrels over, among Gaullists, 178-79
Incentive analysis: explains hard work of program Deputies, 133; and French politics, 26-27; and intraparty conflict, 21; leads to expectations about career patterns, 143;

presentation of, 2-6, 197n, 198n; and role analysis, 20-21; used to explain French National Assembly, 153-67; used to explain French political parties, 169-80; utility of, 6-12. *See also* Incentives; Mission incentive; Obligation incentive; Program incentive; Status incentive

Incentives: definition of, 2-3; distribution of, in France, 26-27, 169; explain aggregate behavior, 153-67; explain career patterns, 143-52, 200n; explain legislative behavior, 127-42; explain party politics in France, 169-80; explain political behavior, 3, 6-12; identification of, 13-15; short description of seven, 4-5. *See also* Incentive analysis; Mission incentive; Obligation incentive; Program incentive; Status incentive

Independent Republicans. *See* RI

Index of Disruptiveness, 139-40, 185-86

Index of Legislative Leadership and Initiative, 140, 141, 187

"Indifferent," 8

Inkeles, Alex, 205n

"Inside-dopester," 8

Institutionalization, 209n

Interview: attitude of Deputies toward, 16, 20; attitude of mission Deputies toward, 69; attitude of obligation Deputies toward, 103; attitude of program Deputies toward, 87; attitude of status Deputies toward, 118-19; in-depth, to discover incentive, 13-15, 189; questions asked during, in France, 189-93

"Inventor," 8, 81

Ippolito, Dennis, 199n

Issue-orientation, 7, 81

Jaurès, Jean Léon, 63

Job-orientation, 7

Journal Officiel, 127, 128n, 131, 132, 134-35, 137, 185, 187, 207n, 210n

Keniston, Kenneth, 204n

Koestler, Arthur, 200n, 211n

Kornberg, Allan, 199n

Kriegel, Annie, 201n

Kunz, F.A., 209n

La Fontaine, Jean de, 33

Lasswell, Harold, 198n

Laurent, Xavier (pseudonym for French obligation-motivated Deputy): interview with, 43-51; persuaded to run for Assembly, 99-100

"Lawmaker," 4, 7, 11, 81, 87, 96, 207n, 209n

Leaders (political): attitude of French Deputies toward, 17, 20; attitude of mission Deputies toward, 69-72; attitude of obligation Deputies toward, 104; attitude of program Deputies toward, 87-88; attitude of status Deputies toward, 119-120; classification of, by incentives, 3; definition of, 198n; of mission parties, 66-67; money and power not incentives for, 6; observation of, leading to formulation of incentive analysis, 2. *See also* Types of political leader

Leadership, 18, 140-41, 165-66, 187

Left (in France), 22, 23, 73, 170-73; and obligation incentive, 175-77

Legislatures: incentives help explain norms of, 10-12; typology of, based on incentives, 153-67. *See also* Behavior, legislative; Assembly, National

Leites, Nathan, 1, 123-24, 165-66, 167, 197n, 206n, 211n

Lenin, V.I., 63

Lindon, Denis, 197n

Liste des députés, 25n

McCarthy, Eugene, 105, 203n, 204n

McClelland, David C., 8, 9

McCullough, Michael, 5, 197n, 209n

McFarland, Andrew S., 200n

Macridis, Roy C., 197n

Main identifying characteristic: definition of, 14; of mission participant, 61-67; of obligation participant, 97-102; of program participant, 81-85; of status participant, 112-15

Manley, John F., 199n, 207n

Marx, Karl, 63, 65, 71

Marxism (or Marxism-Leninism), 61, 66

Mass party, 8, 167

Matthews, Donald R., 8, 9, 165, 199n, 205n, 211n
"May Events," 23, 44, 49, 89, 98, 100, 170
Mayors, French: Schweitzer's attitude toward, 40; number of, in each legislative district, 150-52
Melnik, Constantin, 197n, 206n
Meyer, Frank S., 201n
Ministrable, 139, 163
Mission incentive, 3, 4, 7, 16-19, 20, 21, 26-27, 183; absence of, in other incentive types, 67-69, 85-86, 102, 115-16; and attitude toward interview, 69; and attitude toward leaders, 69-72; and attitude toward legislative role, 76; and attitude toward other political activists, 72-75; and attitude toward party, 76-77, 141-42; and attitude toward voters, 75-76; description of, 61-80; distribution by party of, 62; found mainly among Gaullists and Communists, 66-67; and French political parties, 170-71; interview with Deputy typical of, 29-35; main identifying characteristic of, 61-67; orientation toward politics associated with, 77-80; relation between conflict-provoking behavior in the legislature and, 153-67; relation between legislative activity and, 127-42; relation between political career pattern and, 143-52; relation between urbanism and, 150-52. *See also* Incentive analysis; Incentives
Mitterand, François, 176
Mix: of incentives in a legislature, 153-67
Moch, Jules, 79, 170
Mollet, Guy, 54, 88
Monde, Le, 51, 137, 208n
Money: not an incentive, 6
"Moralizer," 8, 97, 203n
Morazé, Charles, 197n
Motivation (for politics). *See* Incentive analysis; Incentives
Muhammed, Elijah, 201n

"n Achievement," 9
"n Affiliation," 9
Needs, inducing political activity. *See* Incentive analysis; Incentives

"Neutral," 8
Newcomb, Theodore M., 166, 200n, 211n
Non-inscrit, 25, 27, 62, 82, 98, 112, 169
Norms, 10-12, 92-93, 106, 134, 138; and the incentive mix in a legislature, 153-67; in the National Assembly, 165-66
Nowlin, William, 199n
"n Power," 9

Object appraisal, 9, 81
Obligation incentive, 3, 5, 7, 12, 16-19, 21, 22, 26-27, 183-84; absence of, in other incentive types, 69, 87, 102-03, 118; and attitude toward interview, 103; and attitude toward leaders, 104; and attitude toward legislative role, 105-06; and attitude toward other political activists, 104-05; and attitude toward party, 106-07; and attitude toward voters, 105; description of, 97-109; distribution by party of, 98; and entry into politics, 204n; and French political parties, 175-77; interview with Deputy typical of, 43-51; main identifying characteristic of, 97-102; orientation toward politics associated with, 107-09; relation between aggregate legislative behavior and, 155; relation between legislative activity and, 127-42; relation between political career pattern and, 143-52; and sporadic bursts of activity, 200n. *See also* Incentive analysis; Incentives
Orientation toward politics, 17, 21-22; of mission Deputy, 77-80; of obligation Deputy, 107-09; of program Deputy, 94-96; of status Deputy, 124-26
Oversight, administrative, 164-65, 210n

Parodi, Jean-Luc, 187n, 210n
Party, political, 17, 19, 21, 67, 72, 167; activity within, by the four incentive types in France, 148-49; attitude of mission Deputy toward, 76-77; attitude of obligation Deputy toward, 106-07; attitude of program

Deputy toward, 93-94; attitude of status Deputy toward, 124; incentive analysis used to explain, 169-80

"Patrician," 8

Patterson, Samuel C., 199n

Payne, James L., 2, 4, 5, 7, 9, 10-11, 22, 81, 111, 112, 126, 134, 143, 144, 146, 153, 197n, 198n, 199n, 200n, 201n, 202n, 204n, 205n, 206n, 207n, 208n, 209n

PCF (French Communist Party), 21, 23, 25, 27, 32, 62, 65, 68, 71, 76, 77, 79, 82, 98, 112, 169, 170-71, 173; Deputy in, quoted, 61, 62, 65, 66, 67, 68, 72, 74, 75, 78; interview with Deputy in, 29-35; leaders of, prevent change in ideology, 66-67, 170; nondemocratic and disciplined nature of, 201n; no status participants found in, 174, 175; and obligation incentive, 175-77. *See also* Communism; Communists (French); Marx, Karl; Marxism; Mission incentive

PDM (Centrists), 25, 27, 62, 82, 98, 112, 169; Deputies in, quoted, 63, 113, 117, 120, 121-22, 122-23

Peabody, Robert L., 199n

"Peyrane," 105-06, 205n

Philippon, Alexandre (pseudonym for French status-motivated Deputy): interview with, 51-59

Poher, Alain, 71, 88

"Policy incentive," 7

"Policy-influencing behavior," 8, 81

"Policy-making incentive," 7, 81

Politics, France, 1, 22-23, 26-27; explanation of, through incentive analysis, 153-80. *See also* Assembly, National

Polsby, Nelson W., 199n, 209n

Pompidou, Georges, 24, 31, 41, 70-71, 72, 103, 174, 178

Pool, Ithiel de Sola, 199n

Popular Front, 43, 176

Power: not an incentive, 6

Prefect, 56

Prestige. *See* Status incentive

"Prestige incentive," 7

Prewitt, Kenneth, 199n

Private-member bills, 140, 187, 207n

Program incentive, 3, 4, 7, 10, 15, 16-19, 20, 21-22, 26-27, 183; absence of, in other Deputies, 31-32, 67, 85-87, 102-03, 116-18; and attitude toward interview, 87; and attitude toward leaders, 87-88; and attitude toward legislative role, 91-93; and attitude toward other political activists, 89-90; and attitude toward party, 93-94; and attitude toward voters, 90-91; description of, 81-96; distribution by party of, 82; and French political parties, 171-73; interview with Deputy typical of, 35-43; main identifying characteristic of, 81-85; orientation toward politics associated with, 94-96; relation between conflict-reduction in the legislature and, 153-67; relation between legislative activity and, 127-42; relation between political career pattern and, 143-52; *See also* Incentive analysis; Incentives

"Professional," 8

Publicity, personal: sought by status participants, 11-12, 18, 123-24, 125-26, 136-37, 156

Public speaking: status Deputies' enjoyment of, 123-24, 125-26

"Purists," 5, 7, 97, 105, 203n. *See also* Obligation incentive

Queuille, Henri, 79

Questions (National Assembly), 129, 136-38, 208n

Question time, 129

Radical: Deputy quoted, 88, 93, 123-24

Rapporteur, 130-34, 140

Rapports, 128, 131n, 132, 133, 134, 187, 207n

Reciprocity: norm of, 10, 156, 157

Referendum (France, 1969), 24, 89

Reliability: of incentive classifications, 14-15, 199n

"Reluctant," 5, 7, 12, 97, 105, 146, 203n, 204n, 207n, 209n

Rémond, René, 197n

Republican Party (U.S.), 5, 203n

Resistance (France, World War II), 32, 77, 97, 101
"Resister" (to pressure groups), 8, 204n
Responsibility: norm of, 10
Revolution, 61, 65
RI (Independent Republicans), 25, 27, 62, 73, 82, 98, 112, 169, 171, 172, 173; Deputy in, quoted, 85, 86, 88, 89, 90, 91, 92, 94, 95, 99, 101, 102-03, 105, 107, 108
Riesman, David, 8, 9, 203n
Right (in France), 170-73
"Ritualist," 8, 204n
Roig, Charles, 210n
Role analysis, 20-21, 199n-200n. *See also* Role, legislative
Role expectations. *See* Norms; Role analysis; Role, legislative
Role, legislative, 10, 17, 20-21, 30; lack of consensus on, in National Assembly, 165-66; mission Deputy's conception of, 76; obligation Deputy's conception of, 105-06; program Deputy's conception of, 91-93; status Deputy's conception of, 105-06. *See also* Norms
Rossi, Peter H., 205n
RPF (Gaullists), 68, 79
"Rules of the game." *See* Norms
Russell, Bertrand, 63, 71, 201n
Russia, 33-34

Salisbury, Robert H., 199n
Sample (of French Deputies): how drawn, 24; representativeness of, 25
Satisfactions (in politics). *See* Incentive analysis; Incentives
Schweitzer, Jean-Claude (pseudonym for French program-motivated Deputy), 32, 83, 84; interview with, 35-43
Scoble, Harry M., 198n
Sectarianism, 89-90, 173
Senate (Canada), 156-57
Seniority: norm of, 10, 19, 133, 145-47
Shonfield, Andrew, 210n
Siegel, Paul M., 205n
"Significant others," 17, 20; attitude of mission Deputies toward, 69-76;

attitude of obligation Deputies toward, 104-05; attitude of program Deputies toward, 87-91; attitude of status Deputies toward, 119-22. *See also* Activists, other political; Leaders; Voters
Silverman, Corinne, 199n
Smith, Frank E., 202n
Smith, M. Brewster, 9, 81, 202n
Snowiss, Leo M., 199n
"Social adjustment," 9
Socialists, 35, 51, 63, 201n; Deputy in SFIO, quoted, 84, 86, 88, 89, 92, 114, 120, 121, 125. *See also* FGDS
Sorauf, Frank J., 7, 9, 81, 198n, 202n
Soule, John W., 203n
Soviet Union, 33-34
Speaking (in legislature), 127-30
Specialization: norm of, 10, 130-34, 156, 157, 166. *See also* Expertise, legislative
"Spectator," 5, 7, 12, 157, 198n, 209n
Speech-making, 127-30
Spender, Stephen, 104n
Staff, 150, 163-64
Stalin, 71, 211n
Stalinism, 33-34
Status incentive, 3, 4, 7, 10-12, 15, 16-19, 20, 21, 22, 26-27, 184; absence of, in other incentive types, 68, 86-87, 103, 115-18; and attitude toward interview, 118-19; and attitude toward leaders, 119-20; and attitude toward legislative role, 122-24; and attitude toward other political activists, 120; and attitude toward party, 124; and attitude toward voters, 120-22; description of, 111-26; distribution by party of, 112; and French political parties, 173-75; interview with Deputy typical of, 51-59; main identifying characteristic of, 112-15; orientation toward politics associated with, 124-26; relation between *cabinet* position and, 150; relation between conflict-provoking behavior in the legislature and, 153-67; relation between legislative activity and, 127-42; relation between political

career pattern and, 143-52. *See also*
Incentive analysis; Incentives
Style (in politics), 100-02, 109
Suppléant (alternate), 24n

Tacheron, Donald G., 199n, 210n
Talleyrand, Charles Maurice de, 33
Tarrow, Sidney, 203n
Time in politics, 19, 21, 147-48. *See
also* Career, Political
Thorez, Maurice, 71, 72
Touchard, Jean, 24n
Totalitarianism, 61, 71, 75
"Tribune," 8
"True believer," 8
Tucker, Robert C., 8, 9, 200n, 201n
Turner, Ralph H., 166, 200n, 211n
Turnover, 21, 22, 23-24, 146
Types of political leader, 3, 6-9, 11-12,
143, 198-99; comparison of, by
incentive, 20-22; differences among,
in legislative activity, 127-42; differ-
ences among, in political careers,
143-52; identification of the incen-
tives of, 13-15; and the incentive
mix in a legislature, 153-67; profile
of four, by incentive, 16-19. *See also*
Deputies, French; Incentive analysis;
Incentives; Mission incentive; Obligation incentive; Program incentive;
Status incentive

Udall, Morris K., 199n, 210n
UDR (Gaullists), 21, 23, 25, 27, 62,
68, 73, 77, 82, 98, 107, 112, 159,
169, 170-71, 172, 173, 175, 177-79;
Deputies in, quoted, 64, 65, 68, 69,
70-71, 73, 74, 75, 77, 78, 82, 83,
85, 86, 88, 89, 92, 95, 99, 100, 101,
104, 106, 107, 108, 113, 114, 115,
116, 117-18, 120, 121, 122, 125.
UNR. *See* UDR
Urbanism, 150-52
USSR, 33-34

Vallon, Louis, 178
Virginia: Payne's study of city councilmen in, 197n
Voters, 17, 20; attitude of mission
Deputy toward, 75-76; attitude of
obligation Deputy toward, 105; attitude of program Deputy toward,
90-91; attitude of status Deputy
toward, 120-22
Vote bloqué, 95, 203n
Vote sans débats, 160

Wahl, Nicholas, 210n
Wahlke, John C., 8, 9, 81, 165, 199n,
200n, 202n, 204n
Ward, Robert E., 197n
"Warfare personality," 8
Washington, D.C., 5
Waterman, Harvey, 197n
Weill, Pierre, 197n
Weimar Republic, 79
White, Robert, 9, 202n
Who's Who in France, 208n
Wildavsky, Aaron, 5, 7, 9, 198n, 199n,
200n, 203n, 204n
Williams, Philip M., 161, 162, 165,
167, 202n, 203n, 209n, 210n, 211n
Wilson, Frank L., 211n
Wilson, James Q., 7, 9, 198n, 203n
Wolfe, Bertram D., 200n
Wood, David M., 201n
Work: norm of, 10, 11, 92, 131, 146,
155, 156, 157, 158, 166, 209n
Woshinsky, Oliver H., 2, 4, 5, 7, 9,
112, 197n, 198n, 201n, 202n, 204n,
205n, 206n, 207n, 209n
Wylie, Laurence, 105-06, 205n

X, Malcolm, 200n, 201n

Yalta, 64
Yarmolinsky, Avrahm, 200n

About the Author

Oliver H. Woshinsky is Assistant Professor of Political Science at the University of Maine at Portland-Gorham. He obtained the B.A. from Oberlin College in 1961 and the Ph.D. from Yale University in 1971. He has taught at Allegheny College and has served as Department Chairman at his present institution. Mr. Woshinsky lived in France for over a year in 1968-69 conducting the research which forms the base for this book. He is co-author (with James L. Payne) of the 1972 WORLD POLITICS article, "Incentives for Political Participation."

Mr. Woshinsky lives in Falmouth, Maine. His wife is also a published scholar, specializing in seventeenth-century French literature.